PERGAMON INTERNATIONAL LIBRARY
of Science, Technology, Engineering and Social Studies

*The 1000-volume original paperback library in aid of education,
industrial training and the enjoyment of leisure*

Publisher: Robert Maxwell, M.C.

LB 1027.55 .C66 1982
Conoley, Jane Close.
 School consultation : a guide to
practice and training

rary
for
days
or
sale
nts.
new

Pergamon Titles of Related Interest

Amabile/Stubbs Psychological Research in the Classroom:
Issues for Educators and Researchers
Apter Troubled Children/Troubled Systems
Cartledge/Milburn Teaching Social Skills to Children:
Innovative Approaches
Liebert/Sprafkin/Davidson The Early Window: Effects of Television
on Children and Youth, Second Edition
Monjan/Gassner Critical Issues in Competency Based Education
O'Leary/O'Leary Classroom Management: The Successful Use of
Behavior Modification, Second Edition

Related Journals*

CHILDREN AND YOUTH SERVICES REVIEW
EVALUATION IN EDUCATION
EVALUATION AND PROGRAM PLANNING
STUDIES IN EDUCATION EVALUATION

*Free specimen copies available upon request.

PERGAMON GENERAL PSYCHOLOGY SERIES
EDITORS
Arnold P. Goldstein, *Syracuse University*
Leonard Krasner, *SUNY at Stony Brook*

School Consultation
A Guide to Practice and Training

Jane Close Conoley
Texas Woman's University

Collie W. Conoley
North Texas State University

PERGAMON PRESS
New York   Oxford   Toronto   Sydney   Paris   Frankfurt

LB
1027.55
.C66
1982

Pergamon Press Offices:

U.S.A.   Pergamon Press Inc., Maxwell House, Fairview Park,
                     Elmsford, New York 10523, U.S.A.

U.K.   Pergamon Press Ltd., Headington Hill Hall,
                     Oxford OX3 0BW, England

CANADA   Pergamon Press Canada Ltd., Suite 104, 150 Consumers Road,
                     Willowdale, Ontario M2J 1P9, Canada

AUSTRALIA   Pergamon Press (Aust.) Pty. Ltd., P.O. Box 544,
                     Potts Point, NSW 2011, Australia

FRANCE   Pergamon Press SARL, 24 rue des Ecoles,
                     75240 Paris, Cedex 05, France

FEDERAL REPUBLIC Pergamon Press GmbH, Hammerweg 6
OF GERMANY   6242 Kronberg/Taunus, Federal Republic of Germany

Copyright © 1982 Pergamon Press Inc.

Library of Congress Cataloging in Publication Data

Conoley, Jane Close.
    School consultation.

    (Pergamon general psychology series ; 111)
    Includes bibliographies and index.
    1. Psychiatric consultation. 2. School children
--Mental health services. I. Conoley, Collie W.
(Collie Wyatt), 1949-   . II. Title. III. Series.
RJ499.C6385   1982   362.2   82-3837
ISBN 0-08-027566-4   AACR2
ISBN 0-08-027565-6 (pbk.)

*All Rights reserved. No part of this publication may be reproduced,
stored in a retrieval system or transmitted in any form or by any means:
electronic, electrostatic, magnetic tape, mechanical, photocopying,
recording or otherwise, without permission in writing from the
publishers.*

Printed in the United States of America

TO:

Our beginnings, The Closes and Doyles
                The Conoleys and Wyatts

Our futures, Brian Thomas
                Colleen Adele
                Collin Malcolm

Contents

Contents

Preface

It has seemed to us that people who have just one overriding theme or idea are either brave idealists or very dull. What follows, this book on delivering consultation services, will allow the reader to assign us to one of these categories or, perhaps, some other more appropriate one.

Very early in our careers we became convinced, through the knowledgeable guidance of our graduate faculty at the University of Texas at Austin, that psychology needs to be given away in order to be kept viable and influential in today's world. In addition, we came to see preventive programming for children as our top professional priority. These two connections led us to the study of consultation, particularly in school settings. We have had basically one theme for six years.

As university faculty we have been given the privilege of sharing in the socialization of new psychologist colleagues. This book is a product of that privilege. We have collaborated on other writings about consultation, but nowhere have we put down, in detail, how we taught it or how *we* thought it should be done. This, therefore, is a book representing six years of "shoulds" that have withstood the test of many personal and trainee experiences. Background theory and research are provided, but not exhaustively. There are other sources for research and theory that are mentioned throughout this text for interested or otherwise coerced readers to investigate.

Chapter 1 describes consultation as a professional activity and explains some of the major models of consultation. Chapter 2 focuses on generic skills needed for every model, while chapter 3 discusses the particular skills needed for each model. Chapter 4 reviews ways to assess the effectiveness of consultation practice and training. In chapter 5 the entry process and related issues are examined. Chapter 6 is a review of issues associated with training endeavors attempted by young consultants. Chapter 7 presents guidelines for moving from direct to indirect service delivery systems. Annotated transcripts representing consultation from a number of models are presented as chapter 8; and chapter 9 highlights some ethical considerations associated with consultation that have not been covered in other chapters.

.Although we have taught consultation courses, we are aware that many graduate programs do not provide specialized training in the area. Consultation has been seen as something we just "do." With increasing experience (or perhaps increasing egocentrism) we have decided that few of us "just do" consultation well, just as few of us "just do" psychotherapy, research, or teaching well. Every professional function seems to benefit from some information and practice under supervision. As a professional function, consultation has been receiving increasing attention. A number of sources can be identified. There is increasing consensus that professional caregivers will never be able to meet the demand for services using the traditional one-to-one or one-to-small-group clinical methodologies. Preventing mental health difficulties rather than merely treating them remains philosophically, if not practically, a high priority among mental health workers. Theoretical understandings of pathology have shifted from intrapsychic to ecological causes. The appropriate role of the mental health worker has evolved from authoritarian "blank page" to a more collaborative ally in the pursuit of personal adjustment. And, finally, the political upheavals of the 1960s, with the resulting visibility of many special interest groups demanding services, have literally pulled some professionals out of their offices and into the streets to meet people face to face on their own ground. All of these events have suggested that the repertoire of the psychologist, psychiatrist, social worker, special educator, etc., be expanded beyond remedial therapeutic intervention. Only the limits of our creativity should hold us back from envisioning and evaluating new roles and functions for those who call themselves helpers. Professional territoriality, revered traditions, and personal uneasiness must not stand in the way of innovative service delivery systems and strategies.

We see consultation, so often talked about but so rarely done, as one of these innovations. We do not see it as a panacea or as inevitably the correct strategy, nor do we believe it to be inherently superior to other strategies. We simply know that consultation is an effective and efficient method to use when the situation calls for it. We also know that many situations, ripe for consultation intervention, are overlooked because mental health workers' visions are narrowed by traditional problem formulation strategies. Our intent in this volume, therefore, is to provide a helpful explanation of alternative ways of conceptualizing the problems that surround us. The problems are pervasive and potentially overwhelming. The technologies to get us out of trouble have not kept abreast with those that now threaten us. We hope that in a few years we may look back on this work and have a whole new understanding of how best to help others. But we must start somewhere. This is, we hope, only the beginning.

The list of people who deserve thanks for the volume is quite long. The number of professors and colleagues who, through their words and writings, knowingly or unknowingly contributed is very large. The reference list is, we hope, some acknowledgment of our professional debts. The members of our graduate program faculties at the University of Texas at Austin are especially thanked for their wise counsel. The colleagues we have had since then in New York State and in Denton, Texas, have been continued sources of learning. Dr. Arnold P. Goldstein's (Psychology editor at Pergamon Press) continuing faith in our abilities was actually what made this volume a reality. Ranee Beaty's editorial assistance and general support were invaluable for this and many, many other tasks. Our children, Brian, Colleen, and Collin did *not* help us write. In fact, they interfered whenever possible. They deserve special mention, however, because, over their complaints about babysitters, quiet times, and general parental preoccupation, their messages of love and their witness of the simultaneous vulnerability and potentiality of childhood were strong and compelling. Because of them, any other child's needless pain or dysfunction has seemed all the more unbearable.

1

Consultation: What Is It? Why Do It?

WHAT IT IS

Definitions and rationales for consultation are plentifully scattered in the literature. In subsequent chapters it will become clear that a simple definition or rationale would be misleading when considering such a broad professional function as consultation. However, it is possible to present a definition and rationale that can serve as working generalizations. Caplan (1970), in his benchmark volume, *The Theory and Practice of Mental Health Consultation*, gives the basic components. Consultation is a voluntary, non-supervisory relationship between professionals from differing fields established to aid one in his or her professional functioning.

The rationale for a mental health professional (consultant) spending time with a teacher, minister, or probation officer (consultee), instead of the child, parishioner, or prisoner (client), is based on the efficiency, impact, and prevention aspects of the intervention. The consultant hopes that the consultee will generalize the insights and skills learned in the discussion of a single client case to the other clients (now or ever) under the care of the consultee. The benefits of consulting about a single case while the benefits spread is the efficiency of consultation. The impact rationale is the consultant's belief that clients are best treated by those who have high duration or intensity contact with them. Because most specialists have adopted some organizational variation of the 50-minute-hour-per-week treatment modality, the most highly trained among us spend the least time with those we were trained to treat. That being the case, the regular caregivers in a client's life should be helped to be facilitative of treatment goals because they spend the most time with the clients.

Table 1.1. Important Aspects of Consultation Services

1. Consultee initiated.
2. Consultee has complete freedom to accept or reject services. (The relationship can be terminated by the consultee at any point.)
3. Confidentiality of relationship.
4. Peer-professional collaborative relationship. (Consultant viewed in a *facilitative* role, not in an *expert* role.)
5. Indirect resource service.
   a. Economy of service
   b. Generalizability of service
   c. Long-term effects
6. Work related problems only.
7. Primary prevention orientation. (Acute and chronic problems are dealt with as well.)
8. Goals of the consultant:
   a. Provide an objective point of view.
   b. Help to increase problem solving skills.
   c. Help to increase coping skills.
   d. Help to increase freedom of choice.
   e. Help to increase commitment to choices made.
   f. Increase resources available to bring to bear on persistent problems.

In addition, it follows that if generalization and transfer of skills occur because of consultation, there is the potential for the primary prevention of adjustment problems. The possibility of using consultation as a preventive intervention is very encouraging. Rudimentary reports that appear in the literature lend some credence to consultation's preventive potential (e.g., Meyers, 1975; Ritter, 1978). In table 1.1 is a summary of consultation that may serve as a useful overview.

WHAT IT IS NOT

The term consultation has been applied to so many professional functions that it is traditional to further define consultation by mentioning what it is *not*. For example, consultants are different from supervisors, program developers, collaborators, teachers, and psychotherapists. While it is true that consultants are none of these exactly, it is also true that they do some of what each job title suggests. In the next few paragraphs are some of the similarities and contrasts that are apparent when consultation is compared with other professional roles.

Supervisors give advice and are mainly interested in facilitating the work accomplishment of their supervisees. In these ways they are similar to consultants. Supervisors are usually the primary source of evaluative data about supervisees and the relationship between the two roles is a required one. The requirements usually include mandatory meetings and mandatory acceptance of supervisors' "suggestions." Supervisors make decisions about the careers of their subordinates: hiring, firing, raises, promotions, and so on. The supervisory role has inherent in it, therefore, certain facets that make honest self-disclosure about work performance difficult for the supervisee. It also contains elements that make it difficult for the supervisor to adopt a completely non-threatening developmental stance toward supervisee difficulties. The wise consultant, therefore, avoids some supervisory functions as completely as possible in order to facilitate a mutually beneficial relationship with the consultee. Those functions to be avoided are evaluative comments, reporting career-relevant data to supervisors, insisting that recommendations be followed (even if you do this only indirectly) and overly structuring the amount of meeting time or contents of meeting.

When new programs (computer-assisted instruction, values clarification, behavior modification) are being introduced into an organization, consultants are often hired to enhance the implementation. In this volume we will take the position that if you are selling a particular technology, you are not a consultant. If you are helping people decide what fits their needs and helping them utilize whatever new technologies have been jointly chosen, you are a consultant even if you make some money out of the interaction. Consultants sell their problem-solving services. *Program developers* sell their problem-solving services and a particular product. Along with their services, the initial concern of the program developer is to convince the potential customer/consultee that the product being sold is right for whatever client or organization problem has been identified. For the program developer, the problem must lead to the product being sold. Every consultant has a limited repertoire of responses for a particular consultee concern. The best consultants do not know everything, but also do not close their minds to any potential set of solutions. Program developers *must* close their minds to certain alternatives while promoting the alternatives that sell their product.

Professional *collaboration* involves sharing the work and responsibility for some activity. Consultation theorists differ on the limits of collaboration in a consulting relationship. Caplan (1970) describes mental health consultation as a situation in which no real client-work is done by the consultant. Bergan (1977) and Meyers (1973) describe consultation applications in which the consultant implements part of the remedial plan or views him or herself as partially accountable for the results of the consultation. The key element here that differentiates the two perspectives seems to be, what are the goals of consultation? If doing *for* the consultee results in dependency and no new skills, collaboration would be a mistake. However, if working side by side is seen as a way to model skills, increase behavioral repertoires, ensure first-attempt successes, or show concern and investment, then the overriding goals of consultation are approached. Practically speaking, however, in order to increase efficiency, only so much actual collaboration can be done. The skills of knowing how much involvement to offer and how to fade out of implementation plans are important ones to develop.

Teaching is a process of imparting, in a planned systematic way, a specified body of information. Consultants impart information, but not in a planned or structured way. In addition, consultants must be ready to supply data pertinent to a wide variety of concerns. Though always mindful of ethical considerations, consultants will not be very helpful if they "do" only behavior modification or psychoanalysis, or if they are willing to speak only of academic difficulties of a child while screening out emotional or social concerns. Consultants, like teachers, must be aware of the many ways in which teaching is accomplished. Modeling, relationship building, nonverbal reactions, and presentation of alternative world views have the potential of serendipitously teaching a consultee. All of these will be elaborated on later in this book.

Finally, *psychotherapy*, with its emphasis on helping people adjust, opening up new alternatives, and developing beneficial relationships, is very much like consultation. However, therapy also involves probing for personal emotional information over a broad spectrum of the client's life situation, past and present. Therapist and client must at some point come to agree that the client has a problem that requires some personality or behavior change. Most therapies (but not behavior therapy) seek to weaken a client's defensive structure so that more valid information is available to consciousness. Consultation, on the other hand, limits the focus to work-related problems, does not involve much emotional probing (certainly none about a consultee's past emotional history), and generally works to keep the consultee from experiencing a loss of typical coping patterns. Clients in psychotherapy often report a crisis phase in which they are unable to integrate new insights with old behaviors and attitudes. They have a tendency to experience intense dependency upon the therapist. Consultants, while working to add to a consultee's behavioral repertoire and provide new ways of seeing old problems, do not wish to throw a consultee into a crisis that demands continuous consultant support. Of all the consultation models, mental health consultation comes closest to skirting the boundaries between therapy and consultation.

POPULAR MODELS

Consultation can be more specifically understood by considering the currently utilized models. These include mental health, behavioral, process, and advocacy. There are variations on these such as transactional analysis consultation (Fine, 1981), consultation from a number of social psychological perspectives (Hughes & Falk, 1981; Martin, 1978), relationship consultation (Gross, 1978; Meyers, 1981), and ecological consultation (Jason, Ferone, & Anderegg, 1979). What follows are overviews of each of the major models. Each of these will also be mentioned again in subsequent chapters and in annotated transcripts which are presented in chapter 8.

Mental Health Consultation

Mental health consultation is probably the best known, though most difficult to implement, of the consultation models. Comprehensively described by Caplan (1970) and also developed by Alpert (1976), Altrocchi (1972), Berlin (1969, 1974), and Meyers, Parsons, and Martin (1979), this model is based on a number of psychodynamic assumptions about human behavior.

Caplan suggests that there are predictable areas of consultee deficits. Consultees may lack skills, self-confidence, knowledge, or professional objectivity in dealing with particular client problems. He describes four approaches within mental health consultation: client-centered, consultee-centered, program, and administrative. Program and administrative consultation are further subdivided as client and consultee-centered program and administrative consultation.

The important distinctions among these approaches are goals and targets. In the client-centered approaches, the consultant plays a mainly educative function around an issue. This occurs when the consultant assesses the situation as demanding skills and knowledge about a client, programmatic issue, or administrative problem that the consultee simply does not possess. In contrast, the consultee-centered approaches are utilized when, in addition to informational needs about a particularly puzzling issue, the consultee evidences a broad area of skill deficit or an emotional entanglement with the issue (or person) making successful coping difficult.

Caplan emphasizes the consultee's loss of professional objectivity as a particularly important problem area. He offers reasons for the loss in objectivity ranging from the consultee's simple identification with the problem (e.g., client reminds the consultee of someone else) to characterological disorders on the part of the consultee (e.g., antisocial, paranoid, schizoid, schizotypal, histrionic, narcissistic, borderline, avoidant, dependent, compulsive, or passive-aggressive). Caplan's most developed problem area, however, is that of theme interference. This is a situation in which the consultee's competence is impaired because of the activity of some unconscious dynamic. Essentially, the consultee fits the client into a category and then assumes an inevitable outcome. For example, the consultee "sees" the client as a loud, aggressive, controlling female (loud, aggressive, controlling females lack the necessary feminine traits to maintain satisfactory heterosexual relationships) and, therefore, this woman's marriage is doomed to failure. The source of this unconscious syllogism is buried in the consultee's repressed past. Because the result of the theme interference is a deficit in work performance, Caplan sees it as a legitimate target for mental health consultation. His technique, called theme interference reduction, is explained in chapter 3.

Mental health consultation demands a very high skill level from the consultant. Consultants must become experts in the organizational, interpersonal, and intrapersonal variables of consultees. They must walk a thin line between therapy and consultation when the problem is adjudged by the consultant to be caused by the consultee's emotional relationship with the case, and finally, they must sell an organization on the benefits of a model that are somewhat ambiguous and long range.

Despite the difficulties, mental health consultation is in many ways the prototype of consultation models. The model's focus on the process concerns of each member of the consultation relationship—consultant, consultee, and client—is basic to all other models. In addition, Caplan's (1970) emphasis on environmental awareness on the part of the consultant was a leap from the traditional psychodynamic roots of the model, and anticipated the growing ecological awareness in psychology.

Behavioral Consultation

The behavioral model of consultation is, like mental health consultation, a problem solving framework (Bergan, 1977). Unlike the mental health model, however, it is based on social learning theory. Client and consultee problems are conceptualized from a learning perspective; that is, consultee or client may exhibit faulty learning or skill deficits based on idiosyncratic reinforcement histories. The task of the consultant is to determine exactly what the problem is, isolate those environmental variables that prompt and support the target behavior, and devise environmental manipulations that will reduce the probability of the continuance of the behavior. In addition, the consultant must be able to implement programs designed to produce new behaviors through shaping, chaining, successive approximations, or modeling techniques. Most "behaviorists" now allow for the importance of certain cognitive variables and so might suggest skill acquisition programs like Goldstein's (1981) that rely on learning principles, role play, feedback, and homework assignments.

There is no focus on the unconscious dynamics so prevalent in the mental health model. Consultees may become emotionally entangled with clients; however, the reason behind the entanglement is that consultees have not learned the appropriate skills in distancing from clients or have aversive associations with some aspect of the client's behavior.

The literature gives ample evidence as to the usefulness of behavioral techniques in schools and in many other settings (see especially a review by

Keller, 1981) but limited attention has been given to the process of behavioral consultation. The research program of Bergan and Tombari (1975, 1976; Tombari & Bergan 1978) is a notable exception to this generalization. Behaviorally oriented consultants are just beginning to examine the complexity of their relationships with consultees as predictive of consultee utilization of behavioral techniques. Many teachers shudder at the term "behavior modification." As Abidin (1975) points out, the teachers may not be simply resistant to innovation, but actually find the implementation of behavioral plans to be quite personally disruptive. The teachers need consultants who suggest reasonable classroom alternatives and who reinforce teacher efforts.

The techniques involved in behavioral consultation are very diverse but are based, obviously, on the assumption that environmental manipulation will change behavior. The behavioral model is used extensively in elementary schools and in other environments that are mainly under the control of the caretakers, for example, prisons, in-patient units, and partial hospitalization units.

Process Consultation

The theoretical roots of the process consultation model lie in social psychology. It is a problem solving approach that seeks to make people more aware of the interpersonal transactions that are continually affecting their work productivity and morale. Process consultation is frequently employed in organization development efforts. Organization development is a collaborative program between consultant and consultees to enhance organizational functioning through improved use of organizational data. It is a program aimed at creating renewed and renewing systems that optimally utilize the talent of participants (employees, managers, etc.) while maintaining humane, growth-enhancing environments.

Because the work of most organizations is done in small groups, process consultants concentrate on helping members of the group to see interactional patterns that are interfering with task accomplishment. Such patterns might include: poor agenda setting, inconsistent decision making styles, hidden personal agendas, inappropriately high levels of competition, scapegoating of one member or one other group, or poor leadership skills on the part of the chief administrator.

Process consultants might also examine the system for structural or procedural problems. Rarely are process consultants content experts about products per se. They use such techniques as agenda setting, survey data feedback, confrontation meetings, administrative coaching, and process analysis of meetings to improve *how* things are done in an organization.

Schein's (1969) work emphasizing business organizations and the work of Schmuck and associates (1972) in schools are basic readings for this model. It is not, unlike mental health and behavioral consultation, as frequently used or asked for in schools. This occurs for a number of reasons:

1. School-related professionals are rarely trained in the process consultation model.
2. School systems are run (like many other systems) with a pervasive denial that the emotions of the staff (i.e., maintenance concerns) have any effect on work with students ("Professionalism" standards).
3. The benefits to the students from process consultation are usually indirect. Such benefits have been documented in some cases, but not in others (Bassin & Gross, 1978; Keutzer, Fosmire, Diller & Smith, 1971; Schmuck, 1968; Tollett, 1971). The goals usually involve improvement of staff-to-staff relations. Teachers and administrators feel more press from child concerns.
4. A fear is present in every organizational setting of honest direct encounter between peers and between staff and administration.

There are forces, however, that indicate that process consultation may become more common in schools. For example, the rise in teacher unions has forced school administrators to deal more evenly and more frequently with teacher demands. In addition, the emerging team approach to instruction, remediation, and special services has highlighted the need for effective group functioning to better serve children.

Like mental health consultants, good process consultants are highly skilled. They must have a grasp of a number of content areas and have excellent interpersonal skills. Unlike mental health consultation, there is no reliance on unconscious dynamics as an explanation of work-related difficulties. The site of the pathology is not within the persons involved but might be conceptualized as existing in their social interactions. This behavioral-group-dynamic orientation does not suggest, however, that human motivation is ignored by the process consultant. Wise consultants recognize the diversity of need that exists within a group (e.g., cooperation, competition, inclusion, punishment). The simplistic notion that honest encounter necessarily solves all organizational problems is just that—simplistic. Process consultation is oriented toward making manifest the many levels of communication that exist within an organization and examining the effects of communication on each level of the organization as it pertains to the attainment of group goals.

Advocacy

Almost any group of consultation trainers can be sent into instant debate by the suggestion that advocacy is a form of consultation (e.g. Amos, 1981). Advocacy, unlike the other models, is typically seen as highly political—one group is fighting another for a greater share of the resources. The advocate consultant is usually identified as the ally of the underpowered group. Therefore, the advocate, while aiding one group, is necessarily working to limit/change/destroy another group. Our view (shared by others, e.g., Chesler & Arnstein, 1970; Chesler, Bryant & Crowfoot, 1976; Chesler & Crowfoot, 1975; Chesler & Lohman, 1971) is that all consultants are advocate consultants. Whenever a consultant assists a school, business, or agency in solving client or organizational problems, the consultant is facilitating the consultees' goals. The consultant is implicitly or explicitly espousing a set of political values.

In child-related work some predictable issues arise that may help clarify the meaning of advocacy. For example, a school psychologist whose code of ethics defines him or her as a child advocate is employed for years in a district that systematically withholds information about due process procedures from parents of handicapped children. The district is the school psychologist's employer and typically deserves the psychologist's support (American Psychological Association, 1979) but who is the client? Is the school psychologist to risk being fired by organizing parent groups in which the safeguards of Public Law 94-142 are explained? Should information be sent to parents in "plain brown wrappers"? How long should attempts to cause change *within the system* be maintained before going outside with public disclosure? There are no hard and fast answers to these questions. Only a personal decision about overriding values and the belief that every decision broadcasts a value will give guidance to those wishing to pursue advocacy.

The basic theory behind advocacy differs from the other models. Advocates believe in power, influence, and politics as motivating forces behind human behavior. People change when (1) their resources will be increased by the change, or (2) their resources will be decreased if they do not change. Alinsky (1946) points out, however, that although many people change, or contribute to a cause for selfish reasons, once involved in a worthwhile effort they become concerned for the good of others. Advocate consultants must have all the generic consultant skills plus those involved with organizing people and publicizing events.

The heart of the controversy surrounding advocacy consultation is this: Can you portray yourself as a consultant to a human service agency as you simultaneously (a) aid groups who have adversarial relationships with it, or (b) actually implement acts within the agency that are agency stressful?

One of special education's best known advocates, Douglas Biklen (1976), argues that one cannot combine service delivery and advocacy functions. The service provider—teacher, case-worker, ward attendant, psychologist, or administrator—is not in a position to evaluate his or her own services. It might be useful, however, while wholeheartedly agreeing with Biklen's position, to view advocacy functioning on a continuum of roles, functions, skills, and techniques. In moments of decisions when the good of one group is clearly *not* the good of the other, some service providers will desire the information and skills to ally themselves with a vulnerable underpowered group. At some point in a consultative relationship, consultants may realize that continuing to facilitate actual organizational goals is contrary to their values. Most people in human service delivery agencies would agree that they want to deliver services in a humane, just, and legal way. Consultants aware of discrepancies between beliefs and behaviors can be a very valuable resource. They can also be thorns in the system. Finding and keeping jobs may be one of the difficulties inherent in the decision to work as an advocate for underpowered or disenfranchized groups.

OVERVIEW

The models briefly presented above can be contrasted across a number of dimensions. In essence, each strives to increase the problem-solving capacity of the consultee. The relationship is always a triadic one, with consultant and consultee working on some troublesome issue. The issue may be a single person, a group, a communication process, or an institutional injustice.

Implementers of the models tend to work on somewhat different operational levels. For example, most mental health and behavioral consultation is done one-to-one or in small groups. (We are not including in-service training workshops as consultation per se.) In contrast, process consultation is primarily implemented in group settings. Advocacy is quite variable, but the probability of occasionally working with very large groups is higher in this model than in others.

Although in each model the role of the consultant is mainly that of a facilitator of others' work, there are some subtle differences. Caplan (1970), while arguing for a co-equal relationship, still presents the clinical expert consultant who entertains hypotheses about consultees and chooses targets for work without full disclosure to his or her "partner." Behavioral consultants have worked often as content experts with consultees and collaborators on implementation plans. The best behavioral consultants have learned to modify textbook procedures to fit classroom realities and teacher repertoires. This modification maximizes the behavioral consultants' influence, while minimizing their expert role. Process consultants also bring particular expertise into a relationship, but are committed to collaborative problem identification and strategy planning. They are mainly collaborators throughout the consultative relationship, although other roles such as administrative counselor, researcher, or conflict manager (third party consultation, Walton, 1969) are possible. The advocates' role dimensions vary greatly, but their role might be most generally described as that of ally. Typically, the relationship between consultant and consultee is more personal within the advocacy model than the other models. While mental health consultants will be watchful for transference, behavioral consultants for resistance, and process consultants for hidden agendas, advocate consultants are often friends. There is no therapy in progress, only a common cause.

The values and explicit awareness of values differ across models. Mental health consultants and behavioral consultants generally do not explicitly take value stances. The mental health consultant often carries the traditional therapeutic orientation that his or her personal values are of no consequence to the consultative relationship as long as adequate supervision is sought if impasses develop.

Many behavioral consultants still see their techniques as amoral, that is, having no inherent values orientation. They typically opt toward moving client behavior to acceptable levels of occurrence. The behavioral consultants act *as if* they value the status quo or norms of behavior as prescribed by those in authority. In fact, some proponents of behavioral techniques have alerted consultants to make more explicit values judgments so that powerful behavioral techniques are not used solely to make children quiet, still, and docile (O'Leary & Wilson, 1975).

Unlike these two models, process and advocacy have very explicit values. Process consultants value human over thing technology (Chin & Benne, 1976), long-range over short-range planning, process over product awareness, and an equalization of attention toward emotional as well as rational communication. As mentioned previously, advocate consultants are best known by their values. They tend most generally to value an equalization of resources among people.

The diversity among models permits thoughtful prescriptive planning on the part of the consultant. Although little is yet known about the relationships among consultant, consultee, problem, or organizational context and choice of model, it seems intuitively obvious that the existing models provide a rich source of world views through which to analyze and reframe problems.

STATUS AND DIRECTIONS

There are complex forces at work in many of the organizations that typically use external or internal consultants. In schools, for example, the effort to educate children in the least restrictive educational environment seems to predict greater consultant use. Simultaneously, the uncertain funding base plaguing many schools makes consultant use less likely or at least forces consultants to show some accountability for the funds expended.

Graduate training programs in school psychology, special education, clinical psychology, and social work are beginning to provide course work in consultation (Meyers, 1978). Our experience in training has been that once service providers become convinced of the conceptual rightness of consultative, preventive oriented services, they work hard to implement such a service delivery model. There are increasing numbers of people committed to consultation as one of their professional functions. At the same time, the "clinical press" becomes greater and greater. The pressure to provide one-to-one direct service has never been stronger. Schools, in particular, expect the mental health professional to *fix* the child.

Hopeful and dire signs are therefore appearing on the mental health horizon. The easy money and pro-mental health mentality of the 1960s are probably gone forever. But every problem that was with us then is still with us, usually in some exacerbated form. The need for efficient, thoughtful, innovative service is apparent. We hope to provide such a basis for innovative consultative service in this volume.

In the next chapter, the similarities among models will be highlighted again, this time in terms of core personal and interpersonal skills and qualities that all consultants must possess.

SUGGESTED READINGS

Engleberg, S. Open systems consultation: Some lessons learned from case experience. *Professional Psychology*, 1980. **11**, 972–979.

This paper is an attempt to conceptualize consultation in systems terms. An intersystem model is used to describe entry problems encountered by consultants. The first main topic discussed is the boundaries of systems. The second major topic involves input constituency and output constituency. The third topic in this paper is intersystemic relations.

Gutkin, T. B. Teacher perceptions of consultation services provided by school psychologists. *Professional Psychology*, 1980, **11**, 637–642.

The purpose of this study was to investigate whether teachers felt that their professional skills would improve as a function of working with consultants. One hundred seventy-two teachers at 12 different schools served as subjects. Twelve graduate students served as consultants. Consultation consisted of defining the task, analyzing the problem, devising alternative solutions, choosing a solution, implementing a solution, evaluating the solution, and recycling into the problem-solving sequence when results were not positive. At the conclusion of the 14-week intervention period, teachers were asked to fill out a questionnaire related to their feelings about consultation. Results showed that teachers felt it was desirable to have a consultant on the staff, consultation services were viewed as more effective than the traditional testing role, and working with a consultant would improve their professional skills.

Kurpius, D. Consultation theory and process: An integrated model. *Personnel and Guidance Journal*, 1978, **56**(6), 335–338.

It is important to differentiate between the traditional authority figure and today's consultant who is nonjudgmental and noncompetitive in his efforts to help other workers become more efficient and effective. Consultants must be aware of the uniqueness of their role, the various approaches to consultation, and the steps comprising the consultation process. Consultation is, by definition, triadic (consultant, consultee, client). Equal power, authority, and respect characterize the consultant-consultee working relationship. The author discusses four consulting modes: provision, prescriptive, collaborative, and mediation. The operational functions of consulting are: pre-entry, entry, information gathering, problem definition, determination of solution, statement of objectives, implementation of plan, evaluation, and termination. For individuals, groups, or organizations, it is important for the consultant to state his own definition of consultation, the appropriate mode for the situation, and to clarify the various stages of the consultation, reaching agreement at one stage before moving on to the next.

Kurpius, D., and Robinson, S. E. An overview of consultation. *Personnel and Guidance Journal*, 1978, **56**(6), 321–323.

This article presents a brief introduction to various aspects of consultation, vis-a-vis the setting, roles, and necessary skills, as well as its origins, utilizing an historic, developmental perspective. Orientation in the form of process, outcome, and futures is also introduced. This article, and the references cited, are helpful as initial explorations into the field of consultation. A grasp of the basic concepts included would also serve as a helpful baseline from which a group could work to develop a broader body of knowledge and skills.

Lighthall, F. A social psychologist for school systems. *Psychology in the Schools*, 1969, **6**, 3–12.

The article begins by contrasting two ways of understanding psychological events in the school. Psychological events can be seen as residing in and stemming from individual psychodynamics, or they can be seen as being located between and arising out of the interaction of individuals. Some implications of the social psychological viewpoint are stated and an analysis of the kinds of recurrent person-person and person-task relations that can be found in the social systems of any school is made. Some practical implications of this analysis are drawn regarding permanence in the system, the primary source of problem formulations and solutions, and limitations of change in the system.

McGreevy, C. P. Training consultants: Issues and approaches. *Personnel and Guidance Journal*, 1978, **56**(7), 423–435.

The most common approach to training consultants is analogous to the relationship between journeyman and apprentice; the experienced consultant models skills through on-the-job demonstrations and the novice learns. Universities offer few courses or programs for consultant preparation, but the instructional methods used to prepare human service professionals do much to influence their behavior when they later become consultants. Students are exposed to authority and position power figures, and come to believe that the role of the consultant is that of an expert. The emerging view of consultation, however, is not that of an expert, but toward a process-oriented facilitator role. Consultant training should begin with a consideration of the dynamic relationship between environments or systems and people. The task of the consultant is to assist clients to better cope with or solve problems within their environments, by utilizing the skills of diagnosing, teaching, and counseling. General guidelines for training consultants include exercises and role-playing, under-standing of the person–system interrelationship, concepts of authority–responsibility, utilization of people as resources, knowledge of community values vs. bureaucratic values, positional power vs. personal power, and the importance of (with accompanying skills to) studying change.

Schein, E. H. The role of the consultant: Content expert or process facilitator? *Personnel and Guidance Journal*, 1978, **56**(6), 339–345.

Any human problem-solving activity can be analyzed at the level of both content (the actual task to be performed or the problem to be solved) and process (the way the problem is defined, worked through, and solved). There are subtle connections between the content of what is being done and the process by which it occurs. Often, the content is mirrored by the process, and one of the consutant's most difficult decisions is when and how to focus on the content/process interaction.

2

Personal Qualities: Interpersonal Skills

Some recent research is devoted to developing profiles of good consultants. In the construction of the profiles, both consultants and consultees have described the characteristics that facilitate relationship building and problem resolution (Bergan & Tombari, 1976; Cutler & McNeil, 1964; Mannino, 1969; Robbins & Spencer, 1968; Schowengerdt, Fine, & Poggio, 1976). Consultants and consultees are not in complete agreement but, in general, the personal qualities necessary for good consultation include: friendly, egalitarian, open, good with groups, non-threatening expertise, awareness of and sympathy toward the situations of the consultees, supportive, flexible, efficient, and good follow-up or follow-through skills. Obviously, being a perfect person facilitates your identity as a consultant! In lieu of perfection, however, the possibility exists of practicing the skills associated with each of these areas.

What is striking about the various personal qualities that add to consultant effectiveness is that they seem to describe not a content expert but a process expert. Consultees report valuing positive, supportive consultants as much or more than even very knowledgeable but authoritarian experts. Sarason (e.g., 1969) has frequently written about a "being there" kind of skill that the consultant must have. He reports that, in his experience, there were many teachers who appreciated a sympathetic, understanding listener. They could go back to their classroom problems not with new techniques perhaps, but with increased self-esteem and security. We emphasize this, because it is basic to all of consultation training and practice. *Just knowing something very well does not guarantee that you will help others know it.* Good consultants, good therapists, and good teachers are people who really like other people, who care, not in a primary way about some issue or position, but about the people with whom they seek to relate. Skills important to the

The King's Library

establishment and maintenance of good consultation interactions are presented in this chapter. Training exercises are suggested that might be implemented by teachers of consultation methods or used by individuals seeking to enhance their skills development. The training techniques described have been used in a year-long sequence of training at the graduate level. Each of the strategies has been evaluated by student responses and by effects on field performance (Conoley, 1981; Conoley & Clark, 1980).

PERSONAL PROCESS SKILLS

Consultation trainers must be willing to screen students who wish to enter training and be willing to devise skill-building activities. Those practicing professionals who want to add consultation to their repertoire must be willing to introspect a little and seek feedback from others concerning some of the qualities listed above. Consultants who constantly describe consultees as "resistant" may be in need of some skills acquisition training (e.g., Goldstein, 1981). Table 2.1 is an assessment tool for measuring some important process skills. Aspiring consultants might use the rating form to develop a personal profile, in order to identify areas where skill development could be advantageous. In training sequences, these skills can be practiced and refined. Such practice is easy to build into small group (7-9 people) supervision.

Table 2.1. Self-Analysis Form for Important Consultant Skills

	7	6	5	4	3	2	1
1.	Expresses affection (can say positive, supportive statements to another)						Does not express affection
2.	Accepting (nonjudgmental, nonevaluative)						Not Accepting
3.	Flexible (varies behaviors according to the situation)						Inflexible
4.	Pursues issues (once issues arise, stays with them)						Drops Issues

Table 2.1. (*Continued*)

	5. 7	6	5	4	3	2	1
	Empathic						Nonempathic
	(is sensitive to						
	other's emotional						
	states)						
	6. 7	6	5	4	3	2	1
	Congruent						Noncongruent
	(consistency between						
	feelings and behaviors)						
	7. 7	6	5	4	3	2	1
	Able to confront						Unable to
	(ability to confront						Confront
	group and individuals						
	with salient issues)						
	8. 7	6	5	4	3	2	1
	Self-disclosing						Closed
	(open, clearly						
	states own feelings)						
	9. 7	6	5	4	3	2	1
	Able to live with stress						Unable to
	(able to function						live with
	in the presence						stress
	of intense emotions)						
	10. 7	6	5	4	3	2	1
	Perceptive (level						Nonperceptive
	of understanding/insight						
	and ability to						
	communicate these)						
	11. 7	6	5	4	'3	2	1
	Listens well (ability						Listens poorly
	to grasp meaning and						
	affect in communication)						
	12. 7	6	5	4	3	2	1
	Sums up well						Sums up
	(ability to summarize						poorly
	and facilitate movement)						
	13. 7	6	5	4	3	2	1
	Resilient						Nonresilient
	(ability to hang in						
	and bounce back)						

Continued on p. 18

Table 2.1. (*Continued*)

14.	7	6	5	4	3	2	1
	Caring (concern for others)						Not caring

15.	7	6	5	4	3	2	1
	Views self positively (quality of self-image)						Views self negatively

16.	7	6	5	4	3	2	1
	In touch with own aggressive feelings (ability to admit and check punitive, purely self-enhancing responses)						Not in touch with aggressive feelings

17.	7	6	5	4	3	2	1
	Expresses aggression effectively (confronts others without personal attacks)						Too punitive or too mild

18.	7	6	5	4	3	2	1
	Able to anticipate (intervenes with awareness of possible consequences)						Unable to anticipate

19.	7	6	5	4	3	2	1
	Distancing (appropriate personal involvement that facilitates communication)						Distancing ineffective (too close or too far away)

20.	7	6	5	4	3	2	1
	Takes risks (willing to experiment with new behavior)						Does not take risks

We have used the following activities in our training efforts. The skills that these activities are designed to enhance are listed after each description.

1. Consultation classmates spend 40 minutes together sharing positive feedback with each other. They write the feedback down and return to the group to debrief (e.g., express affection, self-disclosing, caring, views self positively, takes risks).

2. Consultation classmates spend 40 minutes together sharing areas of concern or negative feedback. They write the feedback down and return to the group to debrief (e.g., able to confront, able to live with stress, expresses aggression effectively, takes risks).
3. Classmates prepare behavioral contracts for improved performance in their consultation sites and share these with supervisory group (e.g., pursues issues, sums up well, able to anticipate).
4. Each class member plans, implements, and evaluates a group process intervention aimed at improving the performance/cohesiveness of the supervisory group (e.g., pursues issues, perceptive, able to confront, able to anticipate, takes risks).
5. Two all-day laboratory sessions are held during which consultation skills, especially careful listening and problem identification, are stressed. The second laboratory also emphasizes process consultation, teambuilding and organization development (e.g., accepting, flexible, empathic, congruent, perceptive, listens well, sums up well).
6. When consultants present cases during supervision, they play the role of the consultee, while the instructor or other member of the group acts as the consultant (e.g., empathic, perceptive, caring, distancing).

GIVING FEEDBACK

In addition to the skills already mentioned, feedback skills are critical in consultation. The consultant maintains a nonjudgmental attitude toward consultees, but must be skilled in sharing important information with them. Consultants must also seek and respond nondefensively to feedback from the consultee. Effective giving and receiving of feedback models skills for the consultee, as well as increases the impact of the services provided by the consultant.

Feedback is often misunderstood as implying only negative information. In fact, feedback is any information that can be shared with another that informs that person about the effects of his or her behavior on us. The information is shared as a way to help another consider a behavior change. Feedback is, therefore, not simply "what I saw you do and my evaluation of it." Rather, it is a process that should be initiated among people who really care about one another and who are not *demanding* a behavior change but, rather, trying to facilitate one. Clearly, this is one of the consultant's critical roles. In assessing feedback skills, the following guidelines might be useful.

1. Make a decision as to the usefulness or potential influence of your communication on your *relationship* with another. Be sure you are not seeking to punish the other.

2. *Describe* what you have observed the other do in terms that are not evaluative, demeaning, or judgmental. Describe the way the behavior has affected you.
3. State the feedback in a somewhat *tentative way* so that the listener feels free to probe for more information. Also, the consultee should not feel pressured because you, as consultant, tell him or her to change.
4. Focus feedback on *aspects* of the other *that can be changed.* Telling someone that his or her "blackness," for example, makes you uncomfortable cannot facilitate change in the ethnicity of the consultee. Such a statement says more about you than about the consultee. Consultation is not undertaken for the personal growth of the consultant.
5. *Timing* is important. Optimally, give feedback when it is asked for; when the person seems able to hear (i.e., is not preoccupied with something else), when the person is not overwhelmed with feedback from others, and as close to the occurrence of the target behavior as possible. Do not give feedback because *you* have had enough or are angry or punitive.
6. Check the *listeners' understanding* of the feedback by asking them to repeat what you have said.

When doing consultation, direct feedback (especially negative feedback) is often seen as a last resort. School consultants we have known (and loved!) have tended to provide classroom management procedures to consultees as a first strategy. They do not focus on the teacher as implementor, but rather *act as if* a good idea will be implemented. Sometimes, exactly that happens. An already skilled, flexible teacher takes a new idea and "runs with it." Great! When that doesn't happen, however, the consultant is placed in the position of coming up with more and better ideas (obviously this can't go on forever) or carefully examining the variables impeding the new program. When observation reveals that the teacher's implementation is incorrect and/or the teacher is emitting very many counterproductive behaviors, the consultant often feels pressed to give the teacher feedback that is likely to be experienced as negative. Direct and indirect confrontation may be necessary. These examples are from tapes of consultant-consultee interactions.

Direct Confrontation

Your frequent use of sarcastic statements (like . . .) with the children makes me feel somewhat intimidated. Do you suppose the children could experience those statements in this way?

I felt that you were anxious about disciplining the class because of the number of times you said you were sorry about telling them what to do. Do you feel somewhat uneasy about controlling the class?

Indirect Confrontation

> There's no way that this child will qualify for out-of-classroom special services. How can I help you cope better with the situation in the classroom?

> The home situation is terrible. But, all we can control are these 6 hours— probably the best, most consistent 6 hours of this child's day. How can we structure a predictable context for _____?

The difference between the direct and indirect feedback confrontations is the focus on the person *or* the issue. "You are making sarcastic statements" or "You seem anxious." Compare these to "Special class placement is impossible" or "The home may be impossible to modify." Using directly confrontive feedback means that you place the site of the problem on the consultee. With indirectly confrontive feedback, you reconceptualize the problem as the issue it represents and place the problem on the issue. We could be tempted to say to a teacher:

> I have not observed you trying the techniques we discussed to facilitate _____'s learning. I'm wondering if you are unwilling to keep him in your class or are hoping that he will be moved?

We *could* say it, but such a direct question about a teacher's professionalism seems clearly relationship-threatening. If possible, it is better to *indirectly* confront. Because consultation is not therapy, you have not been given sanction to talk about the consultee, only the client. Mental health consultants often prepare a teacher during informal contract negotiations by explaining that part of the focus will be his or her feelings. This mitigates the warning against direct confrontation (Meyers, 1981; Meyers, Parsons, & Martin, 1979).

This extended discussion of confrontive feedback should not suggest that we see feedback as the last resort. Right at the beginning stages of problem identification and problem analysis (Bergan & Tombari, 1976), the consultant should be providing the consultee with feedback about how his or her classroom context and style match potential strategies. During a classroom observation, for example, the consultant can develop well conceptualized feedback about the target children and the teacher. This immediate connection between strategy and strategist opens the way for continuous feedback rather than "last straw" attempts. The following example may be helpful (taken from an actual case study).

> In a second grade classroom, Mrs. Smith, a 28-year teaching veteran, experienced difficulty with classroom management. Two boys were focal, but the teacher described the whole class as being somewhat out of control. The consul-

tant observed that the teacher "jumped" from disruption to disruption in the classroom, made many irrelevant verbal statements, but did make some use of group and individual positive statements. She was also a person who was willing to begin new strategies but who would, after a day or so, lose confidence that they would work and so discontinue use.

The consultant worked on a plan involving the presentation of stars or stickers to well-behaved children. Although somewhat successful (the teacher and principal commented upon a mild/moderate class improvement), the strategy was inconsistently applied, because of the teacher's long-standing habit of responding to disruptive children. The consultant's first impulse was to give the teacher feedback on her poor plan implementation. A further analysis of the problem situation suggested, however, that a plan involving positive attention did not fit the teacher's style. The fact that it was working at all was a credit to the strength of positive consequences. The consultant and teacher worked out another plan involving the two target boys and the classroom. Some of the plan components included (a) positive individual attention to the target children contingent on paper completion (they were already doing some work); (b) classroom rules worked on, one per day, until five or six had been formulated and learned by children; (c) a daily surprise activity (list suggested by teacher) for well-behaving children; and finally, (d) an hour off per month to observe the class as the consultant took over. In addition, the consultant began an effort of consultee-centered consultation, now seeing the teacher's distractibility as a sign of stress or anxiety. This rather "shotgun" approach proved, over the course of 10 months, to be quite successful. It is, of course, impossible to isolate the most influential of the plan components.

The results of this case and many others highlight an important way to incorporate feedback and plan implementation. When the second plan was worked out, each step (except the consultee-centered mental health consultation) was paired with observable teacher behavior. During implementation, teacher feedback was not very risky.

Consultant: Here's something I already see you do. You lean down to Matt and compliment him quietly when you see him working. Did you realize that you did that twice yesterday morning, and he was on-task for 15 minutes following each time you did it?

Consultee: No, I didn't. Of course now, you know Matt. He has his good and bad days. One time when I leaned down to talk with him, he turned so fast that he bumped my face. Now he was nice about that. He said, "Did I hurt you? I'm sorry."

Consultant: So you are already aware of it in some ways—how much impact you have on him sometimes. I wonder if you could do more of what you're already doing to Kent and Matt in terms of quiet positive statements. I'll keep a log of the results.

Consultee: If you think so. Of course now, you know I have some weak ones in here—some like I've had every year, but some others that are really something.

Consultant: You have a lot of experience. I bet you've developed lots of stuff for the kids to do in terms of activities over the past years. I really admire your willingness to try new things.

Consultee: Well, you have to be willing to change. Kids are different. Look at this (points to file). This is my collection of 28 years' worth of activities.

Consultant: What a resource! Would you mind if I looked at that stuff? I'm sure it would give me ideas for other teachers.

Consultee: Some of it is all messed up. I need to organize.

Consultant: I'd love to help you.

Consultee: Well, let's see what we have. . . .

This is an actual excerpt from a taped session with this teacher. The consultant began building on teacher strengths, instead of building plans on her weaknesses. Each component was tied to an openly discussed teacher propensity.

RECEIVING FEEDBACK

It is almost impossible and very undesirable to avoid getting feedback from others. In fact, avoiding feedback is mentioned by Rae-Grant (1972) as one sure-fire way to be a failure as a consultant. Somewhat formal evaluation instruments meant to provide feedback to the consultant are provided in a subsequent chapter. Often, however, the feedback, positive and negative, comes rather spontaneously. Consultants must be able to gracefully accept what is offered. It is good modeling and encourages the flow of valid information (Argyris, 1971) for consultants to elicit feedback routinely and respond nondefensively. Here are some basic guidelines.

1. Develop a relaxation response (for example, deep breathing or muscle relaxation) to use when you become aware that feedback is imminent.
2. Listen very closely to everything the person is saying. Do not begin to formulate a response.
3. Try to catch the essence of the feelings the other is sharing.
4. Before speaking, get in touch with your own feelings. Give your feelings a name.

5. Try to repeat what you've heard. Ask for clarification, if necessary. In a group, check to see if others see you in a similar way.
6. Remember that you have no way to absolutely control the way others see you. You are completely responsible only for your own behavior. Perhaps you will decide to change the behavior. You cannot be sure that another's feelings about you will change concomitantly.
7. Unless there is some clear content misunderstanding between you and the feedback giver, do *not* give reasons why you have behaved the way you did. The person (if he or she read the earlier part of this chapter) is not asking you to change. You are being told how behavior X affects that person. That information is valuable even if you didn't mean to do X or you thought that person asked for X, and so on, and so on.

Here are some examples of actual consultee-to-consultant feedback conversations.

Example 1

Consultee: You are wonderful. I really appreciate your suggestions and support.

Consultant: Thank you. Your openness has made me feel very successful about our work.

Example 2

Consultee: I had the whole class waiting for you. Where were you?

Consultant: I'm sorry you were inconvenienced. Which day are we talking about?

Consultee: Wednesday.

Consultant: Thank you for mentioning this to me. I have to find out why my telephone messages are not being passed on. I called the office Wednesday morning with a message to you, but I guess I needed to be more explicit that you *needed* to know that I was down with the flu.

Consultee: I didn't know you had the flu! We waited only a few minutes before I figured you weren't coming.

In training consultants, it is possible to design exercises that facilitate the occurrence of feedback among members of a class. The activities described earlier in the chapter have feedback as an important element. Additional training or practice strategies include:

1. Classmates rate themselves and then the others, using the form given as table 2.1. Discrepancies in ratings are discussed.
2. After each laboratory activity (e.g., simulations, role plays), a debriefing period is given, so group members can share feelings and observations with one another.
3. Role plays are videotaped and played back with feedback from instructor and other class members.
4. Individual meetings between the instructor/supervisor and each class member can be arranged for mutual feedback. The instructor/supervisor comments on class observations and shares feedback from the field placement. The student shares feedback to the instructor about personal impact and course relevance, organization, etc.
5. Cross-visitation to placement sites. The consultation classmates visit each others' consultation placements and write brief feedback reports to one another.

Once out of graduate school, sources for helpful feedback must be more thoughtfully engineered. Every consultant needs a peer supervisor. It is absolutely necessary to bounce ideas, strategies, and biases off of another knowledgeable person. The most common complaint among independent practitioners is the loneliness and sense of isolation from the professional mainstream that they feel.

LISTENING

Skills in *really* hearing what the other person has said and making the speaker feel *really* heard is another of the generic skills necessary for consultation. Good listening is composed of verbal skills and nonverbal habits. The verbal components of good listening skills include acknowledging, reflecting, paraphrasing, summarizing, clarifying, and elaborating.

Acknowledging

Acknowledging refers to words such as "yes," "umm hmm," "really," "wow," "right," and "good." These words and sounds are helpful in encouraging consultees to speak. They also communicate some awareness of the emotional content of the consultee's message.

Reflecting

Reflective listening is the process of repeating back to the consultee his or her words. The repetitions are not, of course, done in a parrot-like fashion. The consultant can carefully choose the words, phrases, or sentences to reflect back to the consultee, in order to underline the importance of some information or to move the consultation in a particular direction. For example, if a consultee says, "I'm so frustrated that Johnny runs around all day!", the consultant can reflect either the first phrase, "Oh, you're feeling frustrated," or the second, "He runs around all day, huh?" The first choice will direct the session toward the consultee's emotional responses to his or her situation; the second will begin the process of behavioral analysis.

Paraphrasing

Paraphrasing is somewhat more complex than reflective listening. It involves substituting synonyms for the consultee's words and saying those interpretations back. In paraphrasing, the consultant can heighten or reduce the power of what was said, slightly change a meaning, or be very faithful to the message of the consultee. Such a process is used not to test the vocabulary skills of the consultant, but to cue the consultee to slight variations in his or her message. Using the previous example, the consultant might respond, "You seem to be angry at Johnny's activity," or "You're concerned about Johnny's movement." Paraphrases need to be said tentatively, so that the consultee can feel free to challenge the consultant's interpretation. Such challenges are often very instructive. A consultee may dispute the word "angry." Many teachers, for example, do not believe they are supposed to get *angry*. Such an emotion is unprofessional. A consultant can use such an interaction to discuss the indirect effects and costs of suppressed anger. The consultant can do so without disagreeing with the consultee.

Summarizing

Periodically, a consultant can provide summary statements. These might describe what behavioral antecedents or consequents have been thus far described, or what remedial strategies have been suggested. There are different views on the importance of summarizing (e.g., Haynes, 1978, versus Tombari & Bergan, 1978). Its skillful use seems to help decisions be made, information be saved, and meetings end. A consultee will sometimes express pleased surprise that a consultant has listened carefully enough to be able to list back most of the conversation's important points. Written records of the session can be used. The Progress Notes given as table 2.2 are an example of a way to save information through written summarization.

Clarifying

Asking questions that invite elaboration on previously made points is clarification. Consultants should seek to completely understand what the consul-

Table 2.2. Progress Notes in Consultation

Progress Report To _____	
From _____	
	Psychology Consultant
We've met with _____ Date _____	
Regarding _____	

We've discussed these concerns:

Possible strategies:

We've tried these strategies: | *Effective* | *Not Effective*

We are working on the following:

Comments:

---

tee has said about a problem. Sometimes, the consultant understands an issue very quickly. This is good if evidenced through questions that reflect a complex insight. It is not good if the quick insight leads the consultant to make incorrect assumptions, or results in the consultee not getting an opportunity to review the relevant data in his or her possession. Consultants ask questions, not simply to gain information, but also to give consultees practice in putting their information together in helpful, problem-solving ways. Clarifying does not mean rapid-fire questions following from the consultant's agenda. Strike a balance between following the consultee's lead and structuring an interaction to be efficient and effective.

Elaborating

To elaborate means to build upon what has already been introduced into a conversation. Often we can begin an elaboration by saying, "Taking off from what you've said . . ." or "I'm thinking about what you suggested. Would this fit as part of that plan? . . . " Elaborating has a number of benefits in a problem-solving sequence. First, it allows for more complex and comprehensive plans to be formulated. Second, it makes people feel invested in the process, because their ideas have been heard, valued, and used by another. It is critical, of course, to give credit to others when building on their ideas. In consultation, elaboration is especially helpful, because it highlights the collaborative nature of the plans being considered.

PROBLEM-SOLVING SKILLS

Much of what has gone before, in terms of facilitating interpersonal skills, will contribute to effective problem solving. In addition, it is helpful to have a plan or regular steps to follow when faced with a troubling issue. Table 2.3 is a typical seven-step sequence. The sequence deserves some elaboration, because there are special pitfalls at each step.

There is convincing research in consultation (Bergan & Tombari, 1975) that problem formulation or problem identification is the most important part of problem solving. This may seem obvious—you cannot solve a problem before you know what it is. In practice, however, there is a strong tendency for consultants (and everyone else) to jump to generating solutions before they have a clear, mutually understood problem definition. Another way to describe this error is a confusion between "what" and "how" (Conoley & Barnes, 1980). Before struggling with *how* to deal with a problem, people should spend significant energy on *what* the problem includes. Bergan and Tombari suggest an analysis phase during which the environment in

Table 2.3. Steps to Problem Solving

Seven-Step Strategy:

1. Problem Formulation
   State the problem and set goals.
   What do we want to do?

2. Brainstorming
   Ideas to achieve goals; listening skill.
   Follow rules for brainstorming; no judgments made about ideas presented.

3. Evaluate Ideas
   Narrow them down according to some criteria, focus on each idea's pros and cons, prioritize, forecast consequences.

4. Integrate
   Ideas into coherent *plan of action*.
   Develop strategy to implement ideas—What do/How do/ What look like/ Work division-assign roles.

5. Do It
   Go ahead and do your plan.

6. Evaluate Outcomes
   Strengths, weaknesses. Did we achieve our goal?

7. Redo
   Improve design if necessary, repeating all or part of plan.

Answer questions . . . and clarify the plan.

which the problem occurs is investigated: The skills, talents, and deficits of the people involved are discussed; the antecedents and consequences of the troublesome event are specified; and data from others in the child's environment, past and present, are collected. In this way, the problem and its context are completely understood before moving toward brainstorming solutions.

Once a problem is clearly defined, the possible solutions are often obvious. Beginning consultants are most often fearful that they will not have good suggestions to make. This concern will be mitigated if they and their consultees have a clear idea of what they are working on. Brainstorming ideas may not be a guarantee of high quality ideas, but it does set the tone for acceptance and divergent thinking.

When choosing among the solutions generated, it's good to make the criteria for choice explicit. For example, feasible (i.e., easy to implement) solutions are preferable to grandiose, disruptive solutions. Solutions that can be implemented with only minimal guidance from a consultant are preferable to ones that are mostly dependent on consultant involvement. Solutions that build upon existing structures or habits are preferable to ones that entail lots of new learning or procedural changes. Early in the consultation relationship, the consultant may not have too much credibility and, therefore, not inspire the consultee with energy needed to make such changes.

Finally, whatever solution is chosen, the choice should sound tentative. Even if the consultant is positive that this is THE ANSWER, such enthusiasm should not be communicated to the consultee. Consultants can help consultees realize that many different approaches may have to be tried before improvement is apparent. Consultees need also to realize that nothing works forever. They must understand, for example, that changing environmental contingencies may not "cure" a problem. The problem might (will) reappear when it is again sustained by environmental rewards and punishments. This is a difficult concept to transmit. Most of us regard problem behavior, for example, as residing within a person. We fail to see the complex of forces that sustain or inhibit a particular behavior. Lewin's (1951) and, more recently, Apter's (1982) and Rhodes and Tracy's (1972) formulations of ecological theory are important to understand before beginning the problem-solving process.

When developing the plan of action, it is important to be as specific as possible, especially about roles and time lines. Often, consultees leave a consultation session believing that the consultant is about to accomplish most of the plan and do it immediately. Being clear avoids feelings of disappointment later in the relationship. If the plan seems too cumbersome or demanding for the consultee to manage alone, it is probably not a good plan.

During implementation, consultants should keep in touch with consultees. This is true even if the consultant has no active part in plan implementation.

Consultees may need clarification of a point or may simply need reassurance that they are progressing as planned. In some very unsurprising research (Tyler & Fine, 1974; White & Fine, 1976), it was discovered that the consultees greatly prefer intensive involvement with the consultant while they are carrying out jointly developed suggestions. More of a plan will actually be implemented if such contact is maintained.

Evaluation is a very important, yet often neglected, part of the problem-solving sequence. Sometimes the consultant and consultee decide the plan is not working but do not specify whether the plan needs to be changed, abandoned, or tried for a longer period. More often, a strategy is tried, does not seem effective, and is abandoned with no follow-up analysis by the consultant. This reduces the amount of new information available to both the consultant and the consultee. Once again, the consultant must create the expectation that many strategies may have to be attempted, and that the failure of one does not mean that consultation or attempts to improve the situation should be terminated.

AN OPENNESS TO THE UNLIKELY

The problem-solving steps just described are very helpful. There is, however, another dimension of problem solving that is harder to define or sequence. This is problem solving that requires skills in the reformulation of problem statements and seemingly incongruous, illogical solution generation. Watzlawick, Weakland, and Fisch (1974) describe this process as *second order change*. They draw a distinction between second order change (i.e., real change or innovation) and *first order change* (i.e., simply more of the same). It is very important for all consultants to be familiar with their conceptualizations about change. One advantage of knowing the various models of consultation is that it provides various world views with which to examine a problem. Flexibility in applying models is a great consultative advantage, because it facilitates the possibility of second order change. Real change usually depends on the ability to see a problem from an entirely new perspective. Sometimes this new perspective leads us to see the solutions as the real problems. For example, a manager who complains about the untrustworthiness of the staff may put locks on all the phones during lunch hours and after work. The manager may also implement an elaborate surveillance system to monitor arrivals, departures, sick days, etc. The staff may respond with increased attempts to "beat the system" and decreased morale and cohesiveness. A second order change strategy might be to abandon all monitoring procedures (e.g., locks, time clocks) that implicitly suggest that the workers are untrustworthy. A manager may find such advice inconceivable. In other words, do less to accomplish more. The problem may not be unmotivated staff but incorrectly motivated staff. The apparent problems with a staff may not come from *inside* the individual worker, but from the climate of distrust that is projected primarily from the manager.

A mastery of the various models of consultation may help a consultant reconceptualize a problem a number of times, until a helpful problem formulation is attained. This skill, although fairly simple to describe, is extremely difficult to master. All of us tend to get "stuck" in our ways of seeing the world.

In addition, the consultant can practice the process of reframing. This involves casting a problem in a new light, emphasizing the positive aspects of the problem over its negative consequences, and highlighting what adaptive purpose the problem serves. For example, a child's constant talking to the teacher or clinging behavior can be seen as evidence of the child's positive attachment to a teacher, rather than merely as an annoying habit. By emphasizing attachment over irritation, the consultant can show the teacher how influential he or she can be in a child's life. Or, the same behavior could be conceptualized as a normal developmental process necessary for the subsequent appearance of independence. In like manner, consultants may be able to point out how a child's misbehavior is symptomatic of physical problems not under the immediate volition of the child. For example, one child client had been described as exhibiting annoying and somewhat bizarre self-stimulating behaviors in class (e.g., noise making, rocking, hand clapping, head rolling) by a teacher who had cajoled, rewarded, and finally, corporally punished the child. The child was at or above grade level in work but did not hand in all assignments. Careful observation and interviewing led the consultant to discover that the child was experiencing petit-mal seizures. This new understanding of the behaviors led to an immediate improvement in the very strained teacher/child relationship. The improvement significantly preceded the medical alleviation of the child's symptoms. Obviously, the "problem" was not the actual behaviors, but the teacher's perception of the child as a willfully disobedient student. The behaviors had always been of relatively low frequency and duration and went mainly unnoticed by the rest of the class. A similar situation, related to masturbatory behaviors, was described by Robinowitz (1979).

CONCLUSIONS

It is no doubt clear, even by the end of chapter 2, that consulting well is a challenging role. Table 2.4 provides a summarizing checklist of skills. Our experience is that it is very difficult to do a very good job at consulting. Good work seems never accidental or serendipitous. Table 2.5 contains some advice that can be considered by those who may feel there is nothing new to

Table 2.4. Checklist of Consultant Skills

Does the Consultant:

_____ Show respect for the consultee

_____ Set a comfortable climate

_____ Use appropriate terms and language

_____ ʻAsk questions that do not intrude upon the consultee's personal life

_____ Act in a nonjudgmental and nonevaluative way

_____ Keep personal problems out of the consultant-consultee relationship

_____ Demonstrate sensitivity to the consultee's work problem, perhaps by sharing own experiences

_____ Show interest and enthusiasm for the case (e.g., eye contact)

_____ Assure consultee that he/she has the right to accept or reject what the consultant suggests

_____ Assure the consultee that all information is confidential

_____ Ask client- or consultee-centered questions

_____ Demonstrate flexibility dependent upon needs of the consultee

_____ Ask questions that will give the consultant more information about the organizational system

_____ Demonstrate a coordinate relationship

_____ Ask for feedback from consultee

_____ Set a time for the next appointment

Table 2.5. Twelve Easy Steps for Failure as a Mental Health Consultant

1. Know it all.
2. Learn nothing about consultee.
3. Be unaware of your own motives.
4. Be definite, dogmatic, unyielding.
5. Sulk when your advice is not taken.
6. Use ambiguity to your own advantage.
7. Avoid feedback mechanisms.
8. Keep professional status in the forefront.
9. Conspire to cause unwanted, unsanctioned change.
10. Form alliances with subgroups.
11. Pick a few consultees as therapy patients.
12. Interpret consultee's motives with all available jargon.

Source: Adapted from Q. Rae-Grant, "The Art of Being a Failure as a Consultant," in *Practical Aspects of Mental Health Consultation*, edited by J. Zusman and D. L. Davidson (Springfield, Ill.: Charles C. Thomas, 1972).

learn about the consulting role. At times, the unexpected casts us in a particularly positive light; but, more often, diligence and planning (yes, a little compulsivity) are the necessary ingredients for success. Skill acquisition and continued honest attempts to "know thyself" are critical for effective practice. As Rogers (1977) and Maslow (1971) have pointed out so eloquently, we never *become* perfect; it is only in the process of struggling that we make significant personal gains.

SUGGESTED READINGS

Bergan, J. R., and Neumann, A. J., II. The identification or resources and constraints influencing plan design in consultation. *Journal of School Psychology*, 1980, **18**(4), 317–323.

This study examines the effects of four types of consultant statements (plan, plan-tactic, specification emitters, other emitters) on three types of consultee responses (resources, constraints, others). Results from 50 problem analysis interviews shows that plan-tactic-elicitor statements by consultants have a positive effect on occurrence of resource responses by teachers. Consultant statements measured negatively influence the incidence of constraints from teachers. Whether elicitation of constraint statements from teachers would be helpful is open to question. Specifying constraint could be facilitative to the process; however, focus on activities the consultee is unwilling to perform could have a detrimental effect on the consultation process.

Cheney, P. Cognitive style and student programming ability: An investigation. *AEDS Journal*, 1980, 285–291.

The article explores the relationship between cognitive style and programming. It could possibly be generalized as a way of looking at consultee and consultant problem solving as a function of cognitive style. It includes reference to a test of cognitive style.

Fine, M. J., Grantham, V. L., and Wright, J. G. Personal variables that facilitate or impede consultation. *Psychology in the Schools*, 1979, **16**(4), 533–539.

Eleven consultant characteristics were addressed which facilitate or impede the consultant-teacher interaction. They are: (1) consultant ought to be aware of own needs, (2) take care of these needs, (3) try not to cure problems, (4) let go of preconceived beliefs, (5) be comfortable with no closure, (6) try not to be all things to all persons, (7) be flexible in types of response, (8) be explicit, (9) assist teachers' problem-solving abilities, (10) assist teachers to see alternatives to action, and (11) assist teachers to see the consequences of action plans so that they can choose. These variables were identified from the University of Kansas training model.

Hodges, A. How not to be a consultant. *Mental Hygiene*, 1970, **54**(1), 147–148.

This brief essay has two perspectives. The first is a serious statement concerning the significance of the consultant's personal stimulus value on the success or failure of the consultation process. The second is a humorous look at three attitudes guaranteed to undermine the consultation, and seven specific techniques to use to communicate these attitudes to the consultee.

3

Consultation Models: Particular Competencies

In Chapter 2, the generic skills needed to initiate and maintain consultative services were discussed. In this chapter, we will try to examine each model (mental health, behavioral, process, advocacy) more closely to present the particular competencies most strongly associated with each model.

It is difficult to separate out specific skills as unique for each model. For example, although organizational assessment skills are most highly visible in process or ecological consultation, such skills are necessary to some extent in all models. What follows, then, are particular emphases that a consultant would have in a given orientation. Each of the subsequent sections will list and explain needed skills and refer the reader to other sections in the chapter for further discussion of secondary competencies.

MENTAL HEALTH CONSULTATION

In many ways, mental health consultation is the most complex of consultation models. Its complexity is both its strength and its weakness in terms of implementation. The model, as explicated by Caplan (1970), Meyers et al. (1979), and Newmann (1945), emphasizes the intrapsychic, interpersonal, and organizational facets of change possibilities. It is most often characterized as the most psychodynamic of the consultation models. This is accurate, although to emphasize the psychodynamic aspects to the exclusion of its other facets greatly underestimates the model's breadth.

Some of the particular skills associated with the expert use of mental health consultation are specialized diagnostic and decision making skills, theme interference reduction, one downsmanship, avoidance of therapy, and relationship building.

Diagnostic and Decision Making Skills

During an initial interview, mental health consultants must choose the type of consultation to use for a particular problem and the primary target of their interventions. Consultees are rarely sophisticated enough to specify exactly what kind of help is needed and often have conceptualized the problem in a way that defies resolution. Very often, the parts of consultees' problem formulations that are missing are their contributions to the maintenance of the problem itself. A common example is the situation in which the consultee's attempt at solving a difficulty is really the problem. The teacher may report that constant reminding does not facilitate the student's completion of work. The consultant may notice that the consultee is agitated about the problem and exhausted from the frequent attention directed at the child. The best immediate strategy to attempt is to establish logical consequences for failing to accomplish work and suggest that the teacher refrain from any reminding. The consultee may have unwittingly reinforced the child's non-work habits by constant prompting and essentially rescuing the client from the contingencies associated with no production. Few of us have the flexibility to see how we maintain behaviors in ourselves and others that we find objectionable. The consultant's new perspective on a problem, even if not brilliant, is invaluable.

Consultants can choose among four possibilities, that is, client-centered, consultee-centered, program-centered, and administrative or consultee-centered administrative. Further, consultants must decide if the program or administrative work will be mainly client or consultee centered. As you may recall, this distinction refers to consultants' major target for change.

The consultant needs to retain the flexibility of moving among the mental health models as the situation demands. This presupposes, however, that the consultant is constantly conceptualizing and testing hypotheses about the sources of the problem between the consultant and the client. Typical sources of consultee difficulty are deficits in information, skills, self-confidence, or professional objectivity. These four troublesome areas can be improved by consultants providing information or suggestions about remedial techniques to the consultees and by using the consultation relationship as a means of increasing consultee confidence. The relationship is one in which the consultee should experience acceptance, encouragement, and respect for personal expertise. The concern for respect of the consultee is similar to a collaborative relationship rather then an expert relationship. In the expert relationship, the consultant retains most of the self-esteem enhancement. The problem solving nature of the collaborative relationship enhances the hopefulness and personal power that consultees may experience. Some problems cannot be solved in any final form but all can be worked on.

Theme Interference Reduction

Another source of consultee problems, loss of professional objectivity, is considered by Caplan to be the most salient of consultee problems. The prevalence of loss of objectivity is contested in a study by Gutkin (1981). Nevertheless, when loss of objectivity does occur, it can be caused by direct personal involvement, simple identification, transference, characterological distortion, or theme interference. Problem solving, clarification, modeling appropriate affect, and reality testing with the consultee are appropriate strategies to deal with all but the final two of these problems. Characterological distortions might require referral outside the consultee's agency for therapeutic help.

The problem of theme interference was first developed by Caplan (1970). This problem (defined in chapter 1) is handled through theme interference reduction. Theme interference reduction is accomplished in three phases: assessment of the theme, consultant intervention, and follow-up and ending (Caplan, 1970). The first problem facing the consultant is knowing whether an interfering theme is present. Caplan suggests assuming the existence of a theme unless the simpler areas of lack of skills, knowledge, or low self-esteem become evident. Themes may be operating in a consultee's handling of a case for the reasons given above. The clues to the consultant include strange lapses in competence in handling client problems by consultees who are typically quite skilled; intense emotionality in describing cases; unusual fascination with the details of a case; relating personal or somewhat tangential information in the problem description; and discrepant nonverbal cues indicating anxiety during the case discussion. Consultants aware of any cues that the consultee has somehow gotten personally involved with the client must formulate a tentative theme statement.

One seemingly obvious example of theme interference involved a teacher who was having significant difficulty managing a young boy in her classroom. She freely volunteered to the consultant that this boy resembled her own adolescent and quite wayward son. The consultant initially formulated a theme: *Boys who, like my son, are hard to manage, will be troublesome and uncontrollable into their adolescence.* Because the teacher was conscious of the identification, the consultant talked openly about its potential effects on the teacher's attempts to modify the child's behavior. No improvement was evident. The consultant then modified his hypothesis about the underlying theme: *When faced with hard-to-manage young males, I become incompetent—just as I was incompetent to handle my own son's difficulties.* This slight change in emphasis changed the consultant's strategies from providing alternative behavior management strategies for the teacher to focusing on the consultant's relationship with the teacher. The consultant talked of the teacher's many successes in the classroom, and indicated his respect for her skills by asking for advice on cases and listening to her very carefully. He verbally and nonverbally showed his estimation of her as a very competent teacher. The teacher's problems with the child began to diminish although, interestingly enough, behavioral observations showed that the child was still being disruptive at approximately the same very average level after consultation as before.

Interventions for decreasing the theme include verbal focus on the client, verbal focus on an alternative object—the parable, nonverbal focus on the client, and nonverbal focus on the relationship.

Verbal focus on the client.   Verbal focus on the client simply involves the consultant providing alternatives not present in the consultee's inevitable outcome. Without disputing the consultee's apparent problem formulation, the consultant adds other possibilities for endings.

A female supervisor reported her "panic" at confronting, again, a male special education teacher. She was sure that he would defy her, solicit and receive his principal's support, and that she would "fly off the handle" and not behave appropriately. Agreeing that all this was possible, the consultant suggested that if the teacher were approached with very concrete suggestions, he might also ask for clarification, try out some of her suggestions, and come to see her as a valuable resource. In addition, the consultant said that the consultee might want sometimes to use her anger strategically to show her own convictions and also at other times model calmness when put under stress. The themes involved here seemed to include: *Men in subordinate positions to women will always be rebellious and receive covert support from the powerful men. Female supervisors are hysterical and ineffective in the face of male defiance.*

or perhaps

Women who seek supervisory positions are always unsuccessfully trying to emulate men which is against the natural order of things. The consultee was a member of a religious group that valued women in traditional homemaker roles and emphasized the superiority of male decision making.

The parable.   Caplan's (1970) psychodynamic orientation causes him to warn against bringing the consultee's unconscious material into consciousness and the consultee's realization of the personalized interfering theme. If the consultant feels that focusing on the case too specifically will cause the consultee's personal involvement to become apparent, the consultant can tell a story. A well designed story accomplishes the same goal as verbally focusing on the client, that is, it provides alternatives to the inevitable outcome. The story moves the consultee away from the present case, and prevents the consultee from becoming the focus of the problem. The displacement of the problem from the consultee to the client is retained.

> In the case just described involving the female supervisor, the consultant hesitated to delve into the supervisor's feelings and strategies too much because of the consultant's assumption of the presence of deeply ingrained religious conviction. The consultant, also a female, decided a parable might be in order. She jokingly told the consultee of her own efforts to supervise young, bright, male and female doctoral students in psychology. The consultant recounted some of her own misadventures, how she had to learn supervisory skills—they had not been specifically taught—and finally how, although there had been one clear failure on the consultant's part, there had been fifty or so seemingly successful relationships. The consultee relaxed immediately, agreeing that a lot of trial and error learning was unavoidable but most mistakes were not irreconcilable.

A further note on parables may be appropriate. Some students of consultation have objected to story-telling when the story is in whole or part fabricated. The strategy has seemed dishonest or ungenuine to some. After a little experience, most consultants have a store of true stories to tell that may serve the purpose. In addition, the parable is never told to mislead or provide incorrect information to a consultee. It is told as a way to communicate more effectively. Young consultants may wish to use the parable sparingly as its face validity may be questionable given their obviously limited experience. On the other hand, some young consultants are expert in developing very believable and useful stories that metaphorically "hit the nail on the head" (or the theme on the head).

Nonverbal focus on the case or the consultation relationship. In addition to words, the consultant expresses an estimation of the case severity and an estimation of the consultee in every action and reaction to the consultee. A calm, respectful manner in reaction to the problems examined and to the consultee as a skilled professional can have a significant effect on a consultee's handling of a case. The skills listed in chapter 2 regarding careful listening, egalitarianism, and maintenance of appropriate anxiety levels are critical for reducing consultee emotionality toward a case and toward a consultant. These skills also accomplish what Caplan calls one-downsmanship. This is a process of keeping the relationship an egalitarian, peer-oriented interaction by down-playing consultant *a priori* knowledge while emphasizing consultee expertise and resources to handle a problem. Consultants must be aware, however, of the possibility of a consultee developing a "transference" (that is, symbolic emotional attachment) relationship no matter how skillful they may be.

After several consultation meetings with a principal and his staff, the consultant (female) noticed a pattern of covert coy sexuality between the principal and his female staff members. The staff rarely disputed him directly but made humorous remarks to his suggestions that made above-the-board problem solving difficult. The consultant characterized the school as a "harem" in which the principal was blocked from getting valuable staff input because of the intense level of sexual role playing. Away from the school environment, by chance, the principal was introduced to the consultant's husband who so identified himself. The principal showed obvious confusion and embarassment acting as if he did not remember the consultant. Somehow, it seemed, the consultant had also been placed as a member of the "harem." The unexpected appearance of the rival "sheik" was inordinately disruptive to the principal. Aware of the possible transference taking place between the principal and herself, the consultant closely monitored her reactions to the principal and sought additional supervision to remove any of her contributions to the issue. In a final evaluation of the consultant, the principal characterized her as a person able to get his faculty really working together, sharing lots of important information. He saw her, in other words, as a leader—very differently from the way he had been conceptualizing his other female staff members.

Theme interference may or may not be an outgrowth of the consultee's unconscious conflicts. Some consultants might prefer Ellis's and Grieger's (1977) conceptualization of irrational beliefs rather than unconscious dynamics. Ellis's Rational Emotive Therapy (RET) involves the therapist in continued confrontation of the client's distorted beliefs or catastrophizing. Meyers and his associates (1979), in describing their views on theme reduction, suggest more direct confrontation of the consultee than Caplan (1970) recommends. Like Meyers et al. and Ellis, we feel that consultees are often able to hear somewhat personally threatening things about themselves. However, care must be taken not to damage rapport with consultees as consultants must work within the constraints of somewhat brief relationships. In analysis of three years of consultation activities involving almost 700 sessions, we found that the greatest number of consultation sessions around a single case was 11 interviews. The time for such interviews is variable, 5 minutes to 60 minutes. Our observation is that consultants and consultees do not spend too much time together. This fact alone suggests a heavy reliance on some of the more indirect methods suggested by Caplan, regardless of what we consider to be the source of the problems. The indirect methods require less of a stable relationship to implement and are less threatening to the relationship once implemented.

Other Mental Health Skills

In the mental health model, consultants probe tentatively for consultee's feelings. Consultants do this to capture the essence of the consultee's particular problem or theme. Such a stance, however, causes them to come close to therapy-like activities.

The consultant, no matter how skillful, will occasionally face the issue of giving psychotherapy to a consultee. The consulting relationship is warm, the consultant is looked upon as a mental health expert and role model, so it is natural for the consultee to turn to the consultant for help in personal matters. Caplan's formulation regards this as antithetical to the purposes of consultation. Some techniques to avoid a therapeutic involvement with a consultee are:

- explicit consulting contract that makes it clear that therapy is not part of the service
- skill of the consultant in keeping the sessions on work related problems and displacement of the consultee's personal awareness
- referral to outside sources in cases where therapy is clearly indicated

Our experience is that consultees can be counseled briefly during a session if the consultant is adept at shifting the focus back to the work related problem. Personal problems and unresolved issues do interfere with work.

A male teacher sought consultation regarding his problems in controlling his female junior high school students. He reported that they would hover around his desk, giggle at his directives, write him notes, and generally disrupt his classes. He said that he had probably acted unwisely by bringing groups of these students to local baseball and football events. He was, however, quite lonely because he and his wife had recently separated leaving him with too much empty time. The consultant asked some questions about his separation realizing that this approach was skirting close to a counseling interview. The approach was taken, however, to 1) show empathy and interest in the consultee; 2) discover the possible contribution of the separation (not just the loneliness) to the classroom problem; and 3) make a possible connection for the consultee between unresolved marital issues and seemingly unresolvable classroom issues. The consultee revealed his strong ambivalence about the separation and his fear of further rejection from his wife. The consultant drew tentative parallels for the consultee between the consultee's increased need of emotional support from the students and his marital disruption. The consultant suggested counseling resources for the consultee when asked for some appointment time just to discuss marital issues. The cost evident in this consultant's strategy was that the teacher was once again "rejected" by a female.

Thus, in order to avoid therapy, consultants must be assertive in their preferences but not offend or blame the consultee for seeking therapy. The consultant must also resist the temptation to be all things to a consultee. This takes some professional humility.

Other dual relationships must also be avoided. Consultants must not "date" or become sexually involved with consultees. Social events that have consultee and consultants in attendance are acceptable as group events. Successful love affairs between a consultant and consultee put the consultant in a different organizational niche. The consultant becomes aligned with a certain person or group in the system. Unsuccessful love affairs can be disastrous if scorned lovers decide to provide the rest of the system with all the gruesome details of the relationship. This advice has been ignored twice (to our knowledge) by our consultation students. Both times resulted in a systemic upset. Psychological consultants should follow American Psychological Association ethical guidelines in reference to psychologists and their clients. In short, *do not* attempt dual relationships.

Summary

The mental health consultant must be adept at the various modes within the model and be prepared to choose a particular mode quite quickly. In addition, the consultant should be familiar with the concept of theme interference and be able to assess potential themes and plan interventions accordingly. If consultants find theme interference theoretically unacceptable, it is still useful to try some of the strategies described in that section.

BEHAVIORAL CONSULTATION

A superficial knowledge of behavioral consultation makes it appear as simple as mental health consultation appears complex. First impressions are, however, misleading. Expert use of the behavioral model requires an intimate, flexible knowledge of behavioral programming and learning principles with all the interpersonal skills and sensitivities mentioned in previous sections.

The definition of behavioral consultation is similar to mental health consultation as it involves the consultant in a problem solving relationship with a consultee. The methods used, however, spring from social learning theory. Users of the model target amelioration of client problems, increases in consultee skills in handling problem behaviors in clients, and the linking of psychological research to educational application.

Behavioral techniques are met with resistance in some agencies because of the dogmatism of some of the behavioral proponents. The waves of "born again behaviorists" began invading schools and other child-related agencies in the late 1950s and early 1960s. Their intolerance for competing models and apparent insensitivity to the amount of change that was demanded of consultees in order to effect client change led many consultees to reject behavioral consultation in an *a priori* fashion.

Another reason that the use of behavioral interventions encounters difficulties is the misinformation possessed by many persons using behavioral techniques. Many professionals, in their enthusiasm to make use of effective strategies, applied examples of behavioral interventions without understanding the theory. The lack of full understanding led to lack of success.

A teacher stated that she had attempted to control the child's anger outbursts through behavior modification. When asked what the intervention consisted of, the teacher responded in surprised manner. "Just the usual behavior modification. I ignored the child when he was not doing what he should and praised him when he did what he should. It didn't work because he never did what he should and went wild when I ignored him."

Other concerns about behavioral strategies include the ethics of behavioral manipulation; the use of material reinforcements for behavior *expected* of children; and the potential for the abuse of aversive conditioning. Because these problematic areas are voiced by consultees, many consultants have learned to substitute behavioral jargon with more neutral vocabulary in order to make a particular suggestion.

In contrast, many child-related agencies are completely organized according to operant, and observational learning principles. Such places are often in great need of consultation to keep the staff members aware of new research developments and to correct distortions of the techniques. However accepting the culture of the organization, the techniques associated with behavioral work are well-researched and very successful with many, heretofore, recalcitrant problems. All consultants benefit from in-depth information about this area.

Skills

The two areas of skill development particular to this model are content knowledge of behavioral techniques and principles along with the verbal skills in structuring the consultant/consultee interaction. In table 3.1 are brief definitions of important behavioral concepts. Behavioral strategies are well researched (e.g., O'Leary & O'Leary, 1976; O'Leary & Wilson, 1975). Expert practitioners of behavioral consultation must stay current with the literature as journal articles appear continuously reporting refinements of well known techniques and brand new procedures. Keller (1981) provides an exhaustive review of articles and sources for up-to-date behavioral knowledge. Table 3.2 is a summary of the behavioral consultation process.

Table 3.1. Behavioral Techniques and Terms

Concepts	Definitions
Chaining:	Moving from one step (behavior) to next in learning a sequence of skills.
Forward Chaining	Start with first step (one foot forward) and work up to "walking."
Reverse Chaining	Start with last step (making a bow) and work up to "shoe-tying."
Contingency Contracting	The development of an agreement between two or more parties that stipulates the responsibilities of each as related to a specific item or activity; i.e., the relationship between a child's appropriate behavior and the provision of an agreed-upon reward.
Extinction	The withholding of reinforcement from undesired behaviors in an effort to decrease the frequency of such behaviors. The removal of adult attention, planned ignoring of specific inappropriate behaviors can be very powerful, though some behaviors can't be ignored. It is also likely that targeted behavior will increase at start of the program before extinction can take hold.
Fading	Slow removal of cues until child can perform behavior with no prompts.
Generalization	Process by which children learn to transfer skills learned in educational programs to real-world settings. Can be eased by: efforts to make training setting resemble living/working settings, training in many different settings with multiple trainers, teaching different forms of same skill or concept.
Modeling	Provision of a simple appropriate behavior for the purpose of encouraging the patterning of a child's behavior. Three major positive effects may occur: (1) *The modeling effect*: Children may acquire behaviors from the model that were not previously a part of their repertoire. (2) *The inhibitory effect*: Unacceptable behaviors for which the model is punished may be inhibited in the child. (3) *The eliciting effect*: Behavior is elicited from within the child's repertoire that approximates the model.
Negative Reinforcement	Environmental response that, when removed, causes increase in strength of behavior (i.e., removal from timeout room increases appropriate behavior in classroom).

Table 3.1. (*Continued*)

Concepts	Definitions
Overcorrection Restitution	Correcting the results of the inappropriate behavior thoroughly. (Clean up the paint you splashed *and* wash the entire wall.)
Positive Reinforcement	Environmental response with the effect of maintaining or increasing level of the behavior that it follows (i.e., praise for good work).
Premack Principle	Given two responses A & B, if B occurs with greater frequency than A, it can be used as a reinforcer for A.
Punishment	Removal of a positive reinforcer or the presentation of a negative reinforcer with the aim of decreasing specific behaviors. Punishment may involve the direct presentation of an aversive stimulus and it should not be used until more positive approaches have been tried.
Reinforcing Incompatible Behavior	Reduce frequency of undesired behavior by rewarding a more appropriate incompatible response. (Reinforce sharing instead of taking toys.)
Repeat Positive Practice	Close the door properly *several* times.
Schedules of Reinforcement:	Rates at which positive reinforcers are delivered.
Fixed Interval	Reinforcement is delivered according to specific and consistent periods of time (1 every 5 seconds, 1 every 10 minutes, etc).
Variable Interval	Reinforcers are provided after varying amounts of time.
Fixed Ratio	Reinforcers are consistently delivered after a fixed number of behavioral acts (1 every 2 acts, 1 every 20 acts, etc.).
Variable Ratio	Reinforcers are provided after varying numbers of acts.
Shaping	Procedure used to move child through small steps or successive approximations to a terminal goal. Example: Dressing, putting on coat. Full physical prompt—Give child complete assistance. Partial physical prompt—Get coat ready for child. Gestural prompt—Show coat to child. Verbal prompt—"Time to get your coat on."
Task Analysis	Procedure used to develop efficient skill sequences for shaping new behaviors. Careful programming of complexity and sequence of skills to be learned according to following outline: (1) *Determine Behavioral Objective* A statement of the skill the child will attain, the

Continued on p. 46

Table 3.1. (*Continued*)

Concepts	Definitions
	level of performance expected, and the conditions under which the skill will be performed.
	(2) *Identify Sequence of Skills* Break terminal objective into small, discernible steps.
	(3) *Identify Prerequisite Entry Behaviors* What specific cognitive, verbal, social, motor skills are needed as basis for learning new target behaviors?
	(4) *Determine the Order for Teaching the Subtasks*
Time Out	Reducing inappropriate behavior by removing the child from the reinforcing situation (class, play yard, etc.) to a space where no opportunities for reinforcement are available.
Cautions	1) Longer periods are not more effective than short ones.
	2) Less intensive measures should be tried first.
	3) Children must be supervised.

Source: S. J. Apter, *Troubled Children/Troubled Systems*. New York: Pergamon Press, 1982.

Phases

Bergan and Tombari (1975, 1976) and Tombari and Bergan (1978) have reported a fascinating research program in behavioral consultation. They propose a four-step (or four-interview) framework. Behavioral consultants can structure interviews in phases: problem identification, problem analysis, intervention, and evaluation/follow-up.

Problem identification involves a mutual understanding between consultant and consultee of exactly what the problem is in behavioral, observable terms. The process of gaining this mutual understanding is more difficult than most consultants believe. It is the most critical element in the four-phase framework. Once the problem is behaviorally described, the consultant and the consultee decide upon a way to collect baseline data. This may involve the consultant in a few classroom visits, or it may be left entirely to the consultee. In either case, the procedure to collect the data must be carefully explained to the consultee. It is an error to sit in a classroom taking mysterious notes. Even self-confident teachers can experience some concern with an unexplained data collection method. At the very least, consultants can provide teachers with copies of their checklists or some form of immediate feedback before leaving the classroom. If the teacher is establishing the

Table 3.2. Behavioral Consultation—Step by Step Approach

I. *General*
    A. The consultant works with the *teacher.*
    B. Remediation, help, or therapy must take place in the environment where the problem is (e.g., classroom, not psychologist's office).
    C. If you're overloaded, select the teacher with whom you have the best relationship or chance of success to work with first. (Then you can have a model case.)

II. *Establish Rapport*—start even before the teacher asks for help.
    A. Set initial meeting at time convenient for the teacher, not just you.
    B. Let teacher freely express complaints—respect that the teacher has a problem.

III. *Ask* the teacher to list 1 or 2 biggest concerns.
    "If you could change 1 or 2 things. . . . "

IV. *Help* the teacher pinpoint the concerns. Specification.
    "You said Johnny is lazy. What does he do that makes you say so?"

V. *Ask* teacher to select one target behavior.

VI. *Explain* measurement rationale.
    A. To evaluate usefulness or success.
    B. Difficult to see small changes without data.
    C. Target behavior may not really be a problem.
    D. Data are helpful to reinforce the teacher.
    "It would be good to know how often —— occurs. This will help us evaluate the approach we try."

VII. *Decide* with teacher on a specific measurement procedure.
    Explain baseline and make it clear that after the baseline you'll discuss the intervention.

VIII. *Maintain* contact with the teacher.
    A. Modify measurement procedure, if necessary.
    B. Reinforce teacher.
    C. Make sure teacher isn't doing anything to invalidate the baseline. "You said you've been scolding him, make sure to continue."
    D. When data is stabilized, set up another meeting.

IX. *Develop* intervention with the teacher.
    A. Go over basic behavior therapy principles.
    B. Try to have teacher develop the program—suggest alternatives, but the teacher decides.

X. *Maintain* contact, especially in the early stages.
    A. Modify program, if necessary.
    B. Reinforce the teacher.
    C. Make sure teacher keeps measuring.

Source: J. Halfacre, and F. Welch, "Teacher-Consultation Model: An Operant Approach," *Psychology in the Schools*, 1973, *10*, 494–497.

baseline, the consultant should suggest the least time consuming, easiest to understand data collection method. Additionally, the consultant should phone or drop by to support the teacher's efforts and provide suggestions to resolve unforeseen difficulties.

In the *problem validation* interview, baseline information is used to establish the existence of a problem and to begin designing an intervention strategy. Occasionally, a consultee's focused attention on a target behavior will result in the behavior no longer being seen as problematic. Either the frequency of the behavior is actually quite low, or its precipitant becomes very obvious so that the consultee can make the necessary adjustments in the classroom without further consultation. The baseline data should also shed light on the *antecedents* and *consequents* of the target behavior. What precedes the behavior in terms of social context, teacher behavior, time of day, and subject matter must be specified. In addition, what follows the behavior must be analyzed so that the contingencies maintaining the undesirable behavior may be modified. The consultant or consultee may observe, for instance, that the child emits the target behavior most frequently when sitting alone, assigned to written work. They may also notice that this one child's disruption is frequently followed by disruption from another small group leading to teacher reprimands and a lengthy interruption of regular classroom activities. A child might find any part of that sequence reinforcing. The intervention plan designed by the consultant and consultee can make use of this information by altering antecedent and/or consequent conditions in hopes of altering the unacceptable behavior. The problem analysis phase must also include careful consideration of the resources available to bring to bear on the problem. These resources include the general organization of the classroom (small groups, learning centers, peer tutoring, movement, individualization, scheduling) and teacher skills or propensities (positive attention, games, artwork, attention to detail). In addition, resources outside the classroom might be identified such as parent involvement, other teaching or school staff support, or reinforcements associated with visits to other classrooms or people and places in the community. The problem analysis ends with a designation of an intervention in addition to a continued data collection process. The consultee and consultant delineate the discrepancy between actual and desired behaviors (in terms of kinds of behaviors or frequency or duration of behavior) along with establishing some tentative goals for the intervention to be deemed successful. These goals or desired behaviors deserve careful consultant attention.

It is important to compare a consultee's expectations of client's behaviors to developmental realities. First graders do not sit quietly for hours and hours working alone on purple ditto sheets. To design a program meant to accomplish such an anomaly invites frustration for everyone who is involved. Further, a child who has *never* been observed to emit a desired behavior (e.g., playing cooperatively with peers) is unlikely to suddenly display the entire behavior with frequency.

Not only should consultees receive information about shaping and chaining behaviors, but they should also be encouraged to assume that change will take considerable time and effort. Surrounded as we are with very rapid technological change, it is tempting to wish for instant successes with carefully planned interventions. It is all right to wish, but not all right to give up on a strategy after only a few days. Most troublesome behaviors have been nurtured by unfortunate contingencies for years. It is unreasonable to assume that change will be rapid on a behavior that has already defied attempts to extinguish it.

During *implementation* of the mutually developed plan, the consultant should make contact with the consultee to offer support, suggestions for revision, and continued problem solving. Data collection must, of course, continue during the intervention phase.

Finally, after a specified time has elapsed, the consultant and consultee meet to *evaluate* the effectiveness of their efforts. This meeting may result in a decision to extend the strategy, modify the plan, or completely recycle through the problem solving process. Even though human service people believe that all problems, if understood, are amenable to change, that does not imply that the first change strategy will be the effective one. An openness to new ideas and even different problem conceptualizations is needed if consultants hope to increase problem solving skills in themselves and others. Persistence and flexibility are the watch words.

Verbal Structuring

Another aspect of implementing behavioral consultation is careful attention to the verbal statements made by the consultant. Such attention to consultant verbalizations is important in every model of consultation, but has been most carefully researched in behavioral consultation (Bergan & Tombari, 1975, 1976; Tombari & Bergan, 1978). Caplan (1970) also reports on the effectiveness of related concepts *unlinking* (a process of splitting the initial category of a theme from its inevitable outcome) and theme interference reduction. Others have analyzed verbal processes as stages of problem solving (e.g., Cossairt, Hall, & Hopkins, 1973; Freidman, 1978; Isaacson, 1981; Robbins, Spencer, & Frank, 1970; Wilcox, 1977).

The Tombari and Bergan (1978) research illustrates how consultants' verbalizations affect consultee beliefs about a case. When given behavioral cues about a case, consultees reported more favorable impressions of prognoses than when given medical model cues. Such work points to the importance of the verbal influence process occurring during consultation. Other work by Bergan and Tombari (1975) suggests the importance of focusing on each of the consultee's topics thoroughly before moving on to new topics. Although more research is needed in this area, it seems accurate that consultants who can influence the content and direction of an interview in such a way as to stay on topic will be more successful than those who cannot do so.

Based on the *Consultation Analysis* developed by Bergan and Tombari, there are several areas deserving verbal attention from the consultant. The consultant can *elicit* information from the consultee regarding the *background environment* of the client, the overt and covert behaviors of the client, and the present setting of the *troublesome behavior*. The *individual characteristics* of the child, that is, supposed personality "traits," intellectual abilities, and physical descriptors can also be investigated by the consultant. Behavioral consultants may tend to downplay verbalizations of individual characteristics in favor of eliciting the consultees' *observations* concerning the behaviors under discussion. The consultant will also likely *emit* statements concerning observational techniques to consultee.

Finally, verbalizations associated with plan development are also necessary components of consultation. One finding of the Bergan and Tombari research program was that successful problem identification was highly related to plan implementation. In cases where plans were actually implemented, 95 percent were reported as successful. Thus, it is clear that effectiveness in eliciting and emitting verbalizations is critical to successful consultation experiences.

Common Pitfalls

The beauty of behavioral work is that there are many "tried and true" strategies that lend themselves to empirical validation. Successful interventions are easy to identify because behavior change is the ultimate test of effectiveness. The rationale behind behavioral work is very logical and easily explained.

Problems arise in the consultant's overenthusiasm for the techniques in the face of consultee reluctance. What seems obvious, easy, logical, and well-published to the psychologist may appear completely *wrong* to a consultee. Consultants must soft-pedal their allegiance to a particular theoretical orientation. They do this for pragmatic reasons (and perhaps theoretical reasons if they are "systems-thinkers").

The other pitfall associated with behavioral consultation was alluded to earlier in the chapter, but deserves further elaboration. There is a tendency for consultants to overlook the collaborative aspects of consultation because of the straightforward nature of many behavioral interventions. The consultants observe client problems and present detailed behavioral plans to consultees for implementation. They have engaged in a kind of expert or clinical consultation; however, there are problems with the expert consultation model. First, there is no way of knowing if the diagnosis points out the problem that was most troublesome as judged by the consultee. Second, the plan may or may not match the skills, knowledge, or preferences of the consultee. And finally, even when the plan involves major behavioral changes on the part of the consultee, no attention may be given to support the implementation efforts. When the consultant makes these errors, it is unfortunate that even after successful behavioral programs some consultees will not use the strategies again for new cases. Behavioral consultants must be sensitive to the needs of their consultees and devote some of their planning time toward supporting consultee efforts. The right answer is not enough. The consultee must be motivated to make continuing use of the right answer. People reject better ways of doing things for many, many reasons. Only one of these reasons is not knowing about the better answer. Others include devotion to traditions or particular philosophies, passive–aggressive life-styles, low investment in the problem, involvement with systems that do not support innovations, or generalized feelings of low self-esteem.

ADVOCACY CONSULTATION

There are a number of specialized skills needed by advocacy consultants in addition to the generic skills mentioned earlier. Advocates may be practitioners of any of the other models and rarely use advocacy, or they may mainly work in the field of advocacy. The role descriptors of child-oriented professionals always contain a call to advocacy (Berlin, 1975; Biklen, 1976; Conoley, 1981a; Conoley, 1981c; Gallessich, 1974; Hyman, 1975; Mearig, 1974, 1978; Stein, 1972). However, rarely is there any pointed training in advocacy for psychologists or educators. Social workers may be better prepared didactically for advocacy work than most of the other helping fields.

The roles an advocate may assume are very diverse, so many skills are needed ranging from typical therapy-like skills to law, public relations, and negotiating skills. This may be the most pragmatic of all models while simultaneously being the most value laden. Advocate consultants are best known by what they believe in, not best understood by the particular methodologies they employ.

Some of the skills or content areas usually ignored in typical graduate sequences but required of the advocate consultant are law, organizing people, organizing events, media use, negotiation, and parent partnership. Important other skills are persuasive writing or speaking, building support networks, and tremendous tolerance for both ambiguity and conflict.

Law

Professional ethics are regulations governing a particular group. They mainly inform the members what not to do (e.g., American Psychological Association, 1979). Often, graduates of professional programs are aware only of these regulations and those affecting licensure, confidentiality, and perhaps involuntary commitment and some child welfare laws. School psychologists are often quite well informed as to the laws affecting the rights of children to pubic education, and due process procedures. Overall, however, it is rare to find a helping professional with a comprehensive knowledge of both the content and process of the law. Such knowledge is indispensable for advocate consultants. This is no small task, however, and requires substantial study and involvement. Taylor and Biklen's (1979) work is a very helpful source. In addition, all state and federal branches will send information upon request regarding each of their functions and on new regulations written to implement new laws. Litigation must also be monitored as this can have a dramatic effect on what seems to be in place. An example was a 1981 Supreme Court decision overturning a lower court to provide treatment and education to mentally retarded persons in the least restrictive environment. The well known lower court's 1977 decision had forced the Penhurst State School to begin a process of deinstitutionalization. This process received support and funding through the 1975 Developmental Disabilities Act. Thus, the process of deinstitutionalization, so highly prized by families and advocates, seemed protected by law and then was overturned in a 6-3 decision by the Supreme Court.

Advocate consultants can seek lawyers as consultants in their study and use of the law, but lawyers tend to specialize within fields. It is imperative to seek advice from lawyers who are actually working in the advocate's area of interest in order to obtain the most up-to-date information. Workshops on legal issues are available but must also be screened. Many workshops focus more on the laws impacting the particular profession than with laws affecting clients.

One important aspect of the law is the guarantee for due process extended to citizens. Advocates are well advised to understand the exact implications of due process procedures for a particular area of concern. When a child is suspected of having a disabling condition necessitating a change in educational programming, certain steps must be taken to ensure that due process has occurred. An outline for the steps involved in due process is in Appendix 3.A. If parties involved in the process of changing a child's placement have failed to document or take the actions outlined in the due process steps, there is cause to contest any decisions reached by the decision making committees.

Organizing People

Of almost equal importance as legal knowledge for advocacy consultation is skill in getting people together to work on projects. This model derives most of its power from sophisticated understandings of how the politics of each situation are arranged. People must be organized to create pressure or lobbying groups to tip the political balance in the direction wanted by the advocate's consumer group. Sometimes large groups are needed for demonstrations, write-ins, sit-ins, work slow-downs, referendums, packing public meetings and so on. Sometimes strategic alliances must be engineered between groups that, although not large, are influential. If a parents' group can gain the support of even a few school board members, it is likely that the group's goals will be met.

In addition, there are basic managerial skills involved in advocacy. Things have to be arranged, for example, publications, meetings, and public relations events. Staff, often volunteer, must be supervised and oriented. The consumer group for whom the advocate consultant works must be monitored closely to make sure that *their* issues are addressed and that their latent resources are being optimally used.

All these things do not just *happen*. They require careful coordination. The consultant may not have coordinating skills, but the consultant must facilitate the effectiveness of someone who does. Often the members of consumer groups are angry and behave as if the force of their emotion and the rightness of their cause will overcome all obstacles. With all its relative meanings, being right is helpful but does not guarantee success. Usually, both groups in a struggle feel that they are right. This leads to a stereotyping and derogation of the opposing group. Advocate consultants are wise to avoid that trap and attempt to see the other group in all its complexity. This will increase the power of the advocate's suggestions for interventions and increase the chances of the groups moving together in an alliance.

There is no logical reason for parents and school districts not to be partners in the socialization and nurturing of all children. However, many districts are locked in adversarial relationships with parents. The goals of each group might be best met if someone could help point out commonalities and shared purposes while understanding the different pressures each group feels.

The lesson for the advocate consultant may be that, while working 100 percent for the valued consumer group, he or she should not refuse to understand the strengths and the appropriate motives of the adversary. Alinsky's (1946) warning, "In order to be part of all, you must be part of none" (p. 204) should be kept in mind while organizing individuals for action. Consultants are friends and allies but one of their strengths to a group may be their somewhat marginal position in the group (Browne, Cotton & Golembiewski, 1977). They are at a boundary or interface and may have a clearer picture of each group's contributions to the present troubles.

Cormick and Love (1976) describe some role possibilities open to those interested in facilitating social change: activist, advocate, and mediator. The activist is directly involved in the movement. Advocates are facilitators of change or maintenance of status quo but are not actually members of the groups involved (parents of handicapped, or presidents of oil companies). Mediators are individuals who are acceptable in some limited way to all the disputing factors. These people work for mutual improvement as the way to terminate the conflict. All of these roles are available to any citizen. Advocate consultants might move among the roles as the situation warrants. Each role will involve the consultant in direct person-to-person work.

Organizing Events

Much of the work involved in organizing events is accomplished through organizing people. Advocate consultants must be aware of the kinds of events or "actions" that are possibilities (Biklen, 1974). An action is a "planned activity that will lead to social change" (p. 90). Actions will be successful if they:

> reflect short term and long term goals, fit the circumstances of the hour, serve to further your goals, utilize the skills of your constituency, (are) well planned, meet people's expectations, educate others, (are) consistent with your values, lead to other actions. [p. 91]

Within these parameters only group creativity and research will limit the diverse array of possible actions. Public forums or meetings, marches, coordinated letter writing, media coverage or production, symbolic acts (e.g., draft card burnings or arm bands), boycotts, community education efforts, or model programs are all possibilities.

Using Media

Mass media probably represents the single most potent influence on today's world. Access to and skillful use of media channels to create a change in public opinion are vital for advocate consultants to develop in themselves or identify in others.

Possible media projects include press conferences, public service announcements, educational videotapes, newspaper stories, appearances on local talk shows, free or easily accessed information publications, brochures, posters, or thematic children's art. Each of these media projects employs skills in organizing and identifying people and arranging the event or context to increase the effect. The projects depend on careful research and groundbreaking. Newspaper reporters have, for example, some independence in submitting stories for publication. Identifying a reporter interested in or sympathetic to a particular cause and providing that person with information about events may result in "free" publicity. Radio and television stations must broadcast, free of charge, a certain number of public service announcements. Although these announcements are usually aired at odd hours, someone is always listening or watching. It is possible that the announcement could appear at a high usage hour, if it is well produced.

A less dramatic use of media is effective letter writing. The letters may be part of a write-in campaign or simply done by individuals seeking change or clarification from an agency. Some members of constituency groups may rarely write anything. Parents, for example, may need help in both the process and content of letter writing. Some useful guidelines adapted from *Making School Work* (Massachusetts Advocacy Center and Massachusetts Law Reform Institute, 1975) are presented below:

1. Most routine matters between a child and teacher do not warrant letter writing. Telephone calls and notes can be used to keep communication lines open.
2. Letters should be sent and a copy kept when issues important to a child's educational development arise. Examples include: a) a serious disciplinary action or an accusation that a child has broken an important rule; b) a request for an educational service not presently available to a child; c) a request to inspect or receive information from a child's records; d) when a parent believes a child is being mistreated; or e) a request for a meeting or a hearing with agency officials about some issue.
3. Letters should be sent to the person directly involved with the issue. If a satisfactory solution is not accomplished, additional letters may be sent with carbon copies sent to the supervisors of the directly involved persons.
4. Copies are essential. Carbons or photocopied letters are important in verifying what was said to whom on what date.
5. It is often good practice to pay the extra amount demanded to send a letter by certified mail. This establishes proof that the letter was sent *and* received.
6. Follow-up letters are often needed. Times to send follow-up letters include: a) after telephone conversations that have occurred because of an initial letter; b) when an initial letter fails to elicit an adequate response; c) when no response is made to an initial letter; and d) after meetings with agency officials to accurately document what transpired at the meetings and record decisions made verbally.

People should be encouraged to write letters concerning a problem that is affecting them personally. The advocate consultant can be available with suggestions for form and procedure.

Negotiation

Negotiation is a process used when any two groups with conflicting interests meet to discuss the issues that divide them (Taylor, 1979). Negotiation is not an easy or comfortable process. It demands a tolerance for both internal and external conflict. Members of a negotiating team must be in control of their tendencies to become angry, withdrawn, or feel guilty when confronted with opposing viewpoints. In addition, they must be able to continue on a planned course no matter how angry, unreasonable, or accusing the opposite side may become.

Taylor (1979) has described what he considers critical elements in negotiation. Negotiation should occur after informal appeals have failed but before going public with demands. Premature publicity sometimes locks a group into a public position from which they are later unwilling to retreat. After a public stand, a group may feel its image will be tarnished by a compromise or change in policy. A well-timed private meeting might have allowed a change to occur and the powerful group to save face.

Whenever possible, the negotiating team should represent an alliance of consumer groups advocating for change. The group or organization from which change is sought is far more likely to accede if it recognizes a broad-based concern about its policies. We all have used the adage "You can't make everybody happy" to explain why one individual or group is angry with our activities. The more groups that show concern about an issue, the harder it is for an organization to ignore these concerns.

The setting for the meeting should be specified by the consumer group. This group explains the purpose of the meeting and specifies which agency officials should attend. The numbers of representatives at the negotiation session should be equal for both sides. The consumer group, especially, should reschedule the session if many unexpected agency people arrive at the meeting.

In order to negotiate successfully, the consumer group must come well prepared. Knowledge of the budget, priorities, policies, procedures, and goals of the agency is necessary. Discrepancies between stated mission and actual behaviors can be specified.

Emotional control must accompany careful preparation of facts. Anger may be useful if strategically applied, but generally will lower problem solving skills. Members of the consumer group should not feel guilty about making demands, become defensive, or beg for concessions.

If possible, electronically record or transcribe the meeting events. Firm time tables and standards of action should be established. Following the meeting, the consumer group can send the agency a letter describing what transpired and requesting a reply if there are discrepancies between the group's and the agency's memories of the decisions or agreements.

Negotiators must be willing to confront vague promises or generalizations. It is often more comfortable to let items go undiscussed than to deal with delicate or controversial issues. Allowing generalizations or "buck passing" to take the place of specific action plans is a serious mistake.

Finally, all members of a negotiating team must keep a long-range perspective on a problem. This implies being able to see small gains as steps toward desired goals. A coherent plan of action is necessary that uses negotiation as one strategy in overall efforts. In this way, small concessions received from powerful people will not be confused with compromise.

Parent Partnership

A group that is often in need of advocate partnership is parents. Parents are not perfect, romantic or ideal, but they are often a very vulnerable group if they have disabled children. There are numerous situations faced by parents of special needs children that require specialized skills or knowledge. Advocate consultants can be helpful by supplying parents with information concerning new developments in law and suggestions of ways to navigate the somewhat murky service delivery network waters.

Some very concrete suggestions to parents who have disabled children are listed in Appendix 3.B. Another more specialized set of guidelines parents need are ways of evaluating the school programs of their children. Given in Appendix 3.C are suggestions aimed directly at parents seeking appropriate placements for their children.

Once parents have chosen programs for their children, they are still faced with cooperating in the development of the child's Individualized Educational Plan (IEP). In Appendix 3.D is a comprehensive checklist for parent use during the IEP process (Barnes, 1978).

Advocacy Pitfalls

Because advocacy is rarely seriously studied by mental health professionals, substantial attention has been devoted to it in this chapter. It is important to remember, however, that being an advocate consultant is a most difficult task, requiring tireless energy and commitment to values and goals. It is important not to glamorize the excitement associated with the righteous David (you!) taking on the evil Goliath (dehumanizing systems). In the main, the work is hard, alienation from others is always a threat, and the tangible rewards meager. Jobs are hard to find if a reputation for "rabble-rousing" precedes a candidate. Most employees prefer team players. While team players sometimes reduce the effectiveness of an organization (e.g., the "group think" attributed to the Lyndon B. Johnson Cabinet during the Vietnam War), it is understandable that most people in a system value its regularities and resist efforts at change.

The advocates must be on guard, therefore, for distortions of their own motives. They must not inflame situations merely for the attention that it draws to them. They must be sensitive to the real needs of their consumer group—facilitating rather than leading a cause. They must be able to endure hostility and lack of closure for long periods of time. And, finally, they must self-consciously engineer support networks for themselves that serve nurturing and accountability functions.

PROCESS CONSULTATION

Process consultants work at making their consultees more aware of events in the environment and how those events or processes affect work production and social emotional atmosphere of the system (Schein, 1969). Because most people are content- rather than process-oriented, the definition and usefulness of process consultation is often questioned. This is especially true among educators who believe that they work independently of emotion, group cohesiveness, or efficient procedures. This is particularly ironic because, more than most enterprises, education is a *process* not a *product.*

All the interpersonal skills mentioned previously are particularly important to this consultation model because the consultant's goal is more to leave a consultee organization with new skills than with imparted knowledge. This suggests that the process consultant must be a very salient role model for consultees so that the consultees literally do as the consultant has done. Very well developed interpersonal skills are clearly indicated to accomplish this rather tall order. Process consultants must also be adept at identifying important process phenomena, as well as performing certain research and simulation activities.

Process Phenomena

What *is* a process? Essentially process refers to the *way* a certain event happens rather than *what* exactly does occur. We may all arrive at grandmother's house for pudding, but some of us fly over hills, others drive through snow, and some boat down rivers. The *how* and the *what* are both important. It is important to learn the delicate balance between the two phenomena and to adjust the balance depending on the people involved, the task at hand, and the prevailing environmental stress. The first obvious problem for the process consultant is becoming free from merely the content of what is occurring in order to observe and interpret process events. In table 3.3 are listed some common processes that could be evident during any small group activity.

The processes tend to facilitate either the task accomplishment of a group or the maintenance of a positive morale among group members. The people who assume such processes are, thus, described as doing task or maintenance functions, respectively (Schein, 1969). Upon studying the enumerated pro-

Table 3.3. Group Process Phenomena

Emerging Leadership	Disagreeing
Gate Keeping	Encouraging
Time Keeping	Harmonizing
Agenda Setting	Consensus Testing
Listening Skills	Nonverbal Cues
Information or Opinion Seeking	Feedback Skills
Information or Opinion Giving	Clarifying
Communication Patterns	Summarizing
Elaborating	Decision-Making
Diagnosing	Initiating
Calling for Attention or Action	Defending
Offering Help	Agreeing
Blocking Action	Arguing
Diverting	Compromising
Recording	Standard Setting and Testing
Observing	Following
Tension Releasing	Expediting

cesses, people rarely have difficulty "seeing" the processes when they do occur. Consultants must, of course, make some hypotheses concerning the relative usefulness of certain processes for a group and the costs or benefits derived from some processes being emphasized or ignored. While process consultants focus on the problems recognized by the organization, there is an additional focus because of the values associated with attention toward process. Some of these values include attention to human concerns at the work place, a focus on the way work is done, emphasis on long-range rather than short-run planning as well as effectiveness, and an acceptance of perpeptual diagnosis as an alternative to reliance on generalizations or principles as modes of operation (e.g., "We've always done it that way"). Often the values espoused by process consultants are products of research on improving the quality and quantity of work (e.g., Baker & Wilemon, 1977; Burns, 1977).

The process consultant who observes no gatekeeping functions during staff meetings will, therefore, look to see what is going wrong for that group and decide if the lack of gatekeeping may be part of the problem. Consultant attention to gatekeeping is influenced by a belief that shared interaction during a meeting is a good thing.

Another dimension for the consultant to consider when interpreting group processes is the developmental stage of the group or individual group members (Schein, 1969). People seem to have qualitatively different needs surrounding group membership over time. The needs, in developmental order, have to do with clarity about membership, influence, feelings, individual differences, and productivity.

The first struggle a new member faces when entering a group is learning what it means to be a member. What are the norms, the advantages, and the costs? During this period, the consultant might observe a participant to be involved in relatively few initiating processes and far more information and opinion seeking activities. This pattern should not be overinterpreted by the consultant as indicating low initiating skills on the part of the new member. The particular pattern may be quite appropriate given the person's developmental moment.

After getting clear on group acceptance issues, many members turn their attention to influence issues. Who are the power "haves" and "have-nots"? Is power seen as more important than the good of the group? During this phase, members may attempt influence strategies which parallel the existing patterns or question the decision making structures that are currently in place. Effective group leaders accept this as a predictable pattern and try not to respond defensively to questions and suggestions for change. New members are likely to make "mistakes" about going through channels and getting required approvals. These behaviors would probably not be signals to the consultant of authority problems in the staff unless they were part of long-tenured members' repertoires.

The affective response of the group to individual members is another issue that commonly surfaces during group life. Will the group be supportive and constructively critical? Are feelings considered appropriate topics for discussion? Do honest appraisals of agenda items occur only after meetings are over? Members who suddenly confront a group with many unresolved issues may be reflecting a newly discovered understanding that feelings will be taken seriously. A group may appear helplessly bogged down in maintenance functions at a certain point in history. Consultants must use their understanding of the group's time frame to decide whether to push for more task functioning or simply facilitate the affective events as they happen.

In some ways, the three previous stages have emphasized becoming an integral, influential member of the group by learning its norms and responding to its structures. A more difficult stage accomplished by few individuals or groups is coming to appreciate members' differences. It is common for groups to be further divided in smaller units that coalesce because of shared attitudes, experience, and values. Group leaders may require coaching and support to attempt to maximize a group's differences. Different talents, levels of involvement, and ideologies could be openly accepted as part of the group's strength. They should not automatically elicit pressures to conform.

The final issue members and groups face is that of productivity. All groups have some purpose. The way in which that purpose is lived or accomplished depends in great measure on how the previous stages have been resolved. If members feel that membership in a particular group is not self-enhancing and that their attempts at influence and displays of feeling are rebuffed, it is unlikely that productivity will be high. Some groups spend inordinate amounts of time arguing about what is "better" or who is "right." This indicates that group production is likely to reflect the least common denominator rather than creative synergy. Lack of organizational values associated with diagnosing situations, working issues through, and receiving reactions for new ideas should be apparent to the consultant. Inordinate competition in an organization makes these standards unlikely guidelines for group life.

Process observation is best done when the consultant is not heavily involved in the meeting under scrutiny. It is not impossible to be participant and observer, but it is difficult, especially for new consultants. Even consultants who exclusively observe must be aware that their presence is a part of the group process of which they are mainly unaware. The questions consultants ask themselves when doing their process observations are:

- Who is talking with whom?
- Are the verbal and nonverbal messages congruent?
- Who is systematically ignored or attacked?
- How does the group make decisions?
- Are there group data that are ignored (e.g., the angry tone used by some members while verbally acquiescing)?
- Do the participants seem to know what to expect?
- Is the time allotted to each agenda item sufficient to allow discussion, and reasonable given the total meeting time, number of agenda items, *and* importance of particular agenda items?
- How effective is the leader in keeping the group on task and setting standards for accomplishment?

Process consultants and their consultees work collaboratively. The consultant relies on the consultee for the details of the organizational structure, climate, and norms, and is constantly involved in a process of mutual problem identification and solution generation. Of course, there is more to process consultation than observing a staff meeting and then presenting the participants with a detailed list of process observations and interpretations.

During a three day workshop on process consultation, the group of three presenters added an unplanned activity. One presenter went unannounced and unexplained from one small workshop group to another jotting down observations about each group's task and maintenance processes. When the activity was over, the one presenter rather smugly detailed his very sophisticated observations. He was greeted with relatively stony silence as the participants reported later great feelings of defensiveness and unexpected vulnerability to observation.

Such reactions are typical, even when process consultants have been invited to make their observations known. It is tempting to establish an expert position by showing off special sensitivities, but, in the long run, this is quite counterproductive. It is better, if asked to share observations, to ask questions of the group about how they experience a certain process, for example, decision making. A consultant might share a single observation and ask the group to decide if the process described is functional or dysfunctional to group goals. In the end, the consultant wants the group to be able to diagnose and change its own process. It is best to start the self-analysis and self-renewal activities as soon as possible. Nothing is gained by positioning the consultant as the expert observer and interpreter.

Consultants often suggest and facilitate process observation periods at the end of regular work meetings. In addition, the consultant might provide mini-didactic inputs on agenda setting, gatekeeping, or decision making. Often some administrative coaching of the leader is called for if she or he is deficient in certain leadership skills. Skills particularly important for leadership are abilities to give credit to others very generously, to be task oriented, to display facilitative concern toward the staff's personal issues, to actively initiate issues, to be eager for feedback, and to model risk taking. In addition, the leader should be able to move flexibly among the various task and maintenance processes listed in table 3.3 at the appropriate occasion.

As staff meetings take up a substantial portion of time, energy is well spent to make them as efficient, effective, and enjoyable as possible. What follows are rather generic guidelines for well-run meetings. Not all of these guidelines are applicable to every group, but all should be considered when planning the procedures used at staff meetings. Although every group member is responsible for the quality of a meeting, it is especially important for the leader to be aware of these suggestions.

1. Physical setting
   a. comfortable chairs
   b. round table
   c. good light
   d. quiet
   e. uninterrupted by calls or visitors
2. Amenities
   a. coffee
   b. food
   c. smoking? yes or no should be explicit
   d. pencils and paper available
3. Agenda
   a. solicited items from every staff member
   b. circulated *before* the meeting
   c. person in charge of soliciting items and setting time limits is rotating
   d. priorities and times made explicit

4. Chairperson
   a. rotating responsibility (could be agenda person)
   b. facilitator rather than content person
   c. gatekeeper
   d. consensus tester
5. Timing
   a. start and stop at agreed upon times
   b. time left for process analysis at end of each meeting
   c. time keeper times discussion of agenda items to keep group on schedule
6. Roles in a group
   a. task roles:
      initiating, clarifying, opinion and information giving and seeking, summarizing
   b. maintenance roles:
      harmonizing, encouraging, gatekeeping, summarizing

Decision making styles are particularly important for the consultant to investigate. The group will have a preferred style, for example, voting, consensus, or minority rule (Schein, 1969). The leader will also have a particular style, for example, selling, telling, or consulting (Tannenbaum & Schmidt, 1958). Each style or pattern has costs and benefits that are more or less useful given the participants and the task. When the group members have an expectation that they will be involved in a decision or the task is complex enough to benefit from collaborative problem solving, the leader is well advised to govern in a relatively group-centered fashion. This involves delegating certain tasks, consulting, and joining with group members about problem diagnoses as well as problem solutions and continually allowing the group to have decision making functions. In certain groups, for example, the military, there is no expectation for participatory leadership. Therefore, group morale and leader evaluations will suffer if the leader does not adopt a more leader-centered decision working style. The leader might test ideas before a group but generally arrives with a problem formulation and asks for input concerning a circumscribed set of possible solutions.

When tasks are quite simple, leaders in either culture are expected to make decisions alone. They are also expected to act independently if the group is faced with a serious emergency. Procedures to be used in an emergency might be a product of group action, but no one expects a vote to be taken on whether or not to leave a burning building.

Consultants can use their observation time to discern if decision making styles are interfering with high level group functioning. One common problem is the "plop" decision. This has to do with never really making a decision—just allowing the last comment to be seen as a group mandate. If consultants can direct participants to an analysis of their styles and preferences, positive change may occur.

Data Gathering and Simulation

It is convenient to separate a data gathering stage from an intervention stage. Actually, the process of collecting information is in itself a form of intervention. Process consultants must be sure, then, that their research methodologies are consonant with their values and reflective of procedures the consultant would like to establish as aids to ongoing organizational self-analysis. Straightforward procedures that are protective of people's privacy and other group norms are best.

Typical data gathering methodologies are observations, questionnaires, surveys, interviews, and simulations. As with all other consultation modes, the process consultant must be as certain as possible that all the consultees are willing participants and informed as to the purposes of the activities. They must also be made aware of the limits of confidentiality. These conditions cannot be taken for granted. It is most embarrassing to arrive at an organizational subsystem and realize that the members are totally in the dark as to what the consultation effort is all about. Ignorance often facilitates resistance and paranoia. Neither of these, obviously, is helpful to the consultative goals.

There are many published sources for organizational data gathering instruments (e.g., Blake & Mouton, 1976, 1978; Halpin & Croft, 1963; Lippitt & Lippitt, 1975; Schmuck et al., 1972). If questionnaires or surveys are a preferred methodology, these sources for developed tools are efficient guides. The process of gathering data can be conceptualized as another entry problem. Consultees must be identified, and prepared to complete the instruments. They must be informed as to how they are likely to benefit from candid participation in what might be a time-consuming process. Do not believe that any instrument is "fake-proof." The consultant must devote time to planning ways of motivating people to cooperate with survey procedures. The best way, of course, is having the particular methodology chosen in a collaborative effort between the gatherers and the providers of information.

The previous discussion is equally applicable to interview techniques. In small organizations, it is helpful for the consultant to talk with each member. This way, the consultant can try to see the system from a number of perspectives in discovering the incongruities between stated goals and actual organizational behaviors. The consultant should be willing to answer questions from consultees in order to model openness and begin the process of mutual problem solving. It is best to discuss the surveys, questionnaires, and interviews with the primary consultee. If interviewees appear reluctant to answer questions, the consultant must be prepared to provide a rationale for the anxiety-provoking questions and ask for alternative ways for investigating troublesome organizational issues.

Most interviews are best done in a semi-structured manner. All the consultees must be asked the same questions, but this may be done in a relaxed and friendly manner. The consultant can follow the consultee's lead to new content areas, especially if this suggests formerly undiscussed problems. Great care must be taken to ensure confidentiality across consultees. It is important for the consultant not to share information learned in one interview with another consultee. All the information will eventually be fed back to the participants with the pervasive issues highlighted for possible problem solving action.

Another data gathering/intervention device is the simulation. Usually, there are plentiful naturally occurring events for the consultant to observe. Occasionally, however, the consultant might design an activity for the participants that highlights particular aspects of group functioning. The advantages of simulations over regular activities are that the group processes are sometimes more apparent to participants when they are dealing with equally unfamiliar content, and the focus on a few processes allows for some in-depth learning to occur. Of course, there is always the danger that the discoveries in the simulation will lack, or at least appear to lack, any relationship to the problems in the situations regularly encountered by the consultees. Because participation in simulations is somewhat anxiety-provoking, consultees are likely to find fault with even well-designed attempts. Consultants, beware of "hokey" games, activities, and simulations. Be wary also of activities that have substantial potential to raise many personally troubling issues for consultees. Third party consultation, as described by Walton (1969), is an appropriate way to handle strong personality or ideological conflicts that are interfering with organizational effectiveness. Essentially, Walton recommends three-way or small group meetings to creatively deal with conflict. Implementing a simulation that results in everyone yelling is not a creative way to deal with conflict. The yelling probably substantially preceded the simulation to no one but the consultant's surprise.

Information from chapter 9 on training may be helpful for process consultants preparing to use simulations. There are numerous published examples of simulations (e.g., Abt, 1970; Gamson, 1978; Guetzkow, 1962; Pfeiffer & Jones, 1969, 1970). Many simulations were created by personnel working at the National Training Laboratory (NTL). This organization is a continuing resource for process consultants in terms of training experiences and publications. In addition, articles published in the *Journal of Applied Behavioral Science* are often relevant to process consultants. Consultants must often design their own activities in order to capture the exact processes that are under scrutiny.

The debriefing period following the simulation is probably the most critical in terms of consultee learning. Nothing is gained if consultees do something (e.g., decide what to carry to the moon or create a new organization) and then do not get a chance to discuss their experiences. The consultant must allow sufficient debriefing time in order to facilitate positive learning.

> One group abruptly aborted a simulation that involved two organizations which were negotiating for the use of resources, and one team of process consultants. One of the process consultants cried after receiving very negative feedback from one of the organizations. After delaying the negotiations, the other organization tried to begin the negotiating process by staging a get-acquainted social gathering which went very badly. The invited organization had built up suspicions of possible "manipulations" taking place. The remaining process consultant insisted that the simulation be stopped because "people were getting hurt." She wanted to get out of the roles that seemed to her to be distorting the group process. A long debriefing session revealed the strong themes of conflict avoidance and low trust that had plagued this group for almost six months. These very issues in their real group life interfered with their getting on to the creative tasks of which they thought themselves capable. The group was somewhat horrified at the idea that one of its members would get hurt by other members. They basically did not believe, however, that they all had each others' best interests at heart. They avoided dealing with tough issues because they did not trust that each cared enough about the others.

If debriefing is not complete after group experiences such as the one described, participants are likely to leave confused and upset rather than enlightened. Not all confusion and upset can be discussed away, but process consultants must make strong efforts at dealing with each person before allowing the group to break or move to another task.

Many process consultants and other organization development (OD) specialists have made use of sensitivity training or encounter groups as part of their training endeavors. These experiences are not simulations but, rather, activities that tend to focus participant energy and attention very sharply. The usual strategy is for members to deal with each other only about issues currently existing in the group. The goals are often to facilitate members learning about their impact on others and learning new ways to express their impressions of others. Well-run groups are often intense experiences and are literal laboratories of interpersonal phenomena. Learning about personal styles stemming from group experiences can be significant.

Process consultants should be wary of overusing an encounter group strategy. Very early in the history of encounter groups, it became apparent that personal change made by group participants faded as they returned to a nonsupportive environment. Family groups (i.e., entire staffs, or naturally occurring work groups that attend encounter groups) tend to be more successful in generalizing the new skills back to the original situation. It is questionable, however, whether interpersonal issues among colleague workers should demand *so* much attention, and whether trust and openness (the hallmarks of encounter) are the only or best predictors of organizational behavior. People are also motivated by greed and competition. Training groups are, therefore, necessary that focus on maintaining competition at tolerable levels rather than intervening as if honest encounter will solve all organizational ailments. Consultants must stay aware of their own biases when planning strategies. The consultee organization should not be fit into a particular package because the consultant likes running encounter groups (or any other trick from the proverbial bag).

DO WE KNOW ENOUGH?

The skills described as associated with each consultation model are designed to provide the consultant with some basic tools for facilitating change. Each model deserves further investigation. What seems clear is that all change agents must possess enough conceptual and skill flexibility to respond to the myriad human situations that confront them. In a world as complex and pluralistic as ours, dogmatic adherence to any one world view that denigrates the legitimacy of all others is foolhardy. People in the business of helping people are really just beginning their professional journeys. There is much more unknown than known.

SUGGESTED READINGS

Alderfer, C. P. Organizational development. *Annual Review of Psychology*, 1977, **28**, 197–223.

OD aims toward improving the quality of life for members of human systems and increasing the institutional effectiveness of those systems through the use of behavioral science methods. The article is a comprehensive review of the literature in the 1970s. It is divided into four major sections: value conflicts, new settings and new techniques, review of OD research, and the current status of OD.

Alpert, J. L. Conceptual bases of mental health consultation in the schools. *Professional Psychology*, 1976, 7, 619–625.

Consultation as a profession is viewed in its historical perspectives and conceptual bases. Historically, consultation was the preferred mode of treatment (prevention) at the turn of the century, specifically with Witmer and his first mental health clinic. However, economics and demand made it necessary and possible for the main thrust of psychological services to be in a therapeutic therapist-client modality. Now the same two pressures of economics and need require the expansion of consultation services, particularly in the schools. Caplan and Sarason are identified as the two authorities supplying the predominant conceptual basis of school consultation.

Alpin, J. C. Structural change vs. behavioral change. *American Personnel and Guidance Journal*, 1978, **56**, 407–411.

This article traces the historical roots of the Behavioral–Structural controversy and tries to show how these two approaches toward organizational change are not mutually exclusive but have the potential to complement each other. Although the emphasis seems to be on structural change, the author points out in detail how structural problems have related behavioral manifestations which, in turn, influence structural systems. The focus is on structural interventions because the author feels that most consultants lack adequate knowledge in this area and need to better understand the interrelationships of elements within organizations.

Aponte, H. The family-school interview: An eco-structural approach. *Family Process*, 1976, **15**, 303–311.

This article describes the family-school interview, an intervention with a child, family, and school, taking into account the dynamics of each system in that ecological context and the structural interrelationships of these systems relative to the problem presented by the child. According to the author, the challenge to mental health professionals is to develop methods for intervening where the systems touch together. An actual interview is described within the context of an ecostructural framework. An excellent article describing a means by which to conduct combined home-school consultation.

Berlin, I. N. *Advocacy for child mental health*. New York: Brunner-Mazel, 1975.

This book reports the findings of the Joint Commission on the Mental Health of Children. The Joint Commission describes many areas where children's rights should be expanded, and suggests ways of advocating for those rights both individually and systematically.

Goodstein, L. D. *Consulting with human service systems*. Reading, Mass.: Addison-Wesley, 1978.

This book is divided into two major sections. The first four chapters are an overview to organizational and consultation issues, including the following major topics: differences among private-public-volunteer sectors; models of consultation (Caplan's Mental Health Model, Blake & Mouton's Consulcube, Schein's Process Consultation Model, and the Prescriptive Model); and an overview of organizational theory (Systems Model, Psychoanalytic Integration Model, Weisbord's Six-Box Model). Also included in this section on theory is a thorough description of the Process Consultation Model, which is emphasized throughout the book.

The last four chapters deal with the consultation process itself, from entry to diagnosis to intervention to termination and evaluation. Methods of data collection (i.e., observation, interviews, surveys) and two general classes of interventions (technostructural and process) are discussed.

Harvey, J. B., & Albertson, D. R. Neurotic organizations: Symptoms, causes, and treatment. In W. Warner Burke (Ed.), *New technologies in organization development: I*. La Jolla, Calif.: University Associates, 1975.

A condensed "physicians' desk reference" for OD. Presents interviews with employees of an organization from which to diagnose that organization's illness. Discusses common symptoms, typical organizational coping mechanisms, causes, and treatment.

Mearig, J. On becoming a child advocate in school psychology. *Journal of School Psychology*, 1974, **2**, 121–129.

The 1970 Joint Commission on Mental Health for Children recommended a national to local level system of child advocacy be organized. There are many activities which may be classified under child advocacy. Training for child advocacy must be part of professional development. Individual school psychologists must help children develop maximally and see that all necessary steps to this end are followed. Training programs must combine orientation and practical experience so graduates may become child advocates.

APPENDIX 3.A
CHECKLIST FOR DUE PROCESS
FOR HEARING OFFICERS

Was Board of Education notified in writing of a possible handicapping condition by child's parent, professional staff member, local school district, or a licensed physician?

Was evaluation completed by appropriate school district personnel?

Was all evaluation information sent to the district Committee on the Handicapped?

Did the Committee on the Handicapped meet to decide on eligibility for special educational services, or to change, modify, or continue an existing program?

Was parent *notified* of scheduled meeting and invited to address the Committee in writing and/or in person?

Did parent address Committee on Handicapped in writing and/or in person?

Was parent notified in writing of scheduled meeting *before* any action was taken or recommended by Committee?

Did Committee determine eligibility and make placement recommendation to the Board of Education?

Was written notice given to the parent of this recommendation to the Board?

Did this written notice:

(a) describe in detail the proposal classification or change in placement and the reasons why such an action is appropriate for child;

(b) specify the test or reports upon which proposed action is based;

(c) state that the school files, records, and reports pertaining be available for inspection and interpretation. Such records shall be available for review and duplication at reasonable cost;

(d) describe in detail the right to obtain an impartial formal hearing if there are objections to a proposed action;

(e) state procedures for appealing the decision of a formal hearing;

(f) indicate that the parent is entitled to an independent evaluation of the child and the school district shall provide names, addresses, and telephone numbers of appropriate public agencies and other resources within the county where such services can be obtained; and

(g) indicate that during pendency of any proceedings, unless school officials and parents otherwise agree, the child shall *remain* in the current placement or, if applying for initial admission, shall be placed in the public school program until all such proceedings have been completed?

Did Board of Education select most reasonable and appropriate special service?

If residential, private, or out-of-state placements required, did Board of Education notify Commissioner of Education?

Did Board arrange for placement within *30 days* following Committee recommendation?

Did parent request an impartial formal hearing in writing to the Board of Education within *10 days* of the Committee recommendation if not satisfied with arranged placement?

Source: S. McDonald, *Checklist for Hearing Officers*. Unpublished mimeo. Center on Human Policy, 1977.

APPENDIX 3.B
SUGGESTIONS FOR PARENTS
OF DISABLED CHILDREN

1. You are the primary helper, monitor, coordinator, observer, record keeper, and decision maker for your child. Insist that you be treated as such. It is your right to understand your child's diagnosis and the reasons for treatment recommendations and for educational placement. No changes in his treatment or educational placement should take place without prior consultation with you.

2. Your success in getting as well informed as you will need to be to monitor your child's progress depends on your ability to work with the people who work with your child. You may encounter resistance to the idea of including you in the various diagnostic and decision making processes. The way you handle that resistance is important. Your best tool is not the angry approach. Some of your job will include the gentler art of persuasion. Stay confident and cool about your own abilities and intuitions. You know your child better than anyone else could. You are, obviously, a vital member of the team of experts.

3. Try to find, from among the many people whom you see, a person who can help you coordinate the various diagnostic visits and results. Pick the person with whom you have the best relationship, someone who understands your role as the principal monitor of your child's progress throughout life and who will help you become a good one.

4. Learn to keep records. As soon as you know that you have a child with a problem, start a notebook. Make entries of names, addresses, phone numbers, dates of visits, the persons present during the visits, and as much of what was said as you can remember. Record the questions you asked and the answers you received. Record any recommendations made. Make records of phone calls too; include the dates, the purpose, the result. It is best to make important requests by letter. Keep a copy for your notebook. Such documentation for every step of your efforts to get your child the service he needs can be the evidence which finally persuades a program director to give him what he needs. Without concise records of whom you spoke to, when you spoke to him, what he promised, how long you waited between the request and the response, you will be handicapped. No one can ever be held accountable for conversations or meetings with persons whose names and titles you do not remember, or dates you cannot recall, about topics which you cannot clearly discuss.

5. Make sure that you understand the terminology used by professionals. Ask them to translate their terms into lay language. Ask them to give

examples of what they mean. Do not leave their offices until you are sure you understand what they have said so well that you can carry the information to your children's teachers, for instance, and explain it to the teachers in clear, understandable language. (Write down the professional terms too. Knowing them might come in handy sometime.)

6. Ask for copies of your child's records. You probably will not get them, but you could ask that a tape recording be made of any "interpretative" conference. It is very hard to remember what was said in such conferences.

7. Read. Learn as much as you can about your child's problem. But do not swallow whole what you read. Books are like people. They might be offering only one side of the story.

8. Talk freely and openly with as many professionals as you can. Talk with other parents. Join a parent organization. By talking with people who "have been through it already," you will receive moral support and will not feel quite so alone. Get information from parent organizations about services available, about their quality. But bear in mind that a particular program might not help your child even though it has proved helpful for another child. Visit programs if you have the time and energy to do so. There is no substitute for firsthand views.

9. Stay in close touch with your child's teachers. Make sure you know what they are doing in the classroom so that, with their help, you can follow through at home. Share what you have read with them. Ask their advice and suggestions. Get across the idea that you are a team working for the same goals. Make your child a part of that team whenever possible. He or she might have some great ideas.

10. Listen to your child. Your child is giving you a unique point of view that he or she is an expert on in many matters.

11. Work hard at living the idea that differentness is just fine—not bad. Your child will learn most from your example. Help your child to think of problems as things that can be solved if people work at them together.

Source: E. Barnes, "Suggestions for Parents," Unpublished mimeo., Center on Human Policy, Syracuse, N.Y. No Date. Reproduced with author's permission.

APPENDIX 3.C
HOW TO EVALUATE A
SCHOOL PROGRAM

Starting Off

Have some ideas about what you want for your child and don't be afraid to question school officials; don't fall into the expert trap! Think about your child's needs in terms of social development, self-help skills, academic skills—and then look for a program that will respond individually to those needs.

If possible, visit several programs before you decide where you child is going. Certainly, visit as frequently as possible while your child is in a program. It's important for you to know what's really going on in the classroom and also develop enough of a relationship with the teacher(s) to discuss together concerns about your child's education.

Some Questions to Ask About a School Program

What is the philosophy of the program?

What happens to children leaving the program? Where do they go? Does the program prepare a person for a job or for further schooling? For participation in the larger community?

On what basis are the activities chosen? Do the staff members diagnose the individual needs of each child, set goals, and then choose activities to meet those goals? What kinds of goals are set for some of the children in the program who might be like your child? How does the teacher assess what gains children have made? What kinds of records are kept? Let the teacher show you sample records.

Are parents encouraged to be involved in the program and, if so, in what way? How often is contact made with parents? What is the attitude toward parents?

To what extent do children in the program interact with typical children and with the larger community? In what kinds of activities?

What kind of structure is provided for the children to help them feel safe, and what efforts are made to encourage independence?

What is the philosophy of the program with regard to behavior management?

What kinds of support services (e.g., speech therapy, counseling, etc.) are available? Does the school encourage use of volunteers to help in the classrooms?

Do teachers and other staff advocate for children in terms of helping them find programs and get appropriate medical help and recreational activities?

Are children described in a stereotyped way (e.g., "all children with cerebral palsy do that") rather than as individuals?

Some Things to Observe About a School Program

Arrange to spend time in several classrooms (especially of the age group of your child) as well as get a tour of the school. Talk to staff members and with children and young adults in the program. Look for:

a. *the range of materials* in the classroom. Every class should have a variety of materials available to meet the variety of needs the children have. If you do not see much around, ask; some teachers keep things put away but still have a variety of options for children. Materials can be useful without being expensive.

b. *the feeling tone* of the environment. Does the atmosphere seem warm? What kind of relationship does the teacher have with children? Does he/she touch the children, speak loudly or softly, call children by name? Does the teacher seem to respect children's preferences and value the children themselves? For example, are the children's products put up around the room? Do the materials reflect the ethnic backgrounds of the children (e.g., black dolls) so they feel valued? In what way does the teacher control behavior that he/she sees as inappropriate?

c. *evidence of goals and activities* designed for individual children. If you can't see this, ask. There may be folders of planned work for each child as a routine of activities for each child. Do there seem to be both social and academic goals for each child?

d. *kind of interaction among the students.* Social learning is one of the most important functions of school. Is there positive interaction between peers? Are children learning appropriate behavior from each other? In the classroom or in the school building, do children with disabilities interact with typical children? Do the labeled children eat, play on the playground, and have gym, art, and music with the regular classrooms?

e. What is the ratio of adults to children in the classroom? Are there aides and volunteers in the room? Would the teacher be supportive of volunteers? (Ask).

f. Do the teachers and administrative staff seem to talk together and support each other? Is there evidence of teachers working together/ cooperatively with children? When adults feel supported in a school, they are more responsive to children.

Remember that each child's needs are different and so are classrooms. Be active about seeking the kind of school program you think is best for your child. Do not just take what the school offers you; look around for other options that might better meet your child's needs, including private settings. If the school district does not have the right program, perhaps they need to start it!

To get the program you want, you can use the tools of law or the tools of pester power.

State law establishes right to an education for children and appeal procedures for parents. It is possible that your child has a right to the service you want and that the schools or other agencies can be forced to provide the service because the law says they must. So, as a parent, know the law and/or contact other parents, an attorney, or advocacy agencies for support. Use letters, phone calls, conferences, legal hearings, or, finally, lawsuits to get the program you want.

A major force for change is the ability to influence administrators through pester power. Through letters and phone calls and conferences, you can put pressure on officials to do what you would like. If you can organize others to support your idea, then you have even more power.

Source: E. Barnes, "How to Evaluate a School Program," Unpublished mimeo., Center on Human Policy, Syracuse, N.Y., No date. Reproduced with author's permission.

APPENDIX 3.D
A CHECKLIST FOR AN
INDIVIDUALIZED EDUCATION PLAN

In assessing the adequacy or inadequacy of an Individualized Education Plan (IEP), one must look at both its *content* and the *process* of its development. An IEP should facilitate parent-school communication, and provide accountability. It should help a teacher focus learning activities and make lesson plans more relevant. It is to be developed on the basis of the child's needs, without regard to funding or the current availability of such a program.

I. *THE IEP PROCESS*

Timing

_____ An IEP developed within 30 days of the time a child is determined to need special education and related services.

_____ For child currently labeled handicapped, IEP developed, reviewed, and revised at least annually on a schedule determined by the agency. After the initial meeting, an IEP in effect at the beginning of the school year.

Participants. IEP meeting included:

_____ A representative of the public agency qualified to provide or supervise the provision of special education.

_____ Child's teacher.

_____ One or both of the child's parents.

_____ The child, where appropriate.

_____ Others at parent or agency discretion.

_____ For a child evaluated for the first time, a member of the evaluation team or someone knowledgeable about the evaluation procedures used with the child and familiar with the results of the evaluation.

Notification and Scheduling of the IEP Meeting

_____ Parents notified in sufficient time to arrange attendance.

_____ Time and place of meeting mutually agreeable.

_____ Notice included purpose, time, location, participants of the meeting (can be written or oral but agency must keep a record of its efforts to contact parents).

_____ Notice informed parents they could bring other people to the meeting.

_____ Notice in primary language and interpreter provided for parents who are deaf or whose primary language is other than English.

_____ If neither parent could attend the meeting, parent participation occurred through individual or conference phone calls.

_____ If meeting conducted without parent participation, school has record of its attempts to arrange a mutually agreed upon time and place through phone calls, correspondence, home or work visits.

Records

_____ Available data on the child reviewed by parents and school personnel (including physical exam, psychological exam, social history, reports of teacher and outside specialists like speech therapist).

_____ Parents afforded opportunity to examine all records

_____ Additional testing available at public expense.

_____ Confidentiality of child and parents protected.

Content

_____ See Part II.

Completion

_____ Parents received copy of IEP on request

_____ Parents sign a copy of the IEP and return to school.

Review and Accountability

_____ IEP reviewed and revised at least annually with parent participation

_____ Public schools representative initiated IEP process for child placed in private school and participated in review and revision.

_____ Teacher and agency made good faith efforts to achieve goals and objectives of IEP even though agency or teacher cannot be held accountable if child does not achieve projected growth. (Parents can complain, ask for revisions of the program and invoke due process procedures if parents feel efforts not being made).

II. *CONTENT OF THE IEP*

_____ A good IEP is *comprehensive*—it covers all content areas including communication, behavior, socialization, self-help, academics, perceptual-motor and gross-motor skills.

_____ A good IEP is *specific*—its goals and objectives are stated in terms of observable behaviors.

_____ A good IEP is *sequential*—it is based on a developmental sequence of skills and curriculum approaches to teach them.

_____ A good IEP is *realistic* and *appropriate*—its goals and objectives fit the child's current functioning and probable growth rate.

_____ A good IEP is *understandable*—it is written in language that is comprehensible to parents and professionals.

_____ A good IEP is *mutually developed*—that is, it represents a consensus of parents and school personnel in terms of goals and objectives.

The following content should be included in each IEP:

Child's Present Level of Functioning

Accurate information about a child's current level of functioning is necessary for the development of an appropriate IEP. This should reflect the highest level of skill a student has attained in a sequence of skills for each of the content areas included in the IEP. The statements of present level of functioning:

_____ stated in observable behavioral terms;

_____ based on more than a one-shot experience with a child;

_____ covered the major content areas (where appropriate) of:

    _____ communication   _____ perceptual-motor

    _____ socialization   _____ gross-motor

    _____ behavior   _____ academics (subdivided

    _____ self-help   by topics like math, reading, social studies, etc.)

Annual Goals

The yearly goals reflect answers to the question: "What do we want the child to be able to do?" The goals must reflect knowledge of the child's current functioning in each content area, the next sequence of skills in that area, and some estimate of the child's rate of learning. If the learning rate is underestimated, and the child achieves the annual goals earlier, then new goals can be added. Priorities are established in choosing goals based on the student's physical limitations, age, and length of time left in school, and expectations for the future. The annual goals in this IEP were:

_____ stated in terms of observable behaviors;

_____ inclusive of the major content areas:

    _____ communication   _____ perceptual-motor

    _____ socialization   _____ gross-motor (physical

    _____ behavior   education is speci-

    _____ self-help   fically mentioned in the law)

                           _____ academics

_____ based on child's present level of functioning;

_____ realistic in terms of any physical limitations of the student;

_____ prioritized on the basis of student's age and amount of time left in school;

_____ prioritized toward functional skills to help the child live as independently as possible.

Short-Term Objectives and Evaluations

Short-term objectives include a number of steps in the sequence of moving a student toward each annual goal. They can be listed as 3 or 4 steps for each reporting or evaluation period. Short-term objectives are not as specific as lesson plans but, rather, indicate the breakdown of intermediate goals a teacher will teach to help a student reach the annual goal. The short-term objectives must be stated in behavioral terms and the criteria for achieving the objective included. That is, each objective should say *what the student will do, under what conditions*, and *to what criteria*. For example, in a free play situation, John will come to the teacher when called by name ("John, come") and the sign for come is used, 9 out of 10 times (90% of the time). Persons responsible for implementing specific objectives should be noted (e.g., teacher, speech therapist, etc.) as well as dates for beginning and ending work on each objective.

The short-term objectives in this IEP were:

_____ based on annual goals;

_____ based on a commonly accepted *sequence* of skills;

_____ stated in observable behavioral terms;

_____ included the *conditions* under which the students would perform and *to what criteria*:

_____ included persons responsible for implementing objective;

_____ included dates for beginning and ending work on each objective;

_____ (option) stated methods and materials to be used to reach each objective (e.g., DISTAR reading).

Related Services

Related services are those additional services necessary for a child to benefit from special educational instruction. According to P.L.94-142, they include transportation and developmental, corrective, and other supportive services (speech pathology and audiology, psychological services, physical and occupational therapy, recreation and counseling, and medical services (the latter for diagnostic and evaluation purposes only). Special materials (like adaptive equipment) or media (e.g., braille devices) should be listed here also. An appropriate physical education program is specifically mentioned. Who will deliver these special services and for how much time (how often, beginning and ending date) should also be noted. For example, articulation therapy by Jane Stern, Speech therapist, 30 minutes, 3 times a week, 9/78–1/79.

_____ Transportation provided;

_____ Appropriate special services designated. Check which:

_____ Speech/language	_____ O.T.	_____ Medical
_____ Psychological	_____ Recreation	Diagnostic
_____ P.T.	_____ Counseling	

_____ indicated who will deliver service;

_____ included amount of time for each service and beginning and ending dates;

_____ physical education plan included;

_____ listed special media and materials to be provided.

Participation in Regular Education

P.L.94-142 states that (1) to the maximum extent appropriate, handicapped children, including children in public and private institutions or other care facilities, are educated with children who are not handicapped; and (2) that special classes, separate schooling or other removal of handicapped children from the regular educational environment occurs only when the nature and severity of the handicap is such that education in regular classes with the use of supplementary aids and services cannot be achieved satisfactorily. The law also encourages a child's placement in their neighborhood school or as close as possible to home, and the provision of nonacademic and extracurricular services and activities (meals, recess, etc.) with non-handicapped children. The IEP must specify how and when the student will interact with non-handicapped peers in a planful way.

_____ opportunities for interaction with nonhandicapped peers listed;

_____ staff responsible for implementation of program during integrated activities noted;

_____ socialization objectives related to integrated activities and criteria for evaluation indicated;

_____ amount of time and beginning and ending dates noted.

Additional Comments/Concerns

An optional section of the IEP may include *medical concerns* (e.g., seizures and medication); statements of particular important physical or behavioral characteristics; descriptions of learning style or effective approaches (e.g., reinforcers), etc.

Placement Justification and Signatures

A statement must be included indicating the placement of the child and why it is deemed most appropriate. The final IEP must be signed and dated by the participants including parents.

_____ Placement stated;

_____ Justification for placement included;

_____ Signatures by all parties involved (parents, teachers, school representative, child if appropriate, others).

4

Evaluation Issues and Strategies in Consultation

A number of authors have summarized and analyzed the state-of-the-art of research on consultation efficacy (especially Mannino & Shore, 1979; Medway, 1979). These reviews are of particular interest to researchers and trainers. Typical consultation research may provide helpful prescriptive practice ideas, but they have little relevance to the day-to-day work of consultants in the field in terms of evaluating *their* own effectiveness. Few working consultants without university affiliation can spare the time to carefully manipulate one variable in the consultation experience in order to find out what is true about its particular efficacy (e.g., Conoley & Conoley, 1982). All consultants are, however, interested in making judgments about the value of their particular services to a particular host system (e.g., Fairchild, 1976). This distinction between *truth* and *value* lies at the heart of the difference between research and evaluation (Matuszek, 1981). It will make little difference to a consultee organization if the consultant does everything with textbook perfection. The decision makers are interested in positive outcomes in terms of cost, increased services, or staff feedback. Consultants must be prepared not only to provide assistance to others who are planning, implementing, and evaluating programs (i.e., program consultation) but must also give priority to such activities in their own service delivery systems.

In order to accomplish a good evaluation, consultants must, as a minimum, know what their goals are; what the goals of the organization are; what methods or techniques appear feasible and preferable; and what outcomes are expected because of the consultation. These general points are items that also make up the consultation contract (see chapter 5 for further discussion). A well done contract can, therefore, provide the basis for the evaluation plan.

Evaluation is not relegated to the final moment of a consultation venture. In fact, if consultants wait until the last few weeks of a consultation contract to begin data collection, they have missed the points of both consultation and evaluation. Good consultants seek feedback in an ongoing way. Good evaluators plan on collecting data throughout a program so as to be able to answer various evaluation questions. For example:

1. Are consultees aware of the consultation service?
2. Do consultees understand the parameters of consultation?
3. How many requests for consultation are made during specified time periods?
4. How much consultation is going on during specified time periods?
5. What generally are the problems being addressed in consultation?
6. How successful are various cases according to consultee feedback and client outcome?
7. Is the consultant spending the agreed upon time with the organization?
8. Is consultation actually taking place, or are other activities more prevalent?
9. Are time lines attached to certain goals being met?
10. With increasing knowledge about the system, does consultation still appear the most preferable strategy?

Even this abbreviated list may seem overwhelming at first. "When do I provide service," you may be asking, "if I spend all my time in data collection?" Two considerations are relevant. First, the ability to gather such data depends on planning before the consultation begins. Experience will suggest different strategies. And second, it is shortsighted to believe that quality services can be provided in an information vacuum. What is gained by *knowing* the answers to those questions? What is lost by *not knowing*? Our experience indicates that quality services and invitations to return to do more consultation are the results of knowing. The converses are true when the questions go uninvestigated.

PROCESS AND PRODUCT EVALUATIONS

Many writers in evaluation theory and practice point out the complementary aspects of process (formative) and product (summative) evaluations (e.g., Borich, 1974; Hayman & Napier, 1975). Generally, process evaluation refers to data collection that monitors whether or not the program is going as planned. Has the consultant been working four hours every day? In addition, process evaluation keeps abreast of interim time lines or instrumental goals.

Has the consultant met all the important system gatekeepers within the first three weeks of work?

Product evaluation is aimed at determining the final outcomes of the program, that is, were objectives met. Did consultation services result in a decrease in direct service referrals? The two "types" of evaluation are obviously not separate entities because a hierarchical structure is implicit. If the program was never implemented as planned, the chances for outcome success appear very slight. Despite the interdependence of these two, most evaluations are conceived of as product evaluation—wait until the end and see if objectives were met. The problem with this approach is obvious. Self-correcting feedback is a necessity. When consultation services are planned before entry is complete, some of the planning is necessarily hypothetical. Some consequences of action can be anticipated and every effort should be made to do so (Sarason, 1972). Predicting intended and unintended consequences would be, however, far less crucial if data were available for careful analysis and interpretation throughout the implementation phase of a program.

SAMPLE STRATEGIES

A number of process data collection strategies can be employed. If consultants are employees· of a system, they probably already respond to certain data gathering mandates. Much of these data, although they appear to be potentially helpful process data, are either fed back too late or looked at only as product or accountability data. Consultants may have to keep simultaneous records in order to meet their own evaluation needs. They also might target the efficient use of collected data as a consultative goal. Logs of activities are very helpful devices. These might be relatively structured checklists or impression-filled accounts. Table 4.1 is an example of a checklist log. The advantages of this or other checklists is standardized information across all cases and relatively effortless accomplishment. A disadvantage is that no checklist accounts for all that may happen; therefore, important impressions, events, or facts may not be recorded because there are no appropriate categories. Relatively unstructured logs are easy to put off doing and may result in gaps in detail across some cases. On the other hand, writing gut reactions, plans for the future, and vague impressions is a particularly rewarding activity that everyone should try at least for awhile.

Special checklists can be constructed to match particular objectives. Consultants might list all of their potential consultees and then check and date the names as each is met and some preliminary entry is accomplished. The checklist provided as table 4.1 also illustrates how other data regarding problems, efficacy, methodologies, and data gathering can be consolidated.

Table 4.1.Structured Consultant Log

Consultant's name _____	Referral date _____
Consultee's name_____	Interview date _____
role _____	Organization _____
sex _____	Model of consultation:
age _____	Client-centered _____
Client discussed:	Consultee-centered _____
sex _____	Behavioral _____
age _____	Process _____
Case # _____	Advocacy _____
Interview # _____	Program _____

1. Check as many processes as you employed during this interview and rank order the top 3 (in terms of frequency)

   problem identification _____
   problem analysis _____
   plan developed _____
   evaluation of prior plans _____
   offer to share responsibility _____
   share information _____
   probe for information _____
   verbal reinforcement _____
   direct confrontation _____

   indirect confrontation _____
   providing alternatives _____
   summarizing _____
   encouraging _____
   validating _____
   clarifying _____
   empathizing _____
   probe for feelings _____
   other (specify) _____

2. What are some components of the plan you developed:

   parent conference _____
   curriculum change _____
   staff development _____
   inservice _____
   role playing _____
   advocacy _____
   addition of a positive
      reinforcer _____
   removal of an aversive differential
      reinforcement _____
   involved teachers meeting _____
   modeling _____

   prompting _____
   establishing, removing or altering an
      SD _____
   physical response guidance _____
   noncontingent application of
      reinforcers _____
   task alteration _____
   extinction _____
   counseling _____
   classroom observation _____
   other (specify) _____

3. Rate the receptivity of your consultee

   very closed _____quite receptive

       1   2   3   4   5

4. Write one sentence description of the problem:

5. Rate the severity of the problem as you see it:

   severe _____mild

       1   2   3   4   5

Continued on p. 86

Table 4.1. (*Continued*)

As consultee sees it:

severe _____mild

| | 1 | 2 | 3 | 4 | 5 |

6. How are you evaluating your consultative effort?

    feedback from consultee _____

    observation of client _____

    feedback from supervisors _____

    none _____

    other (specify) _____

7. What are the results of your evaluation?

    from consultee

    very poor _____very good

| | 1 | 2 | 3 | 4 | 5 |

    from client observation

    very poor _____very good

| | 1 | 2 | 3 | 4 | 5 |

    from supervisors

    very poor _____very good

| | 1 | 2 | 3 | 4 | 5 |

    other (specify)

    very poor _____very good

| | 1 | 2 | 3 | 4 | 5 |

The progress notes illustrated in chapter 2 are also helpful process devices. These can be kept filed with each child's information, but also as part of data relating to quantity and quality of services.

Multilevel product data should be sought in consultation because it is a multilevel strategy. Positive evaluations from consultees are crucial but probably insufficient. Whenever possible, data should be collected from consultees concerning their use of consultation, their impressions of the consultant, and the perceived effects of consultation on the targeted case. In addition, the consultant should do some direct observation or measurement of client changes. These may take the form of classroom observation and academic standings in school or staff meeting observations and productivity records in businesses.

Numerous occasions in a consultation program occur when supportive consultation is sought. No real problem resolution is being sought by the consultee—just a sympathetic ear and some words of encouragement. These times are not trivial and should figure into an evaluative program. Asking for open-ended comments from consultees sometimes allows some of these positive or negative feelings to surface for interpretation and action.

Supervisors' reactions to consultation are also important to monitor. Such monitoring may take the form of face-to-face meetings during which the consultant asks for feedback, checks if the supervisor has questions, asks if the supervisor has had feedback from other staff members, brings the supervisor up to date on consultation activities, and probes to see if the standing contract is still satisfactory. It is good to establish a norm for open communication of this sort. Consultants must stay aware of the time constraints of

Table 4.2. School Psychologist Trainee Evaluation Form

Date of Evaluation: _____

Trainee: _____

Field Supervisor: _____

University Supervisor: _____

Directions: The ratings of trainees should be based upon actual observation and/or reports received from staff, parents, students, etc., regarding trainee performance. Circle the number of the scale that best describes the intern's competence as given in the description below. Rate each category independently. A description of scale points is provided below.

1—competence considered to be in need of further training and/or require additional growth, maturation, and change on the part of the trainee in order for him/her to be effective in the various skill areas;

2—competence currently considered to be below average but which, with further supervision and experience, is expected to develop satisfactorily; close supervision is required;

3—competence at least at minimal level necessary for functioning with moderate supervision required;

4—competencies assessed to be above average, suggesting a minimal need for supervision;

5—competencies very developed and reflect capability for independent functioning with little or no supervision required;

No Data—insufficient data to make rating at this time.

General Competencies			Rating			
1. *Evaluation—Assessment*						
Intellectual	1	2	3	4	5	No Data
Social-Emotional	1	2	3	4	5	No Data
Interviewing Skills	1	2	3	4	5	No Data
Behavioral Assessment	1	2	3	4	5	No Data
Ability to Integrate Data	1	2	3	4	5	No Data
Other (_____)	1	2	3	4	5	No Data
2. *Intervention*						
Practicality	1	2	3	4	5	No Data
Appropriateness to Problems	1	2	3	4	5	No Data

Continued on p. 88

Table 4.2. (*Continued*)

Specificity of Recommendations 1	2	3	4	5	No Data
Provision for Follow-up 1	2	3	4	5	No Data
Implementation 1	2	3	4	5	No Data
Actual Follow-up 1	2	3	4	5	No Data

3. *Communication and Collaboration*

Teacher Conferencing 1	2	3	4	5	No Data
Parent Conferencing 1	2	3	4	5	No Data
Administrative Conferencing 1	2	3	4	5	No Data
Case Staffing 1	2	3	4	5	No Data
Reporting (written) 1	2	3	4	5	No Data

4. *Consultation*

Problem/Need Identification 1	2	3	4	5	No Data
Plan Formulation 1	2	3	4	5	No Data
Plan Implementation 1	2	3	4	5	No Data
Follow-up and Evaluation 1	2	3	4	5	No Data

5. *In-service Training* 1

In-service Training 1	2	3	4	5	No Data
Planning 1	2	3	4	5	No Data
Implementation 1	2	3	4	5	No Data
Follow-up and Evaluation 1	2	3	4	5	No Data

6. *Research/Program Evaluation*

Planning 1	2	3	4	5	No Data
Implementation 1	2	3	4	5	No Data
Follow-up Communication............. 1	2	3	4	5	No Data
Provision for Individual Rights and Confidentiality................... 1	2	3	4	5	No Data

7. *Interpersonal Style*
   A. Rapport with:

students 1	2	3	4	5	No Data
teachers 1	2	3	4	5	No Data
staff 1	2	3	4	5	No Data
administration 1	2	3	4	5	No Data

   B. General Performances
      Characteristics:

enthusiasm and interest 1	2	3	4	5	No Data
dependability 1	2	3	4	5	No Data
promptness........................... 1	2	3	4	5	No Data
productivity 1	2	3	4	5	No Data
creativity.............................. 1	2	3	4	5	No Data

8. Overall Rating of Trainee 1   2   3   4   5   No Data

On the other side, please summarize the trainee's strengths and weaknesses. Where weaknesses are indicated, indicate the kinds of experience needed to strengthen those areas of weakness.

supervisors, however, and not appear (or be) too demanding of supervisor time. Some supervisors prefer written communications either preceding or following face-to-face meetings. Copies of these can be saved by consultants as summaries of interactions with supervisors. These might be collapsed into part of a final summarizing report presented to the consultee organization. One such report is given as Appendix 4.A.

Table 4.2 is a comprehensive evaluation device useful to gather judgments about mental health service delivery in schools. This type of instrument can be administered toward the middle of a consultation contract and at the end.

Table 4.3. Assessment Form: Consultative and Change Agent Concerns

---

The following areas of concern are common to most consultant-consultee relationships. In using this form, use the following symbols: 1—Little ability; 2—Some ability; 3—Moderate ability 4—Considerable ability, 5—Great ability

---

1. *Self Awareness*: aware of one's own personal needs which might be served in the relationship (perhaps detracting from one's effectiveness). 1 2 3 4 5

2. *Entry*: entering (and re-entering) a consultee system. Able to work out a relationship which has the desired long-run consequences.   1 2 3 4 5

3. *Diagnosis*: examination of the consultee's motives. Definition of problem, assessment of barriers.   1 2 3 4 5

4. *Data Collection*: agreement between consultee and consultant as to kinds of data to be gathered and method(s) for collection.   1 2 3 4 5

5. *Relationship*: working out a constructive mutual acceptance of each other's contribution.   1 2 3 4 5

6. *Resource Identification and Development*: determining those areas where consultant and consultee can be resources to the process.   1 2 3 4 5

7. *Decision-making*: determining how decisions will be made and getting them accomplished and acted upon.   1 2 3 4 5

8. *Boundary Definition*: reaching clear agreement as to where the relationship and roles may proceed.   1 2 3 4 5

9. *Ethics and Values*: establishing and maintaining a set of values which are kept clear to the consultee system.   1 2 3 4 5

10. *Plans and Alternatives*: developing and implementing specific plans which are tangible and mutually accepted.   1 2 3 4 5

11. *Change Strategy*: accurate assessment of consultee's capacity for change; development of strategies which will help the consultee system carry out change plans.   1 2 3 4 5

12. *Termination*: altering the relationship as it progresses and terminating it without undue strain to the system.   1 2 3 4 5

13. *Evaluation*: building in feedback mechanisms which can continually monitor the change experience.   1 2 3 4 5

Table 4.4. Consultant Assessment Form

Name of School _____

Have you used the mental health consultant this year?

Yes _____   No _____

Instructions: For each of the following questions circle *one* response which best fits you or your view of the mental health consultant.

1. I feel free to express my school-related concerns to the consultant.
    a. agree
    b. somewhat agree
    c. neutral
    d. mildly disagree
    e. disagree
2. The consultant understands the important aspects of the problems I bring up.
    a. agree
    b. somewhat agree
    c. neutral
    d. mildly disagree
    e. disagree
3. The consultant offers advice that I do not think is relevant.
    a. agree
    b. somewhat agree
    c. neutral
    d. mildly disagree
    e. disagree
4. With the consultant I see complexities of the problem situation in greater depth and breadth.
    a. agree
    b. somewhat agree
    c. neutral
    d. mildly disagree
    e. disagree
5. The consultant helps me see alternatives I haven't thought of before.
    a. agree
    b. somewhat agree
    c. neutral
    d. mildly disagree
    e. disagree
6. As a result of consultation, I find myself trying out some of my own ideas.
    a. agree
    b. somewhat agree
    c. neutral
    d. mildly disagree
    e. disagree

Table 4.4. (*Continued*)

7. How satisfied are you with the consultant?
   a. very pleased
   b. somewhat pleased
   c. neutral
   d. not particularly pleased
   e. definitely dissatisfied
8. If consultants were available for next year, would you want one assigned to your school again?
   a. very much
   b. probably yes
   c. indifferent
   d. no
   e. definitely not
9. Do you have any suggestions about the mental health consultant's work in your school?

Table 4.5. Open-End Consultation Evaluation Form

1. Compared with other teachers at your school, would you say your contacts with the consultant were:
   considerably fewer
   fewer
   average
   more
   considerably more
2. With what aspect of the consultation have you been happiest last semester? least happy?

3. What would you like to see changed this semester?

4. How might the consultant be more available to you this semester?

5. What comments or suggestions do you have specifically about the consultant's work this past semester?

6. Based on the things the consultant did this past semester, how would *you* define the role of consultant?

7. Based on your experience with mental health consultation this year, you feel that mental health consultation is:

Extremely   Not at
helpful _____ all helpful
         7   6   5   4   3   2   1

The instrument can be modified in many ways to reflect the important activities of the consultant. A somewhat different instrument related especially to organizational consultation is given as table 4.3.

Consultees may not feel able to complete global evaluation devices and so it is important to tailor their devices to reflect a single consultee's experience with a consultant. Examples of such instruments are given as tables 4.4, 4.5, and 4.6. As with all examples given in this chapter, these instruments should be seen as merely suggestive of important consultant dimensions. Each consultation program is unique and the evaluation effort should be individualized in order to maximize the useful information gained.

Table 4.6. Consultative Processes Evaluation

Date: _____

Below, a number of possible consultation processes are listed. Please assess how true each descriptor is of the consultant by checking the appropriate number on the 1–7 (Not at all true or descriptive of consultant—Always true or descriptive of consultant) differential.

EX: Not at all true or   Always true or
     descriptive of   1   2   3   4   5   6   7 descriptive of
     consultant   consultant

1. The consultant is nonjudgmental; nonevaluative.
                      1   2   3   4   5   6   7

2. The consultant varies behaviors according to the situation.
                      1   2   3   4   5   6   7

3. The consultant pursues issues when they arise.
                      1   2   3   4   5   6   7

4. The consultant is empathic.
                      1   2   3   4   5   6   7

5. The consultant is able to confront with salient issues.
                      1   2   3   4   5   6   7

6. The consultant is perceptive and able to communicate insights.
                      1   2   3   4   5   6   7

7. The consultant is able to grasp meaning and affect in communication.
                      1   2   3   4   5   6   7

8. The consultant is able to summarize and facilitate movement.
                      1   2   3   4   5   6   7

9. The consultant anticipates the direction of consultation and intervenes with an awareness of the consequences.
                      1   2   3   4   5   6   7

10. The consultant maintains the appropriate personal involvement which facilitates communication.
                      1   2   3   4   5   6   7

TRAINING EVALUATIONS

In the course of training, it is necessary to monitor the skill development of students. Reproduced below are typical course objectives used in consultation sequences of study. These are taken from shared course outlines of consultation trainers such as Judith L. Alpert, June M. Gallessich, Joel Meyers, and Mark Swerdlick.

1. Increase skills in conceptualizing school (and other) cultures and processes of change.
2. Develop repertoire of interventions with consultees to increase their effectiveness with clients and each other.
3. Develop skills in evaluation of service delivery programs.
4. Knowledge of four theoretical models of consultation: mental health, behavioral, advocacy, and process.
5. Ability to engage in the four theoretical models at appropriate times according to the presenting situation.
6. Ability to synthesize a personal model of consultation intervention.
7. Expertise in listening and feedback skills.
8. Ability to both enter into and terminate smoothly individual consultative relationships.
9. Ability to design and deliver in-service training to consultees.
10. Expertise in design and implementation of preventive mental health strategies.
11. Ability to diagnose organizational variables and design, implement, and evaluate appropriate interventions.
12. Awareness of personal impact in the consultative relationship.

As with any other training procedure, evaluations must be developed to monitor attainment of each of the training objectives. Evaluation methodologies available in training include evidence of information retention (e.g., tests, class discussions); organizational abilities (e.g., papers, reports); consulting skills (e.g., in-class role plays, feedback from consultees or other supervisors); and interpersonal skills (e.g., mutual feedback sessions, teaming abilities, simulations). It may be good consultation training policy to allow students to resubmit written work until the criterion grade (at least a B) is earned. This allows for constructive supervisor consultation to occur and, thus, provides additional modeling examples for the trainee. In addition, consultation instructors should model openness to feedback and evaluation by regularly seeking input from their students. A brief but informative instructor/course evaluation form is given in table 4.7. Regularly scheduled feedback sessions between instructors and students are important for the continued personal and professional growth of both. The ability of an in-

Table 4.7. Teacher and Course Evaluation

Name of Course_____

Name of Teacher_____

Please be specific in your comments:
1) How would you rate the teacher?

2) How would you rate the course?

Circle number: 1-poor, 2-below average, 3-average, 4-good, 5-excellent, 0-not applicable

3) Ability to get information across—adjust to level of student comprehension—
   explanations clear   0 1 2 3 4 5
4) Class preparation—comes to class well prepared   0 1 2 3 4 5
5) Interest and enthusiasm—stimulates thinking—creates desire to learn—
   enthusiastic   0 1 2 3 4 5
6) Speech delivery—speaks clearly—students can hear and understand
                                                         0 1 2 3 4 5
7) Class discussion—promotes interesting discussions—stimulates
   questions   0 1 2 3 4 5
8) Tolerance—encourages independent thought—respects other points of view
                                                         0 1 2 3 4 5
9) Accessibility—available to outside help   0 1 2 3 4 5
10) Efficiency—prompt in returning papers   0 1 2 3 4 5
11) Grading, strictness—too severe or too easy   0 1 2 3 4 5
12) Grading, fairness   0 1 2 3 4 5
13) Teacher's overall rank compared to others you have had (1 = 1-10%, 2 =
    10-30%, 3 = 30-70%, 4 = 70-90%, 5 = 90-100%)   0 1 2 3 4 5
14) General value of course (rate same as above)   0 1 2 3 4 5

structor to present and organize information is critical. Equally important is the ability to excite students about an area. Without appearing (or being) myopic about the importance of his or her own area of academic interest, a professor must convince others how important, challenging, and exciting an area of work is. Fortunately, this is not difficult when teaching mental health workers who are interested in working for children.

J. C. Conoley and Clark (1980) evaluated consultation training from the perspectives of both students and field supervisors. Recurrent student concerns were identified (see table 4.8) through supervisory records, and training strategies were designed to remediate the problem areas. These strategies were evaluated by the trainees (see table 4.9). In addition, the trainees evalu-

Table 4.8. Recurrent Concerns of Consultation Trainees

How to enter

Never knowing enough

Incongruities or disagreements between consultant and consultee

Territorial concerns (i.e., what is consultant role vis-a-vis other helping professionals?)

Is consultation really the right intervention?

Student status of consultants

Table 4.9. Evaluation of Consultation Training Strategies

As psychologists-in-training in schools, you face many problematic areas. University instruction is meant to meet such areas of concern. Listed below are some of the problems you've probably faced in your field placements. Below each problem are listed some strategies that were employed during consultation training to ameliorate these problems. Please rate each of the strategies on the five point scale provided.

1. = not at all effective
2. = only rarely effective
3. = effective about half the time or neutral about the strategy
4. = a moderately effective strategy
5. = an extremely effective strategy

If you don't remember doing or hearing some of the strategies, rate the strategy according to how you judge its potential, but asterisk (*) such ratings.

1. *Entry concerns of new consultants*
   a. entry papers
      1   2   3   4   5
   b. role play interview with principal
      1   2   3   4   5
   c. given concrete guidelines for staff introduction
      1   2   3   4   5
   d. school norms and common pitfalls described
      1   2   3   4   5
   e. relationships/communication between university and field supervisors
      1   2   3   4   5

2. *Lacks in specialized knowledge*
   a. reinforcement for what you *do* know
      1   2   3   4   5
   b. guest speakers
      1   2   3   4   5

Continued on p. 96

Table 4.9. (*Continued*)

c. handouts on particular areas
  1   2   3   4   5
d. sharing information during supervision
  1   2   3   4   5

3. *Consultant/consultee incongruity*
  a. role play practice with "difficult" consultees
    1   2   3   4   5
  b. discussion and lectures on problem identification
    1   2   3   4   5

4. *Territorial concerns*
  a. directions to seek out and coordinate efforts with other support personnel
    1   2   3   4   5
  b. listing of what resources are typically found in school organizations
    1   2   3   4   5
  c. didactic input on role dimensions of consultation
    1   2   3   4   5

5. *Ambivalence over consultation as a role for school psychologists*
  a. communication between university and field supervisors meant to increase field supervisor support of consultative efforts
    1   2   3   4   5
  b. directions and discussion of how to blend direct service and indirect service
    1   2   3   4   5
  c. didactic inputs on the rationale, theories, and research concerning consultation
    1   2   3   4   5

6. *Student status*
  a. Directions not to empathize student role, rather, to focus on professional expertise
    1   2   3   4   5
  b. grading system independent of actual field performance
    1   2   3   4   5
  c. keeping of narrative logs
    1   2   3   4   5
  d. keeping of structured logs
    1   2   3   4   5
  e. small supervisory group with potential for personal attention to needs
    1   2   3   4   5
  f. consultation teammate for support and peer supervisors
    1   2   3   4   5
  g. availability of both field and university supervisors
    1   2   3   4   5

Thanks for your help. Please use the space below for any open–ended comments you have about the training you've received thus far in consultative techniques. Also, if you remember something we did in class that you found useful, mention it here.

Table 4.10. Evaluation of Trainee Field Competence in Consultation

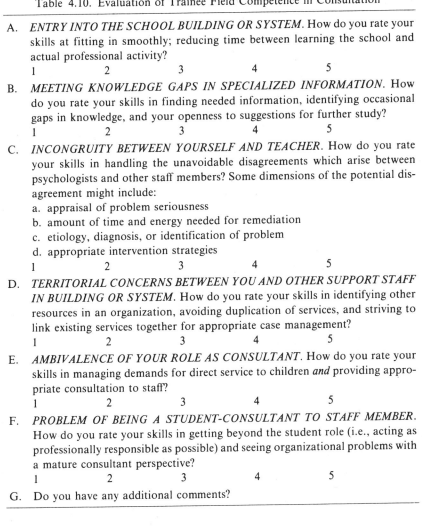

A. *ENTRY INTO THE SCHOOL BUILDING OR SYSTEM.* How do you rate your skills at fitting in smoothly; reducing time between learning the school and actual professional activity?

   1   2   3   4   5

B. *MEETING KNOWLEDGE GAPS IN SPECIALIZED INFORMATION.* How do you rate your skills in finding needed information, identifying occasional gaps in knowledge, and your openness to suggestions for further study?

   1   2   3   4   5

C. *INCONGRUITY BETWEEN YOURSELF AND TEACHER.* How do you rate your skills in handling the unavoidable disagreements which arise between psychologists and other staff members? Some dimensions of the potential disagreement might include:

a. appraisal of problem seriousness
b. amount of time and energy needed for remediation
c. etiology, diagnosis, or identification of problem
d. appropriate intervention strategies

   1   2   3   4   5

D. *TERRITORIAL CONCERNS BETWEEN YOU AND OTHER SUPPORT STAFF IN BUILDING OR SYSTEM.* How do you rate your skills in identifying other resources in an organization, avoiding duplication of services, and striving to link existing services together for appropriate case management?

   1   2   3   4   5

E. *AMBIVALENCE OF YOUR ROLE AS CONSULTANT.* How do you rate your skills in managing demands for direct service to children *and* providing appropriate consultation to staff?

   1   2   3   4   5

F. *PROBLEM OF BEING A STUDENT-CONSULTANT TO STAFF MEMBER.* How do you rate your skills in getting beyond the student role (i.e., acting as professionally responsible as possible) and seeing organizational problems with a mature consultant perspective?

   1   2   3   4   5

G. Do you have any additional comments?

ated their perceived competence in meeting field placement concerns (see table 4.10). The field supervisors of these students rated trainee competence in these same areas on an almost identical evaluation device. The results were quite positive and are explained at length in the Conoley and Clark article. The evaluation devices are provided as other examples of product evaluation efforts. These too, can be adapted to meet the particular objectives/concerns of individual trainers. Table 4.11 is another example of a device used to collect evaluative evidence after a few years had elapsed since the training.

Table 4.11. Two Year Follow-Up Evaluation Device of Consultation Training

Dear _____ :

We are interested in getting some information about the type of activities you are engaging in as a school psychologist. In particular, we want to judge the impact of training in consultation, child advocacy, and systems analysis.

What follows are questions meant to ascertain the effects of "non-traditional" training on your everyday activities.

I.　Can you divide your week in terms of percentage of time spent on various activities?

1. Consultation with teachers _____ %
2. Consultation with administrators _____ %
3. Consultation with other support personnel _____ %
4. Direct service to children:
   Cognitive assessment _____ %
   Social/emotional assessment _____ %
   Counseling _____ %
   Adaptive behavior assessment _____ %
5. Classroom observation _____ %
6. Report writing _____ %
7. Attendence at meetings:
   Committees on handicapped _____ %
   Due process hearings _____ %
   Staff meetings _____ %
   Faculty meetings _____ %

II.　1. Can you identify a number of cases in which you were clearly a *child* advocate rather than a system employee?
   How many in the past public school semester? _____ _____

2. How many due process meetings have you attended in the past public school semester ? _____

3. What was your role at these meetings? _____
_____

4. How many contacts have you had with the families of your clients? _____

5. What services do you regularly offer to families? _____
_____

6. What percentage of your time is spent working with families? _____ %

7. How many home visits have you made in the past public school semester?
_____

8. Do you maintain relationships with community agencies to coordinate services for children? _____
   If yes, which agencies? _____
_____

Table 4.11. (*Continued*)

III. 1. Can you describe the program development or program consultation you have done during the past public school semester? _____

_____

2. What are your long-range goals for the system in which you work? (If you are a "temporary employee" what have you identified as systemic needs?)

_____

3. How many times in the past public school semester have you engaged in process consultation? _____

IV. Now, with the advantage of hindsight and experience, how important do you feel training in consultation is? _____
How important training in child advocacy? _____
How important training in systems assessment? _____

VI. What other types of training would have been helpful to you in the everyday practice of school psychology? Include suggestions in traditional and non-traditional areas. _____

_____

LAST EVALUATIVE WORDS

Collect data for only three reasons: to help facilitate personal change, to help others change, or to help others make a decision. Uninterpreted or thoughtlessly collected information wastes everyone's time. Information that is collected or used for punitive purposes is inappropriate for consultation service delivery or training. Emphases on strength and the capacities of people to change positively are in keeping with good consultation theory and practice.

SUGGESTED READINGS

Cohen, H. A. A comparison of two consultation training programs. *Professional Psychology*, 1976, **7**, 533–540.

Two university training programs resulting in Ph.D.s for consultants are compared and contrasted for efficiency in producing successful consultants. The first program studied is a traditionally oriented approach with two years of study. The first year was basically theoretical and the second year comprised of practica with T group experience for catharsis purposes. The second program, more radical in nature, combined the didactic forums and T group experience along with practica in a one year experience. The conclusion reached was that the second program was more effective in reaching success because the combined experiences resulted in more meaningful cathartic experience within the trainee T group and much of the emotional working out of doubts, fears, etc. of the first group was left to be done on the job, so to speak. In addition, Harvey, Hunt, and Schroeder's (1961) stage theory concerning conceptual systems and personality organization is used to explain why the second training program is more successful.

Colligan, R. C., & McColgan, E. B. Perception of case conduct as a means of evaluating school psychological services. *Professional Psychology*, 1980, 291–297.

The lack of information concerning evaluation of effectiveness of psychological services in the schools was cited. A 40-item questionnaire was devised to determine staff satisfaction of services. This was used in a small rural school setting. The authors believe the questionnaire or a similar one could serve as sensitizing agents for the psychologist in terms of perceptions of the services being provided or seen as needed.

Fox, R., Luszki, H., & Schmuck, R. A. *Diagnosing classroom learning environments*. Chicago: Science Research Associates, 1966.

The purpose of this book is to help teachers understand and identify the attitudes and relations that influence pupils and the classroom climate. The book provides 23 tools for diagnosing the social and psychological factors inherent in the classroom learning atmosphere. The instruments cover the following areas: social relations in the classroom, pupil norms, pupil-teacher interactions, outside influences on pupil learning, parental influences on school adjustment, and the pupil's concept of her or himself. In addition, the book describes ways in which the information obtained can be recorded, interpreted, and acted upon.

Fox, R., Schmuck, R. A., Egmond, E., Ritvo, M., & Jung, C. *Diagnosing professional climate of schools*. Fairfax: National Training Laboratories Learning Resources Corp., 1973.

The purpose of this book is to help principals, teachers, school psychologists, and other school personnel diagnose the existing problems within the school climate. The book presents suggestions about various instruments or types of questions that can be useful in carrying out a diagnosis. Each chapter, while focusing primarily on data-gathering techniques, also attempts to help the reader visualize how the data might be organized for sharing with the faculty, what kinds of interpretations can be drawn, and how these implications might be converted to several alternative courses of action.

Leitenberg, H. The use of single-case methodology in psychotherapy research. *Journal of Abnormal Psychology*, 1973, **82**, 87–101.

Research designs for testing the efficacy of behavioral treatments involving a single subject are presented. The advantages and drawbacks of such designs in psychotherapy could be applied to consultation research, which often tests the effects of one consultant.

Mannino, F. V., & Shore, M. F. The effects of consultation—A review of empirical studies. *American Journal of Community Psychology*, 1975, **3**, 1–21.

In this review of the reports of 35 consultation outcome studies published between 1958 and 1972, Mannino and Shore observe that 65 percent of those articles contain evidence of positive change in consultee, client(s), and/or system factors. In most studies, researchers focused on the consultee; those interested in client change were next in number. Mannino and Shore suggest increased research attention should be given to system change; and they note a need for studies that build cumulatively on prior ones.

Neely, G. Evaluation of the consultation process in schools. *Professional Psychology*, 1974, **5**, 299–302.

This is a philosophical examination of the goals of consultation in the schools. The author suggests that the most important goal is to change the situation of minorities and students in the school. Because the clients are the individuals ultimately affected, clients should be the ones to evaluate the results of consultation.

Reichen, H. W. Memorandum on program evaluation. In French, Bell, and Zawacki (Eds.), *Organization development: Theory, practice, and research*. Dallas: Business Publications, Inc., 1978.

This chapter attempts to provide a common basis for discussing problems and strategies of evaluation. It provides definitions, categories, techniques, and problems with explanations of each; a practical guide to a difficult undertaking.

APPENDIX 4.A
REPORT TO THE FACULTY

The following report is divided into two main sections. One has to do with task accomplishment. The latest version of the grade level criteria are appended. The second section is concerned with recommendations I have as an observer of this process.

Task Accomplishment

As you read this report you will note that the task that the faculty set for itself in terms of developing a coherent, sequential description of children K-4 has been substantially accomplished.

Some work is still needed. The fourth grade academic entry and target skills are missing. There are some minor differences in language or headings in some areas. These differences may be preferable to a uniformity which leaves some people dissatisfied, however.

Overall, the tasks as defined in our first meetings have been accomplished:

1. Faculty members have had the opportunity to talk and work with each other on a topic they deemed important, and

2. A written set of guidelines has emerged.

This was, of course, simply an initial step. Now the faculty must decide what to do with the standards and how to implement changes suggested by those decisions.

Recommendations

What follows are some suggestions about the standards, implications of the existence of such standards, and possible implementation strategies.

Grade Level Descriptions

A small subcommittee of the faculty might take this latest version of the standards and give them a final editing, seek the missing parts, and decide on uniform headings (if desired). This committee might be composed of the former Guidelines for Describing Children Committee members plus a teacher from a special area and a fourth grade teacher. The optimal time line might be for a "final" version to be available before the January conference day.

Implications

The implications of a faculty statement such as you have made are numerous. They include:

1. Close cross-grade-level communication so that changes in one's grade curriculum or skill development strategies are known to the subsequent grade level.

2. Communication of these standards to parents so that they have reference points upon which to evaluate their children (especially attitudes).

3. Some flexible formula for using these descriptions in promotion decisions.

4. A careful check of curriculum and extracurricular activities to ensure that training in the targeted areas is actually occurring.
5. A system for evaluating the standards every few years to ensure that the written document continues to reflect the faculty's beliefs about children.

There may be many more implications; these may not be the most important. However, each suggests the need for an "action plan."

Implementation Strategies

1. I suggest that some regular times be established for grade-level and cross-grade-level meetings. These meetings would be devoted to:
   a) curriculum changes,
   b) entry skill strengths/defects,
   c) discussion about children structured as a staffing.
   (see Case Staffing form).
   These meetings might occur 6 times during the year; e.g., September, grade-level; October K & 1, 2 & 3; November 1 & 2, 3 & 4; January, K, 1 & 2, 3 & 4; February, grade-level; May, K & 1, 1 & 2, 2 & 3, 3 & 4. Special area teachers would attend these meetings by identifying with a particular grade level. Option II teachers would do the same. These decisions would, of course, be flexible.
2. A checklist of the standards could be developed for use in parent conferencing (See Parent/Teacher Conferences handout). This might assume a rating scale appearance. For example:

	Never	*Sometimes*	*Always*
1. Self-maintenance			
ties shoes	_____	_____	_____
toileting	_____	_____	_____
2. Skills in using materials			
replaces materials	_____	_____	_____
uses materials carefully	_____	_____	_____
cleans up	_____	_____	_____
3. Sits in chair	_____	_____	_____
4. Speaks in modulated tone	_____	_____	_____

Each teacher might have this filled out to show to parents and then ask parents to comment on the level of skills or kinds of attitudes shown at home. Discrepancies could be discussed and problem-solving plans made.

During the January conference day, one third of the faculty could be involved in drafting these forms. These checklists would be helpful to share with each other at promotion time *and* to give to parents. The final form might, therefore, be the kind that makes 2 or 3 copies simultaneously.

3. A procedure for decision making about a child's readiness for the next grade-level follows:
   a. Teacher has concerns about social or academic skills of a child.

    b. Teacher alone and/or in collaboration with grade-level colleagues institutes a series of interventions.

    c. If not successful, teacher involves other grade-level (previous year) colleagues, special area teachers, principal, and parents in problem-solving meetings.

    d. If concerns persist, the Special Help Center is involved.

    e. Parents are informed of new developments and data.

    f. Information is summarized. Teacher decides if retention is indicated and has parent conference (with appropriate support personnel) to discuss pros and cons of retention. Parents are given the written reports to study.

    g. Decision is made. If decision is made to promote, despite some weak areas, teacher informs next grade-level of the considerations. Cross-grade-level meetings are planned. Written records are made available. (No doubt a neat flow chart is indicated. Unfortunately, I don't know how to make it.)

Another strategy might be, of course, to do away with grade levels: to have primary (K, 1 & 2) and intermediate (3 & 4). Written information provided to parents and teachers' expectations would suggest that any child would take between 4 and 7 years to complete the primary and intermediate sequences. The steps outlined above would still be appropriate when concerns occurred except that decisions about promotion would be made just once; i.e., between primary and intermediate.

During the January conference day, one third of the faculty might examine this area and make recommendations.

4. Curriculum revision and evaluation is an ongoing process. I'm sure there is already some structure existing at Fayetteville to do this. What needs to be added is that the curriculum be carefully compared to the standards in addition to other criteria. In this way, the learning activities in each class will be tied to an important outcome. It will prevent a targeting of an area with no support teaching going on. An example might be the skill area of "using time wisely." This is important at every level. How is it taught? Or, is it just wished for or assumed? Many adults have trouble prioritizing time. What are ways that we teach it? How can we involve parents in teaching it?

    The existing curriculum committee might tackle this job during a scheduled meeting. Some detective work will be necessary.

5. Finally, the standards written this year (1978) will not perhaps reflect goals for children in 1984. Some method of periodic review needs to be established. I would suggest that, during the January conference day, one third of the faculty develop an evaluation procedure for the standards. This might be a biannual full-faculty meeting where:

a) each grade level reviews its own standards,

b) cross-grade and special areas review their skill interfaces,

c) the faculty comments on the continuing usefulness of the standards.

The evaluation would want to include use of the standards in parent conferences, use of the promotion/retention procedure based on the standards, and parents' reactions to the standards.

Conclusion

There is still substantial work left to do if you wish the time spent, thus far, to be meaningful. I believe, however, that one day's work in January, preceded by a final version of the descriptions, will nearly accomplish the meaningful integration of the standards into your decision making about children. In summary, I suggest:

1. a small committee to facilitate the completion of the written work.

2. division of the faculty into three work teams during the January conference day to:

   a. develop a parent conference checklist

   b. make recommendations about a promotion/retention decision making sequence which uses the standards

   c. develop a plan for evaluating the appropriateness of the standards over time

I have enjoyed my association with all of you. Please feel free to call upon me if I can be of any assistance.

Jane Close Conoley, Ph.D.
Assistant Professor of
Psychology and Education

5

How to Enter: When to Stay

Knowing how to consult does not guarantee an opportunity to do it. The tremendous press in most agencies for direct service interferes with the implementation and maintenance of a consultation program. In addition, even the person who has been invited into an organization to be a consultant may find his or her efforts frustrated. The problem of successfully introducing consultation to an organization from an internal or external base is the entry problem. Entry refers, therefore, to both the physical entry of a consultant into a system and to the expansion of services within a system. (Refer to figures 5.1 and 5.2 for rough graphics of the problem.) Interestingly, the issues concerned with the dual aspects of entry are very similar. That is, the groundwork, observation, and conceptualizations needed to accomplish physical entry are needed again when new services, new people, or new problems become part of the consultation effort.

In table 5.1 is a listing of some basic consultation guidelines associated with entry. Attempting a consultation entry from an external base will be described first, followed by a discussion of consultation entry from an internal point. Issues associated with contracts, organizational assessment, confidentiality, entry failure, and the choice of other than consultation services for an organization are also dealt with in this chapter.

EXTERNALLY BASED CONSULTANTS

Numerous situations will result in a consultant being invited into an organization. Well-known experts, professional consultants, and university professors are all likely to be sought after to assist a system in some matter. These people may also promote themselves as potentially useful in some area through letters, brochures, telephone contacts, and so on. Most federally

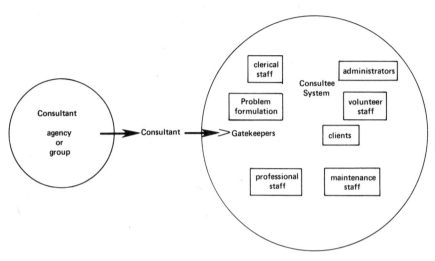

Fig. 5.1. The Initial Entry Problem: Crossing the Organizational Boundary.

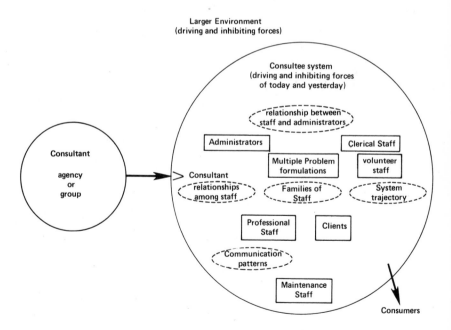

Fig. 5.2. The Continuing Entry Problem: Identifying Top Priority Problems

Table 5.1. Consultation Guidelines Associated with Entry

---

1. Assess personal skills and history of change efforts in the organization before agreeing to consultation.

2. Specify (at least informally) the amount of time, effort, and money that may be expended and the consultation still be considered cost/effective.

3. Be aware of different theories of change in terms of targeting consultation problems. For example, grass roots vs. top level work; crisis situations vs. prevention; affective vs. cognitive strategies.

4. Establish a written or verbal contract with the consultee making explicit areas of responsibility and topics that will be covered.

5. Make long-range plans seeing change as a sequential process aimed at preventing system dysfunction rather than merely remediating current problems.

6. Be clear as to the target and operational levels of consultation. Know who the consultee and client really are.

7. Recognize the potential complexity of the relationship between the consultant and the consultee. These issues include dependency, authority, confidentiality, and competence.

---

funded projects have monies earmarked for consultant use during planning, implementation, and, especially, evaluation phases. Despite the proliferation in the use of consultants, it is a rare system that actually anticipates so diverse a function as real consultation. Most problem formulations that trigger a consultation request are either extremely vague and diffuse (e.g., staff has low morale) or extremely specific (e.g., staff needs training in a new therapy technique). Consultants often find that the host organization not only does not know what to do about a particular issue but, also, is not quite sure what the problem is.

This is, perhaps, the toughest aspect of entry from an outside-the-system base; that is, how to make a quick and accurate assessment of what is troubling this organization. There is pressure for some immediate assessment because consultants must provide some loose description of what their services will look like, how long they will work, what people they need to talk with, and the probability of success of the venture. This is true in every individual consultation interaction, however, and demands some practice and restraint on the part of the consultant. It is very tempting, when the welcome mat is out, to leap into consultation before looking into the realities of the host system.

On the other hand, at times, we attempt entry into a system for ideological reasons that are unrelated to the probabilities for success. Examples of these include some school consultations, mental health department to community agency consultations, and consultations established for training purposes. In cases such as these, organizational assessments are still invaluable, but are not usually used to eliminate consultation sites, but rather to enhance the chances for a successful consultation. Seymour Sarason's *Port of Entry* is an eloquent example of how such ideologically-based consultations might describe their consultation plans:

What do we propose to do? It is easier for me to tell you what we do not intend to do. For one thing, we do not intend to come into a school in order to see how many problem children we can refer out to various agencies. There is no doubt that you know a lot of children who should utilize the services of a child-guidance clinic or family service society. To come in with the intent of referring them out is both unfair and unrealistic because these agencies, particularly the child-guidance clinics, are overwhelmed with cases and generally have long waiting lines. *Even if the child-guidance clinic could take the child on, it would take them quite a while to get to first base with the child and in the meantime you still have that child in your class.* Treatment procedures are neither that quick nor effective, to allow you to expect that *your* difficulties with the child are over once you know he is being seen in a clinic. The question we have asked of ourselves is how can we be of help to the teacher in the here and now with whatever questions and problems she raises with us. In short, we want to see how we can be of help within the confines of the school.

It is not our purpose to come into a school to sit and talk to teachers, however helpful and interesting that might be. When we say we want to be helpful in the here and now within the confines of the school, we mean that in addition to talking with the teacher about a child, *we have to be able to observe that child in the context of the classroom in which the problem manifests itself.* For help to be meaningful and practical it must be based on what actually goes on in the classroom setting. For example, it is in our experience of no particular help to a teacher to be told that a child needs individual attention, a need which differentiates him not at all from the rest of us. What a teacher wants to know is when, how, and for what goals this "individual attention" will occur, and this requires a first-hand knowledge of what is going on.

We do not view ourselves in the schools as people to whom questions are directed and from whom answers will be forthcoming. Life and the helping process are not that simple. We have no easy answers, but we have a way of functioning that involves us in a relationship to the teacher and the classroom and that together we can come up with concrete ideas and plans the we feel will be helpful to a particular child. We are not the experts who can come up with solutions even though we have no first-hand knowledge of the context in which the problem has been identified.

I hope I have made clear that when we say we want to help it means that we want to talk to the teacher, observe in the classroom, talk again to the teacher, and together come up with a plan of action that with persistence, patience, and consistency gives promise of bringing about change. It is not a quick process and it is certainly not an easy one.

I cannot state too strongly that we are not coming into the schools with the intent of criticizing or passing judgement on anyone. *We are nobody's private FBI or counterintelligence service. We are not the agent of the principal or some other administrative officer.* In fact, we are in no way part of the administrative hierarchy or power structure of the school system. We have no special strength or power except that which flows from our being able to establish a situation of mutual trust between teachers and ourselves. To the extent that we can demonstrate to you by our manner, gesture, and verbalization that we want to help, to that extent we make the development of this mutual trust more likely and quickly to occur.

There is one aspect of the way we function that I think needs some elaboration. I have already told you why it is essential for us, if our efforts are to be maximally useful, that we spend time in the classroom. Another reason this is essential resides in the one advantage we have over the teacher, i.e., we do not have the awesome responsibility of having to handle a large group of young characters five days a week for several hours each day, a responsibility that makes dispassionate observation and clear thinking extraordinarily difficult. We can enjoy the luxury of being in the classroom without the responsibility of the teacher for managing and thinking about 25 or more unique personalities. We do not envy you, although I am quite sure that you will envy us for not having your responsibilities. It is precisely because we are "free" that we can observe what is going on in a way not usually possible for a teacher.

. . . We do not know to what extent we can be of help to you. We do not present ourselves as experts who have answers. We have much to learn about this helping process. If our previous work with teachers is any guide, the type of service we want to develop is one that they feel they need. The only thing we can guarantee you is that we want to learn and to help. We have much to learn from you, and together we may be able to be of help to children in school (Sarason, Levine, Goldenberg, Cherlin, & Bennett, 1960, pp. 58–62).

See table 5.2 for a checklist of information that should be included in entry speeches to staffs. There is research suggesting that such introductions result in more and more appropriate requests for service (Chandy, 1974).

In addition to assessing the feasibility of consultation and meaningfully describing their planned activities, external consultants must carefully specify the details of their involvement with an organization. For example, amount of fee, expenses, and time reserved for consultation should be very clear. The amounts that consultants charge vary greatly according to their areas of expertise, and their own renown. Fees should be set with careful observance of professional codes of ethics. The APA code specifies that psychological services should not be denied merely for lack of funds. Although these guidelines were written with the client/psychologist relationship in mind, their spirit should be observed in consultation endeavors.

Whatever the charge, there should be no ambiguity concerning all of the consultant's reimbursements and obligations. Often we work in systems that

Table 5.2. Entry Introduction Checklist

When consultants introduce themselves to a staff they can mention:

1. Something professional about themselves   ———
2. Something personal about background or interests   ———
3. The preventive orientation of consultation   ———
4. The value of being an outsider to the problems   ———
5. Confidentiality   ———
6. Collaboration, not expert but facilitator/colleague   ———
7. Help with work-related problems   ———
8. No cookbook solutions   ———
9. Respect for and interest in consultees   ———
10. Low priority to direct work with clients   ———
11. Consultees' freedom to initiate, accept, or reject consultation   ———
12. What consultant receives, i.e., increased skills and knowledge   ———
13. Desire to visit consultees in their work settings   ———

suffer from lack of clear goal setting and poor communication. At the very least, consultants can model clarity in their negotiations with consultees. Beware of the tendency among some mental health people to find financial dealings rather crass, and thus fail to clearly delineate all aspects of the financial side of the consultation. Such failure usually results in discomfort for both consultant and consultee.

Time spent doing consultation is also an item that requires some clarification. Are the consultants to be paid only for the hours they spend at the site? Or can planning and development time also be reimbursed? Such an understanding is necessary often before a per hour or day at the site charge can be fixed. One three-day consultation of ours involved three separate training sessions along with administrator and teacher consultations. At least three days of work were involved in preparing for the training sessions. Most organizations will understand additional or higher fees being assessed in situations such as this.

Consultants should let people know exactly when they will be on-site. Preplanned schedules should be followed explicitly. This facilitates consultees locating and scheduling with the consultant and creates a sense of predictability in the consultant's behavior. Such predictability may be the only consistency the consultees find in the consultant's behavior. Many administrators are enraged by tardiness and absenteeism among their employees. For some, the concern to have everyone present borders on an obsession.

Consultants may not generally predict obsessional behavior, but should be aware of what things reliably raise the ire of administrators.

> Once while chatting with a rather authoritarian principal in the front hallway of a school, the consultant witnessed the following scene. A teacher entered the building two minutes past the first bell and hurried down toward her classroom. The principal watched her progress from the front door until just before she turned a corner. At that moment, he bellowed down the hall, "It's about time you joined us, Mrs. _____!" Children and other teachers in the area fell silent and the rebuked teacher hung her head and dashed away to her room. After a dramatic moment of quiet, the principal said loudly to the consultant, "This is going into her file right now!" He stalked away.

The example illustrates a number of concerns relative to this school principal. It also would alert the sensitive (and even not–so–sensitive) consultant that rules are *rules* in this particular building, and successful entry may depend on conscientious adherence to small details.

External consultants make mistakes more frequently than internals in terms of breaking the unwritten rules for a system. Such errors are usually very helpful diagnostically, but are not likely to endear consultants to those who are responsible for their presence.

One rule that is easy to break is the "who-talks-to-whom" rule. Consultants who blithely assume that everyone knows they are there and should hear what the consultation assignment is are in for a shock. Ask before talking. Tell the contact consultee what your typical interviewing or surveying needs are and see what reaction is elicited. In addition, it is perfectly good form to ask for a list of people who are not intended for any consultation contact. There may be no one on such a list. In either event and every in-between possibility, the consultant learns important data concerning the consultees and reduces the chance of marring the consultation work by an avoidable error.

INTERNALLY BASED CONSULTANTS

Internal consultants require all the same skills as do externals, but have certain advantages and disadvantages with which to contend. The advantages include: (1) a more thorough knowledge of the host system, facilitating accurate problem identification and reducing system-jarring errors; and (2) an already established rapport with consultees. Disadvantages associated with internal consultation include: (1) a tendency to see problems as do the other members of the system because of the organizational acculturation that takes place in every group; (2) a somewhat diminished status (in contrast to externals) because of familiarity between the consultant and consultees; and, (3) potential difficulty in establishing new role dimensions in addition to the current role. These include both new consulting functions (e.g., survey research) and new stresses on confidential relationships.

It is impossible to provide a general statement about when internal versus external consultants are preferred. The context of the problem and organization and qualities of the people involved as potential consultees and consultants all figure into a decision about from whence to seek or to implement consultation.

There is a suggestion in the literature that internal consultants who are somewhat marginal to their host organizations may be the most helpful (Browne et al., 1977). Marginality refers to a distance from and neutrality toward the home system. Such an attitude of disengagement may preserve the internal from some of the organization co-option difficulties mentioned before.

An interesting point raised by Pipes (1981) deserves reiteration and some expansion. A system's predilection for using internal versus external consultants may be related to other important organizational qualities. Never seeking outside help might indicate: a) a high opinion of full-time staff, or b) a paranoia concerning outsiders' influences. Always going outside the organization might indicate: a) a desire to renew the organization through the planned importation of new ideas and talents, or b) an attempt to avoid chronic conflictual issues by regularly hiring a consultant to be a scapegoat for system failure. There are, of course, many other possible shades of meanings to these particular organizational behaviors. The important entry questions for the consultant to ask are, "Why work on this problem now?" and "Why am *I* being asked to do it?"

Internal consultants will know the history of problems. Although this might limit their creativity, it does give them a sophisticated awareness of which people must be contacted, what procedures be gradually modified, and what special interest groups be mobilized for support. Sarason (1972) has pointed out that few aspiring innovators have taken the time to learn the history of change in a particular system. As in all other human endeavors, those consultants who do not know history are doomed to repeat it. Unfortunately, the history of meaningful change occurring in our human service organizations is somewhat dismal. Americans' and American social scientists' ahistorical stance has been pointed out repeatedly (Levine & Levine, 1970; Sarason & Doris, 1979). Entry is a particularly important moment in consultation. A working knowledge of the critical past incidents of an organization gives the internal consultant a decisive advantage. Examples of what a consultant knows can be shared with the principle gatekeeper through sophisticated questions about the system. It is better to ask good questions that show your complicated understanding of pressing issues than to produce what you know about the consultee. Reeling off information is likely to create paranoia rather than a good impression. This is especially likely if the system is experiencing substantial stress and crisis.

The advantage the internal consultant has in knowing the subtle aspects of the presenting problem can be mitigated if the consultant has become strongly identified as a member of a staff faction. All organizations contain subgroupings that might be defined by their task, age, religious or philosophical convictions, ethnic group, values, status, competence, or ties of allegiance. Inherent in the process of grouping is an identification of some as in-group and some as out-group. If this were not so, groups could not exist. Internal consultants are likely to have been so identified. This has the potential of reducing consultant effectiveness by limiting meaningful access to all factions. It seems that particularly divided organizations who are using a lot of organizational energy on intrasystem competition are motivated to label every newcomer and oldtimer as quickly and decisively as possible. When there are warring camps, each wants to know who is the comrade and who the enemy. This situation provides troublesome challenges to both external and internal consultants. On the one hand, an internal consultant might be seen as a spy for the other side; and on the other hand, an external consultant might simply be unloaded upon with each side fighting to gain his or her seal of approval. Chronically factionated systems must also be seen as places in which at least some of the members derive satisfaction from the conflict.

A consultant was asked by the chairperson of a large academic department to investigate the sources of tremendous faculty unrest and low morale. Rumors, charges and countercharges, and ill will were pervasive. The faculty was ostensibly divided along researcher/nonresearcher lines. Superficial data-gathering revealed, however, that such a descriptor did not accurately classify members of each group. Rather, it appeared there were three groups: oldtimers who had once been powerful (have-nots), oldtimers and newcomers who had always been or were now pretty uninvolved, and newcomers who had arrived with or shortly after the chairperson and were now in positions of power (haves). Valid data gathering was virtually impossible as members of the haves and have-not groups used all interview time to first check on the loyalties of the consultant and then extol their group's virtues while derrogating the other group. The relatively neutral group had stayed so by keeping their mouths, eyes, and ears shut, and so were only minimally helpful.

Numerous issues are involved in the entry process. Even with similar skills, externally-based versus internally-based consultants will deal with markedly different problem presentations. There are advantages and disadvantages to either location and, in most cases, the consultation work can be done successfully from either base. Careful observation and data gathering about a system's use of consultants in the past and historical response to problem solving are critical for eventual successful entry.

CONTRACTS

A substantial amount of literature exists concerning contracts in consultation (e.g., Gallessich, 1974; Pipes, 1981). A contract is a verbal or written agreement between the consultant and the consultee that specifies the parameters of the relationship. These include fees, obligations, times, acceptable activities, time limits, and so on. Despite the large written attention given to contracts, it seems that there are just a few central concerns of which to be aware.

1. Whatever the form of the contract, its particulars must be clear.
2. In addition to whatever the initial contract contains, it should also contain the notion of renegotiation at the request of the consultant or consultee.
3. The contract should be negotiated with the person or persons who actually have the power to see that its terms are carried out.

The need for clarity between consultant and consultee has already been stressed. Below is an example of a marred entry with a new consultee after the consultant had been with a school for about six months.

> The consultant believed that her series of meetings with a new consultee fourth grade teacher had gone very well. Later the consultant heard through another consultee that the fourth grade teacher was quite dissatisfied with the consultant for not being reliable. The areas of responsibility between teacher and consultant had been left a little ambiguous, such that the teacher had expected some direct help with the child. The consultant believed that responsibility for caring for the child was remaining completely with the consultee.

This is an example of the many "mini-contracts" consultants make continuously during the progress of their work. It is very tempting, at times, to let some of the details involved in a planned intervention slide away unclaimed by either consultant or consultee. It may be that each hopes the other will "take up the slack," or simply that precise problem definition has not been attained.

Another important aspect of the contract should be a procedure for evaluation and change. This might be as simple as, "I'll check back with you in three weeks to see if there are changes to be made." Or the clause might be written in the contract specifying a meeting of all interested parties at a certain time to assess and potentially change the focus of the consultation. This need for renegotiation is particularly important in consultation because a well done consultation never ends back where it started. Consultants learn more and more about systems and may completely reconceptualize the problem formulations. When that happens, the consultant may need sanction to perform different roles or activities. The renegotiation process also models feedback skills and, in a microcosm, the renewal process each organization might be implementing to improve its task and maintenance functions.

Finally, the obvious point of making the contract with the legitimate person deserves some elaboration. First of all, when negotiating for a consultation endeavor, it is important to be talking with the people who will actually decide when and if a consultant will be accepted. It is common for decision makers to have "scouts" in the field to suggest potential consultants. It is fine to have a first round of negotiations with such scouts, but do not pack your consultant baggage until something from the decision maker arrives.

Another aspect of this issue is determining who the consultee is. Often consultants are hired by administrators to consult with subordinates. The consultant must have the go-ahead from the administrator, but cannot consider entry complete until a relationship has been established with each of the actual consultees. In this situation, by the way, the consultant is well advised to arrange regular meeting times with the administrator to investigate the need for administrative consultation. Change, elusive as it is, proceeds somewhat more smoothly from the top down rather than in the opposite direction (the difference between a new law and a revolution).

If the consultee agency does not have a formal contractual agreement procedure (many just ask the consultant to sign a purchase order including his or her social security number), the consultant can simply write the agency a letter after the decision to begin consultation has been made. The letter should restate all the particulars and ask for a reply if there are points in need of clarification. A sample of such a letter is given as table 5.3.

Internal consultants must gain the support of their supervisors as they begin the consultation efforts. Depending on the consultation goals and the supervisor, this may be a difficult negotiation. Freeing time for consultation demands imagination on the part of the consultant. The consultant must show how the new interventions will fit with other approaches to reaching the continuing goals. The most persuasive argument often revolves around a more efficient means of carrying out the old roles and tasks, thereby affording time for new projects.

The definition of a clear contract describing the goals, problem formulation, intervention strategies, time line, number of hours a week, and cost is essential. It is important to note the difference between goals and intervention strategies. The professional worker should strive to keep control over the intervention strategies while the setting of the goals is more in the policy realm of the employing organization. Professionals should strive to influence goals as well, but understand that each organization has some particular mission. Part of the definition of the professional is to be able to make the determination of what intervention skills to use for reaching certain goals. If the job defines the techniques, the professional becomes a technician. For the internal consultant, it is important to gain the commitment of the super-

Table 5.3. Sample Consultant-Generated Contract

January 14, 1981

Peggy Frank
Special Education Dept.
Great School District
340 East 3545 South
New City, Nebraska

Dear Peggy,

Thank you for your very helpful letter of January 7th. I appreciate the information regarding your school district.

March 6th and 7th are fine with me. I will make plans to arrive the evening of the 5th. When the flight number and time are confirmed I'll send them to you. I am happy to make my own way to a hotel or be met, whichever is best for you.

In terms of preparations:

1. Let me know which is the most convenient hotel *or* make reservations in my name for the 5th and 6th of March.

2. May I have use of an overhead projector for my large group presentations?

3. May I also have you make copies of materials I send? What I'll do is bring 25–30 manila file folders and put the sets of handouts in one for each participant.

4. Let me know if you have your own evaluation instruments. If not, I'll bring some of my own so that I can learn the participants' reactions. I will share all evaluative data with you.

5. Especially for Saturday, I would like juice, milk, etc. to be available for the teachers. I really appreciate their attendance at something on a *Saturday*!

6. Can you tell me what your perceptions are about the biggest obstacles to using a consultative service delivery system in your district?

For example: a)   lack of skills
                    b)   lack of motivation/commitment to model
                    c)   resistance from regular ed. and principals (you mentioned this briefly in you letter)
                    d)   something else?

This is quite a list I've given you! I've started my preparations for the workshop. Will I still see the coordinators separately? They will receive some additional information from me about supporting the consultation of others and district level consultation.

My fee for consultation of this type is $200 per day plus expenses. I will provide an itemized account of the living expenses as soon as possible after the consultation days.

Thanks for all this, in advance.

Sincerely,

Jane Close Conoley, Ph.D.
Associate Professor of Psychology

JCC/rb

visor to the consultation project. The internal consultant should anticipate decreasing supervisory support as soon as pressure for traditional service delivery increases. Be prepared for loss of support by careful documentation of the positive effects of the consultation project. Collect data continuously and make it available to decision makers. Internal consultants must consider the constant education of their organizations as part of their contracts.

ORGANIZATIONAL ASSESSMENT

It is difficult to immediately grasp how to "know" a system. The complexity of the task may appear overwhelming. There are several important sources of information regarding this process (e.g., Secord & Backman, 1974; Katz & Kahn, 1978; Schmuch et al., 1972). Mental health professionals who wish to function as organization development experts can tap into a huge literature (e.g., Argyris, 1971; Bennis, 1969; Blake & Mouton, 1976; 1978; Cummings, 1980; French & Bell, 1978; Lawrence & Lorsch, 1969; Schein, 1969; Steele, 1973). This section of the entry discussion will provide some basic guidelines for performing an assessment to maximize consultation entry success. The topics contained in this section are helpful also in planning consultation interventions throughout the duration of the consultation work. There is always new information to be learned about a system. An openness to such new information will enhance consultation and serve as a check on initial observation.

The areas to be covered in this section include rationales for organizational assessment, what to look at to do the assessment, and data collection strategies.

Rationales for Organizational Assessment

An important element in the identity of most psychologists is that of skills in assessment. Traditionally, assessment has meant a focus on rather micro units of the person (e.g., personality traits, intellectual skills, vocational aptitudes). There is, however, a growing body of assessment conceptualizations that focus on more macro units (e.g., small groups, entire organizations, suprasystems). Perhaps the work of Kurt Lewin (1951) is the precursor to this area. Certainly the more recent writings of Barker (1978), Barker and Gump (1964), Gallessich (1973), Kounin (1970), Sarason (1981), Sarason and Doris (1979), Schein (1969), Schmuck (1976) and von Bertalanffy (1968) are representative of perspectives mainly interested in larger systems and systems' interactions.

The targets of interest in a systems analysis are not the individuals, intra-psychic lives of the individuals, or even the behaviors of the individuals per se who actually compose the organizations. Rather, behavioral regularities (Sarason, 1981) are extracted from observations. Norms, communication patterns, leadership emergence and style, decision making procedures, uses of time and space, interdependence/cooperation/competition among subsystems, and climate are a few of the areas scrutinized by people interested in organizational assessment.

Organizational assessment seems to have at least three important purposes during entry: (1) understand the organization according to important systemic variables; (2) understand the influence of these variables on the behaviors of organization members; and, (3) design and implement system level strategies to accomplish consultation contractual goals.

As interesting as assessment of organizations may seem to be, clearly the effort would be wasted for the mental health professional if it were not well established that organizational variables do affect individuals within the organizations (e.g., Astin & Holland, 1962; Breer & Locke, 1965; Inkeles, 1960). There are even those who suggest that meaningful personal change is often not possible without systemic change (Chesler, Bryant, & Crowfoot, 1976).

The effort involved in systems assessment would also be wasted on those who conceptualize real change as occurring only after major intrapsychic or personality restructuring. Intrapsychic supremacy adherents would find the contexts in which individuals live and work of only minor importance (Levine, 1973). There are two key assumptions in organizational assessments:

1. There is a need to understand the realities of the organization in order to understand the individual because organizational variables often override personality variables.
2. Human systems should not be self-serving systems but, rather, ones that are established to serve humans. Systemic change and modification are rational and often preferred strategies.

Important Organizational Dimensions

Several major areas of a system must be examined in order to accomplish an assessment. Each area contains a number of important components.

Physical Factors. The physical plant(s) of the system can be examined to ascertain the amount of usable equipment that is available. This includes machinery and office supplies. The maintenance of the equipment and of the facility itself are points to notice. Other important aspects of the physical environment include the existence and quality of staff lounges, the design of the reception area, and the artwork that adorns the halls and offices. It is also possible to make note of the physical marks of status within a system. Such things as paintings on the walls, rugs on the floor, corner offices, drapes, and wooden versus metal desks are often associated with power within a system (Steele, 1973).

The entering consultant can form hypotheses about how a particular building or subsystem ranks in the larger system by seeing how clean and well equipped the facility is. Physical dimensions of the staff lounge (e.g., comfortable furniture, convenient location, coffee available, etc.) may shed light on the concern administrators show for the comfort of their staff and/ or how much the staff values each other.

The office or area reserved for greeting or screening outsiders may be a particularly important area to study and to experience. This area may represent psychological as well as physical entry into a building. Is it comfortably furnished? Are there magazines or system brochures in the area? Is the room physically arranged so that newcomers are recognized immediately? Consultants who are waiting to be received by their gatekeeper are well advised to observe how others who enter are received. Are there differences based on some obvious dimensions such as age, race, or role (e.g., parent versus school board trustee) of the newcomers? Also notice if staff tends to drop by this room for quick chats or just to relax for a moment.

Social-Emotional Climate.   As soon as consultants gain some physical access to a building, for example, the administrator conducts a tour, they should note how the staff seems to relate to one another. Does their conversation seem warm, task-oriented, stilted, or only social? Later, consultants can ascertain if the staff tends to work as a whole faculty on problems or in small groups, and which staff (if any) socializes outside of work.

In addition, the quality of the vertical relationships should be conceptualized: Does the administrator do personal favors for the staff? Does staff share personal concerns with the administrator? Is the administrator first to work and last to leave? How accessible is the administrator? The use of written versus face-to-face communication is important to notice. Often, heavy reliance on written memos reflects a somewhat formal, rigid organizational structure. Face-to-face feedback concerning poor performance is especially important. The exclusive use of written memos in this area may indicate an administrator with no feedback skills or with substantial needs to punish others.

Another indication of the social/emotional climate of a system is how weak members are treated. For example, new, sick, or recently bereaved staff members are at least temporarily vulnerable. Are they offered guidance or support? How does the organization respond—as a whole, in small groups, or individually? Are there procedures in place to support weak members, or is every incident a new problem to solve?

Finally, the culture and norms of the organization must be analyzed. There are already published analyses of certain organizations cultures (e.g., Sarason's *The Culture of the School and the Problem of Change*). Each organization has unique features to be discerned, however, so it is important to enter with eyes open to new possibilities. An organizational culture is made up of many spoken and unspoken rules, habits, attitudes, beliefs, and preferences. Dress, what is discussed, what is not discussed, punctuality parameters, quality of humor (e.g., wit versus sarcasm), attendance at meetings, and quality and quantity of staff meetings are all contributors to an organizational culture.

Power.   Power is a particularly critical variable to investigate during entry and for the organizational assessment. It is important to ascertain who the haves and the have-nots are and what is the major contributor to having power. Some possibilities include power accruing to legitimate structural power processes within the organization (e.g., bosses); power due to competence or seniority; and power built on the allegiance of others or because of connections with others. Powerful people can be identified by observing to whom verbalizations are directed at meetings, whose opinions are sought, who initiates the most at meetings, or who is the most successful in getting a policy adopted.

The way power is used must also be described. It seems common for even people whose role gives power to be somewhat power phobic (see fig. 5.3). Many people who need to act decisively and authoritatively simply do not.

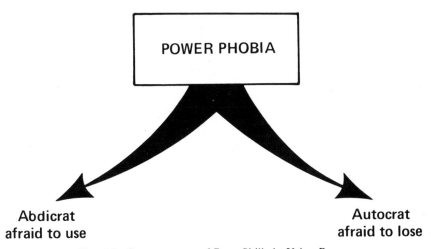

Fig. 5.3. Consequences of Poor Skills in Using Power

Others are so concerned about losing any gram of influence that they hold it close to themselves, allowing no participation in decision making and blocking the dissemination of important information.

> The now-dead president of a large university was remembered as a person with an iron grip on the faculty. No one was hired, given keys, promoted, etc., without his direct and absolute involvement. Faculty remembered even seeing him stop maintenance tasks (e.g., painting a curb) that he had not directly approved. The president would make no figures concerning work loads or salaries public, so everyone worked in a vacuum of information—never knowing if they were doing enough. Years later, when a consultant visited one of the faculties, he was struck by the very low level of faculty power. The faculty, however, felt that they had made significant strides toward decentralization and were quite satisfied.

Because consultants are interested in facilitating change, they must understand the power realities of each new consultee organization. Change is far easier to accomplish with the support of those who are already influential. Martin (1978) has described consultants as having expert and referent power. So, too, do consultees. The relationships among the power "haves" in a system are important to discern. One simple strategy is to draw or obtain an organizational chart (see fig. 5.4 as an example). Sometimes, sketching out the formal lines of authority in a system immediately suggests the site of a

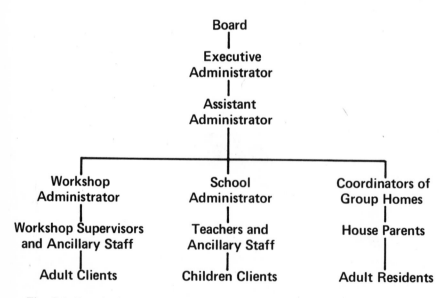

Fig. 5.4. Sample Organizational Chart of an Outpatient Developmental Center

particular problem. People or roles with informal (or referent) power can also be added to an organizational chart to highlight other strong or dysfunctional areas. The organization represented as figure 5.4 suffered from very low teacher morale. A major contributing factor was the strong influence that some workshop supervisors and house parents had on the assistant administrator. Many small decisions consistently favored the adult staffs over the children's staff because of this informal access. The assistant administrator was completely unaware of the bias because no one had carefully confronted it as an issue. Most observers felt that the low teacher morale was due to their low skills, or their very difficult teaching assignments.

Administrative Style.   Obviously, administrative style is closely related to power. Consultants must be able to detail the way in which administrators handle their work. As illustrated in figure 5.3, there are extremes in administrative styles—from those who delegate every task and decision away to those who refuse any input. Most administrators will fall between these two extremes. The consultant wants to understand how best to be influential and so will match the style of the administrator during entry. The consultant may also wish to offer consultation to the administrator and so should be able to formulate some goals for administrative consultation. For example, if the administrator is quite controlling, consultants will appear regularly with progress reports, make sure the administrator knows their arrival and departure times, and is informed as to their consultees. Consultants in this situation may scan the system for dysfunction related to the controlling style of the leader. If none is found, then no administrative consultation is indicated. If issues of dependency, low creative output, or anxiety are present, then the consultant might begin a program of consultation aimed at increasing the administrator's tolerance for ambiguity and openness to decentralized decision making.

Considerable literature is available from social psychology concerning optimal leadership or administrative variables (see Conoley, J. C., 1980; Hare, 1976, for review). There is some disagreement as to whether the traits (i.e., intelligence, charisma, attractiveness) or flexibility (i.e., style matches situation) of the leader is more important. In our experience, it is probably the flexibility of the administrator that will be the consultant's target. Because personal traits (if such things exist) are difficult to change, the consultant is well-advised to try to increase the administrator's repertoires of responses based on the audience, task, and other contextual demands surrounding decisions or events that must be managed. So, for example, in a crisis situation, a staff expects a leader to be decisive and authoritative. If the building is on fire, no one wants or expects the leader to hold a meeting to decide upon the right course of action. Analogously, no one wants or expects a meeting to be called to decide on the brand of wax that should be used to do the floors.

Some groups prefer or expect more input into decisions than other groups do. Educators seem to prefer more democratic leaders than do members of the military. Some tasks are so complex that they demand a group effort to be accomplished, while others are so simple it would be a waste of time for many to be involved.

Flexibility must not be confused with inconsistency. The old saying, "The devil you know is better than the devil you don't know," captures this problem. It seems somewhat better for organizational morale for staff to be able to predict the leader's behaviors. This seems true even when the behaviors are objectionable.

Other factors associated with administrative style that should be investigated by the consultant are the reward system (e.g., is it congruent with stated objectives?); administrator's theory about people (i.e., people are innately good or innately bad); amount of commitment the administrator has to *this* staff (or is this job just a stepping stone?); attitude of administrator to the client population (supportive and caring versus punitive and blaming); and, attitude of administrator to consultant (facilitator versus pipeline or spy). All of this information has effects on the consultation effort. Its relevance may not be immediately obvious, but such an intimate knowledge invariably enhances the consultant's chances for successful interventions.

Health of Organization. The final dimension to consider in organizational assessment is the health of the organization. Many indications of health or dysfunction are available for examination.

Scapegoating is a sign of an organization in distress. It refers to a process by which all organizational or personal problems or weaknesses are blamed on some other system, process, or person. An example would be if the marketing branch of an organization blames its poor performance on the service department while refusing to look at itself for deficits. Scapegoating occurs when there is a discrepancy between what people know they should be doing and what they are doing. Pervasive scapegoating perpetuates irresponsibility among consultees and decreases the number of alternatives to which they are open.

Another indicator of system health is the *integration among the subsystems*. As illustrated in figures 5.1 and 5.2, systems are complexes of units that have some shared purpose or goals. They are, by definition, interdependent. The amount of interdependence may vary, but there is always some. This interdependence demands cooperative coordinated action among and between the subsystems if system goals are to be realized. Consultants must observe interface interactions (i.e., transactions between different subgroups) to determine the quality of the integration (Ferguson, 1968). Often, instead of cooperative efforts, consultants will observe competition, territoriality, expansionism, and scapegoating. Some administrators seem to believe that the system is improved by competition across the subsystems. Mild competition is an enhancer, but often the competition becomes the focus instead of larger purposes.

As the declining birth rate was felt in some Northeastern school districts, elementary schools were being closed. It was clearly the principals' jobs to make their schools seem irreplaceable in the district configuration. The comparisons became heated, however, with trivial differences in floor plans becoming major items of discussion. The faculties were thrown into insidious comparisons of each others' degrees, experience, evaluations, and relationships with parents. The result was a marked decline in morale, even in schools not currently faced with closing.

Related to the integration of subsystems is the *permeability or rigidity of the organizational boundary* to the larger environment. The openness or closedness of a particular system to other community systems should not be a static fact. Permeability should vary according to intrasystem development and particular issues. For example, early in a system's development it might be very open and inviting of new input. Following this phase, the system may shut out new input for awhile in the hopes of testing what has been accomplished thus far. Similarly, a system may allow very open information exchange about some matters, but be quite rigid in relation to others, for example, client or staff personnel files. The consultant must look for strengths and deficits along this boundary and identify the gatekeepers of the boundaries. Some systems merely lack skills in making themselves known or involving others in their functioning. Others have to be supported to open their doors to input that they have labeled adversarial, unsympathetic, or undermining. The examination of differences is a key to change. Rigid systems are in danger of an organizational leveling or entropy because nothing new or challenging is imported. What they contribute to the larger environment may become obsolete or irrelevant if there is no regular monitoring process of the larger environment's needs or new priorities.

Role clarity is another aspect of organizational functioning. Do people know what is expected of them and know what to expect from others? Such shared understandings are imperative. Roles may be so clear as to be rigid, or so diffuse as to be invisible. Flexibility is optimal with people free to change parts of their job descriptions to meet current interests or system needs. Everyone should be willing to do what they can to achieve organizational goals and be allowed to be different from one another in that pursuit. Consultants might notice attitudes of "It's not my job" or frustration attached to not knowing to whom to turn for a certain bit of advice or action.

Clarity and agreement on goals should also be investigated. Sometimes goals are in contradiction with each other. For example, notice the discrepancy between "Promote curious, independent thinking among children" compared with classroom realities that demand conformity and rarely give children encouragement or time to ask questions (McIntyre, 1969). Consultants must ascertain which are *really* shared goals among a staff and the discrepancies between goals and actual behaviors.

Another aspect of organizational health is the *problem-solving patterns* within a system. Does the system avoid confronting problems, over-discuss issues, or squarely face problems and develop action plans? What decision-making style is used: voting, minority rule, administrative fiat, consensus, or unanimity? Each of these has costs and benefits. The consultant must decide if the benefits are outweighing the costs. If not, some coaching on decision-making procedures may be in order. Also, are the *latent resources of the organization* brought to bear on problems and important decisions? Many systems *always* seek outside consultation and never use or discover what is already present in the system. If this is a problem, a consultant can direct and redirect planners toward existing resources in terms of people, publications, experiences, procedures, or equipment.

Gallessich (1974) mentions the *trajectory of the organization* as important organizational data. Is the system or the system's immediate environment on an up or downswing? Many teachers have needed intense consultation to move through an almost grieving process as their white middle class students have been replaced by poor minority students in urban ghettos. Their energy to try new strategies will be most certainly different from the energy of teachers at a brand new school, showered with new programs, and supported by interested parents and bright students.

The final and perhaps most important question to be addressed by the consultant is this: "*Can this organization balance stability with change?*" Every system must be adaptable to change, facing up to what is really happening inside and outside the system. Many systems avoid such self-analysis. Renewal and viability depend, however, on a system's willingness to examine itself, hold steady where possible, and change where needed. If there is sign of system death (e.g., declining enrollment at a university), the consultant might investigate the procedures for self-analysis and correction. If these are lacking, then the facilitation of such procedures is an important consultation goal.

A church-related college had experienced enrollment decline for the last five of seven years. An externally mandated self-study for an accreditation process was initiated. All of the heads of the various committees were untenured. None was given release time to accomplish the work. A representative from the accrediting agency chided the administration for stacking the deck away from meaningful criticism, especially during this period when there was obvious need for some honest analyses of the concerns facing the university.

Pulling It Together

When all these observations have been made, the consultant is in a position to identify:

1. the coping strengths and latent resources of a system;
2. failure areas; and
3. obstacles to success.

These are the generalizations that should be drawn from the assessment and then tested again and again when new data become available. Sources to accomplish an organizational assessment, in addition to observation, are written publications, local news, school journals, system library, and the immediate surroundings of the system.

Before drawing conclusions based on observation and other sources, consultants should consider a few guidelines.

1. Avoid premature judgments. Behaviors that appear maladaptive may serve necessary functions. Some issues are present in most organizations. The consultant should not overreact. Examples are conflict avoidance, resistance to change, authoritarianism of administrators, authority issues, subgroup competition, and confusion because of lack of goal clarity or congruence.
2. Look for patterns of behavior, that is, complementary interactions. Examples are paternalism and dependency, new bosses arousing fear and mistrust, authoritarianism and in-group cohesiveness ("us and them").
3. Become aware of personal biases. Consultants' ideologies or preferences for age, sex, or ethnic group may lead them to overidentify with certain groups or certain (incomplete) information. We cannot completely escape ourselves, but should seek supervision and be willing to introspect nondefensively. In addition, it is valuable to examine whether the consultant is prone to authority issues him or herself. Authority figures sometimes facilitate dependency or counterdependency irrespective of who they are. Consultants should not fall into this particularly frustrating pattern.

As overwhelming as all this information may appear on first reading, be assured that much of the data gathering needed to accomplish an assessment becomes almost automatic over time. Having skills in assessing organizations speeds entry and makes the chances for successful consultation much greater.

CONFIDENTIALITY CONCERNS

The need to keep all consultee communications in confidence has been mentioned several times already in this volume. It is such a critical aspect of
consultation, however, that confidentiality deserves a special discussion, especially as it relates to entry.

The consultant's commitment to confidentiality should be mentioned during the entry process. Administrators need to understand the limits of what
they will learn about specific staff members from consultants. Consultees
must be assured that their interactions with the consultant are completely
confidential or warned of the limits of confidentiality. During a first interview with the top administrator, the consultant can introduce confidentiality
issues. Specifically, consultants can explain their willingness to report to the
administrators the identities of the people with whom they consult. At the
same time, it is best to emphasize their unwillingness to share the exact
content of consultation sessions. What they can share are general impressions, organizational issues they perceive, or specific problems that seem to
be common among most of the staff. Most administrators accept this quite
casually. If the administrator's rights to staff information are raised, the
consultant can explain the difference in roles between the consultant and the
administrator. Administrators should be collecting evaluative information
about their staff on a continuous basis. They must make difficult hire/fire
and salary decisions. Consultants, on the other hand, are not in supervisory
roles and should not be used to do administrative tasks. Consultants are in a
position to learn what administrators need to know, but to act as an administrative spy undercuts the purpose of the consultation. Administrators must
make a decision whether they want effective consultants *or* they want their
evaluative work done for them. The two functions are very different. If the
"consultant" must report specific information about specific consultees to
an administrator, then consultees must be told of that particular contingency
before any consultation begins.

> A brand new consultant was sent in to "set things right" in a classroom for
> seriously emotionally disturbed children. The teacher was painfully inexperi-
> enced and unprepared for the assignment. After a few consulting days had
> elapsed, the consultant was summoned to the principal and asked for a "report"
> on the distressed teacher. The consultant reported his activities in terms of
> teaching, life space interviewing, and behavioral management strategies. He was
> pressed for details of what the teacher was doing. When he replied that the
> teacher was receiving consultation eagerly, the principal angrily said, "You were
> put in there to tell me what is going on. Now, tell me what is going on."

Fortunately, few of us face such blatant demands for breaches of confidence.
The consultant in the example, however, had failed to educate the principal

about confidentiality. The consultant had also failed to explore what expectations surrounded him. If he had known that he was really seen as an evaluator, he could have warned the teacher of his true role rather than assuring her of his consultative services.

The American Psychological Association Code of Ethics may serve as the basis for psychologists in deciding on complex ethical issues. Consultants owe primary loyalty to their clients. The consultee or consultee agency who hires the consultant also deserves complete loyalty, except in instances in which needless injury is being inflicted upon the client.

One consultant was shocked to observe a teacher routinely using corporal punishment and serious verbal abuse on students. The corporal punishment was being accomplished without use of the usual safeguards accompanying the procedure (e.g., certifying parental permission, and securing a witness). The law of the state was being broken right in front of the consultant. The consultant met with the consultee intensively for days, arranged a three-day leave for the teacher to observe in other classrooms, and did extensive in-the-class modeling of positive contingencies. The consultant also confronted the teacher on the infraction and the uncomfortable ethical position it presented to the consultant. The teacher laughed off the consultant's earnestness, reporting that *all* the parents had given her permission to "whip these kids into shape." The consultant checked the appropriate files and found no such permissions. The consultant presented the concern as wanting the teacher to escape parental fury. The teacher refused to consider a change in her policy. The consultant set up a meeting with the principal to clarify school policy as it related to state law and official district policy on corporal punishment. The consultant had correctly hypothesized that the illegal use of corporal punishment was going on because of, at least tacit, complicity by the principal.

The consultant started the meeting by asking for the school procedures for corporal punishment. When the correct procedures were spelled out, the consultant explained her legal and ethical obligations if she saw the law being violated. The consultant explained to the principal, as she had to the teacher, that she wanted to remain helpful and facilitative. In order to do so, probably everyone needed to know when ethical lines would be crossed, forcing the consultant into another role. The meeting ended on a cordial note. Later, teacher consultees reported that the principal had reiterated his support of the official corporal punishment policy at a faculty meeting and suggested that teachers who needed help in classroom management seek collegial, principal, and consultant support. A whole series of mini-workshops were instituted on social skills training (Goldstein, 1981), the use of space and movement in the classroom as it related to management (Kounin, 1970), and life space interviewing (Redl, 1959). Within weeks of the beginning of the consultation, another teacher was suspended without pay for "shaking" a child very roughly. This incident seemed to increase teacher motivation to learn more diverse management procedures as attendance at the workshops increased dramatically.

Many uncomfortable issues can be avoided if confidentiality is carefully explained during the entry process. Obviously, however, confidentiality is an ongoing concern. The best proof of confidentiality is the consultant's behavior. All the assurances will be for nought if breaches in confidence become apparent. Do not even report others' successes without their permission. It is easy to say, "I like your procedure so much! Do you mind if I tell other people about it?" It is permissible to comment on public knowledge about a consultee. "She has the most unusual bulletin boards." "His class seemed so responsible about taking care of the disabled child." "They are great teachers." It is not permissible to describe within-the-class policies that are not within the usual public domain. Teachers who maintain an effective token policy for classroom management may not want other teachers to know of their efforts no matter how successful. There may be a school norm against token economies. The consultant's exuberant praise of the teacher could result in an uncomfortable situation rather than the hoped for positive glow. In general, the fewer evaluative remarks made, positive or negative, about specific consultees, the better the chances for a smooth entry.

If a breach of confidence is made unknowingly, go immediately to the injured party. Explain the circumstances and nondefensively ask for forgiveness. Consultees report liking consultants who show some human frailty and react nondefensively to criticism. In addition, as problems in confidentiality are pervasive in many organizations, consultants may perform an important modeling function even when they are in error.

HOW TO FAIL

It may be helpful to refer back to chapter 2, and reread the ways to fail as a consultant (Rae-Grant, 1972). All of these behaviors will interfere with successful entry. Here are some additional ways to make sure your entry will not be successful:

1. Ignore the norms of the organization. Use phones without asking, be late or unreliable, and dress in whatever fashion you feel comfortable.
2. Talk with one consultee about another or report to administrators about staff behaviors.
3. Wait in your office to be approached for service.
4. Criticize the system whenever possible to insiders *and* outsiders.
5. Fail to build a relationship with the top administrator.
6. Appear somewhat aloof and formal. Do not ask consultees any questions about who *they* are. Rather, spend time describing your own life and accomplishments.

7. Be dependent on administrator support to structure your every activity. Insist on meeting with him or her very frequently.
8. Announce your intention to (and do) engage in activities that fit *your* interests and *your* agendas.

Although we have not empirically tested each of these guidelines, we feel sure of their efficacy.

WHEN NOT TO OFFER CONSULTATION

A well done organizational assessment is used to decide upon the feasibility of consultation as well as provide diagnostic information on consultation targets and operational levels. It is difficult to provide guidelines that give absolutes to use in deciding about when to abort an entry or discontinue consultation. Some signals at entry that may predict an unsuccessful effort include: extremely autocratic or unsupportive administrators, a system in extreme crisis, or a system with an overwhelming need for direct services.

Consultation is best used when it matches the situation. If there are many children in a school coming every day hungry, tired, or abused, the consultant's time might be better used doing advocacy for those children at local welfare agencies rather than offering teachers mental health or behavioral consultation. It is possible, of course, that helping teachers advocate for the children might also be indicated, that is, advocacy consultation.

Sometimes the assessment shows a need for consultation, but not the "brand" you offer. Some professional honesty and humility are in order in this situation. The system might be very well served by a curriculum expert, information flow analyst, or equipment expert. The right thing to do is to facilitate a connection between the system and the best resource for the situation. Private practitioners may find the directive "hard to hear." Our experience has indicated that such referrals are very well received by consultee systems and result in much good will, good public relations, and increased requests for appropriate services at later dates.

Other times not to complete an entry or offer consultation are when the interests or time available from the consultant really do not match organizational needs. Most consultants have accepted jobs that did not match their primary skills or interests and then found it hard to devote the appropriate time to the work. Or, they have simply taken on too much work. Mediocre or poorly done work usually results. No one benefits from the consultant's spreading his or her time too thin as the system receives poor quality service and the consultant becomes known for delivering poor quality service. It is hard to say no. It is best to examine each request and pick only those with some chance for success, in which you are interested, and for which you have appropriate time resources.

Finally, do not enter organizations with hidden personal agenda based on ideologies that run counter to the consultee organization. Stein (1972) makes an important point in suggesting that psychologists should spend more time with groups that have dissimilar values. The problem of becoming involved in unsanctioned change is, however, exacerbated when consultants enter systems knowing that they are not in agreement with even the public goals of an organization. Beware also of consulting with organizations that hold some personal meaning or threat. Consultants who had terrible school experiences in parochial schools and blame it all on a rigid authoritarian church structure may not belong as parochial school consultants.

As mentioned earlier in the volume, the key is for consultants to know themselves. Be open to learning from others and seek advice on situations that arouse intense emotionality or tendencies to blame the consultee.

SUGGESTED READINGS

Harrison, R. Training internal OD consultants in industry. *Industrial Training International*, 1972, **5**, 152–153.

Harrison outlines basic skills needed by organizational development consultants and the training required to generate these skills. There are three main skill categories: diagnostic ability; giving help to enable people to solve their own problems; and getting action taken, i.e., knowing when and how to use your influence. Consultation training involves practical experience, deepened self-knowledge (e.g., T-groups), and conceptual understanding, understanding behavior in groups and organizations, understanding consultancy relationships, and knowledge of basic management techniques.

Patti, R. J., & Resnick, H. Changing the agency from within. *Social Work*, 1972 (July), 48–57.

A "classic" in the social work literature, this article deals with intraorganizational change. When an agency's service delivery system does not meet client and staff needs, the system itself must change. Yet, staff often feel helpless and overwhelmed at the thought of pursuing change within their agency. Patti and Resnick argue that professional obligation necessitates that practitioners challenge agency policies and effect qualitative changes in service delivery. Intraorganizational change is defined as "the systematic efforts of practitioners to effect changes in policies and programs from within their agencies, when they have no administrative sanction for these activities." The authors present a conceptualization of this change process, identifying three crucial phases—goal formulation, resource mobilization, and intervention.

Sandoval, J., Davis, J. M., & Lambert, N. M. Consultation from a consultee's perspective. *Journal of School Psychology*, 1977, **14**(4), 334–343.

The intent of the article is to sensitize consultants to the learning needs of the new consultee so that he/she can anticipate and facilitate the consultee's experience in adapting to the consultation relationship. Basic concepts underlying the consultation relationship are reviewed. This is a useful reminder to consultants that it takes time to become a consultee.

Schroeder, C., & Miller, F. Entry patterns and strategies in consultation. *Professional Psychology*, 1975 (May), 182–185.

Schroeder and Miller illustrate the importance of proper entry to the effectiveness of consultation. They describe three unsuccessful change programs in schools, specifically involving behavior modification training. In all cases, the reasons for failure were traced to improper entry of the consultant, resulting in lack of commitment of key people to the change program. A successful fourth program utilized all their prerequisites for proper consultant entry, and proper relationship in general between consultant and system. Some actions recommended are securing administrative sanction, involvement of personnel at all levels, and preparation of a formal written evaluation. They warn that the consultant should not become an integral part of the system but, rather, should develop resources within the system to carry on his/her role.

Steele, F. Consultants and detectives. *The Journal of Applied Behavioral Sciences*, 1969, **5**(2), 187–202.

As a step toward learning more about the process and practice of organizational change for intervention, this paper explores the usefulness of an analogy between the roles of the detective and consultant. The roles are compared on dimensions such as use of expertise, trust or suspicion creation, action intervention and so on. Two main problems seem to emerge as central: how to obtain valid information from the system, and how to balance personal and professional needs or motives.

6

The Consultant as Trainer

In-service or workshop training is not the same as consultation. Even flexibly formatted workshops have a body of preplanned information to impart to the participants. In contrast, teaching within consultation is relatively unstructured and completely dependent on the issues raised by the consultees.

In-service training for school personnel or workshop training for other agencies is, however, often a valuable springboard for consultation. The workshop gives the consultant high visibility and, if it is well received, gives some initial consultant credibility, thereby increasing early approaches for service. A consultant wishing to become involved with a particular agency might offer very low-cost or free workshop training. Trainers of consultation students might do likewise to open up new practicum sites for students or "pay" for the supervision given to consultation students.

The wise consultant does not believe that a one-hour or five-day workshop will lead to significant behavioral changes on the part of the consultees. In-service training, for the consultant, is a *means*, not an *end*. If expertly-done training was *the* answer to behavioral change, the follow-up studies about in-service would be far more encouraging (e.g., see Collins, Porter, Beam, & Moss, 1979; Walker, 1978). The keys to the in-service process being mutually advantageous are, of course, that the consultant give training that matches the needs and interests of the agency and that the training be of very high quality.

What follows is an overview of issues of which consultants must be cognizant in order to present good training experiences. There are, of course, complete books devoted to training. This chapter is meant to support those whose work is mainly consultation, *not* training. The information presented here has been gathered by us over the past eight years. This information represents what has been helpful to us.

ARRANGING THE TRAINING

Finding out what kind of training an agency desires or really needs may be a straightforward or very complex task. The consultant's base of operation (internal versus external), the source of the request for training (grass roots versus upper administration), the size of the agency, and the status of the agency (in crisis versus coping well) are just a few of the parameters interacting with the needs assessment problem.

If the consultants are internal consultants, they may desire to do in-service training to fill a need they perceive, or may wish to improve their consultation efforts by increasing credibility and visibility. From this base, the consultant can often use a simple checklist form suggesting topics for training, while leaving space for consultees to suggest other important topics. Table 6.1 is an example of such a checklist used by a school psychologist wanting to increase consultation services. Finding out potentially popular topics is,

---

Table 6.1. Survey of Faculty Interests

In order to tailor my services to the needs of the school, I have compiled the following survey to determine what subjects the staff is interested in and/or desires information about. Based on the results of this, handouts and/or in-service training will be done on specific topics.

Please check the categories in which you are interested or about which you would like information:

_____ Reading frustration exercises for parents.

_____ Reading: how parents can help.

_____ The Education for ALL Handicapped Children Act of 1975.

_____ The LD child.

_____ The gifted child.

_____ Identifying children with special needs.

_____ Ideas for coping with stress.

_____ Parent interviewing.

_____ What is consultation?

_____ Mainstreaming.

_____ Strategies for teaching children who need structure.

_____ Psychological testing.

_____ Why children behave as they do and strategies to counter disruptive behaviors.

_____ Feel free to add any topics, not mentioned above, which would be of interest to you.

    1.

    2.

    3.

---

therefore, probably relatively easy for the internal consultant. Actually arranging the in-service training may be more complicated.

When the idea for the training is generated by the internal consultant, he or she must make the arrangements for space and time, and struggle with the "prophet in his or her own land" phenomenon. That is, inside resources are sometimes not as well identified or appreciated as those from somewhere else. This is probably why one of the common definitions of a consultant includes that he or she must be from at least 50 miles away. When consultants work with people all the time, it is probable that their deficits (usually irrelevant to the training area) become apparent to consultees. Externally-based consultants have the advantage of greater control over what is known and not known about them. Perhaps related to this are the complications in obtaining space for the workshop and finding a time for the training.

School districts often have in-service days. Arranging time on one of these days simplifies matters because the district administrators have decided to free teachers from their regular duties while continuing to pay them. The costs involve the possibility of very large groups, relatively generic topics, and no provision for follow-up consultation. In lieu of established in-service times are the options of:

- freeing personnel from work for relatively short times through the use of aides or supervisors;
- paying personnel (with money or graduate credit) for attending evening or Saturday workshops;
- making attendance mandatory through administrative ruling, usually early morning or after work;
- volunteer attendance during times suggested by the consultees;
- use of written materials provided by the consultant to consultees with no face-to-face group meetings; and/or
- on-going, brief meetings with variable attendance held as problem-solving sessions over a particular topic.

Each of these options has built-in costs and benefits and some or all may not be even considered *possible* in some settings, though all have been and are being used in certain agencies. The rise of employee unions has reduced the chances that building supervisors or central administrators will require attendance just because the psychologist, social worker, or nurse has a good idea. Even though this method, when used, guarantees an audience, the consultant might experience all the resistances and hostility such a method engenders, thus mitigating the positive consequences of training. The consultant might be made the scapegoat for administrative arbitrariness. As a general rule, volunteer audiences are much better than mandated audiences. It is impossible to avoid (at least in education and business) training nonvolunteer audiences all the time. It is possible and necessary to ascertain why people are present and strategize accordingly. Sometimes directly confronting the issue, with some humor, deflects the hostility. For example:

I sure felt wonderful watching you all file in here just now, until _____ told me she was docking anyone who did not show. For a moment I *thought* my fame had preceded me. Now I *know* my fame has preceded me.

Also, the consultant can gaze out the window once and say how hard it is to stay indoors on such a beautiful day, putting him or herself in the same situation as the trainees, instead of as the cause of the discomfort. Ultimately, of course, a very well-done workshop will engage all but the most resistant participant (who does not learn from anyone, anyway!).

Arranging for pay or graduate credit can be complicated, but is often not impossible. Many school districts are in Teaching Center arrangements with nearby universities. Gaining access to these may facilitate credit-bearing training. University professors may be able to arrange with their departments for a series of workshops to earn credit, but this could involve the paying of tuition by the consultees unless the agency pays or has a cooperative arrangement with the university.

The mere provision of written materials is unlikely to be very influential in producing change, but it may trigger some consultation requests. In fact, it is important to reiterate that the mere provision of training is unlikely to be very impactful unless follow-up consultation is utilized. Volunteer attendance scheduled at times suited to the trainees is usually the optimal choice for the in-house consultant. This may result in small, variable groups, but may also provide the most motivated audience. These groups are also likely to help the fame of your intervention spread within the organization because of the greater possibilities of change in this energetic group. Often participants in such groups are the very influential, competent teachers.

External consultants who are hired to do training avoid most of the arrangement complications. Rooms, audio-visual materials, and audiences usually appear quite smoothly. Balancing these positives is the problem of identifying the exact training needs of the group or groups in question. External consultants may lack intimate knowledge of a particular system and can. therefore, unknowingly be used by a particular faction or the administration to "push" an unpopular training package.

It is always wise to meet with key potential consumers of the training and learn their concerns. If distance makes this infeasible, some preparatory correspondence is helpful. In addition, consultants can use written needs assessment devices that break a particular topic area into its component parts, thus giving them some planning guidance. An example of such a device is given in table 6.2. This particular device (developed with Dr. Harold

Table 6.2. Needs Assessment

In terms of possible future in-service training concerning the new testing program, a committee of school personnel suggested that the following areas might be of interest. Please indicate on a five-point scale the degree to which the issue/question/need listed is of interest or concern to you. Indicate in the blank provided before each statement a number between 1 and 5, according to the following scale:

5 = this is a major concern/interest to me
4 = this is a strong concern/interest to me
3 = this is a mildly strong concern/interest to me
2 = this is somewhat of a concern/interest to me
1 = this is not a concern/interest to me

General testing issues
_____ 1. What was the process by which tests were selected?
_____ 2. What are the advantages of criterion-referenced testing and of standardized testing?
_____ 3. What is the distinction between achievement and intelligence tests?
_____ 4. Will information from testing be used for accountability purposes or to facilitate positive growth?

Logistics of the tests, testing, and workshops
_____ 5. How long will the tests take?
_____ 6. What is the response format?
_____ 7. How will the tests be scored?
_____ 8. What is the time lag between the test and the receipt of the results?
_____ 9. What will the printout of the results look like?
_____ 10. Are norms provided for grade and for age?
_____ 11. Are national and local norms to be provided?
_____ 12. What are the specific focuses of the content of the tests?
_____ 13. What kinds of scores are provided?
_____ 14. What is the meaning of terms such as raw scores, standard scores, stanines, etc.?
_____ 15. How do we interpret results?
_____ 16. Should we have grade-specific meetings among teachers since needs of teachers/children are different at the various levels?
_____ 17. Concern with attaining specific skills that can be used in the classroom as a result of participating in workshop(s).

Issues relating to the testing process
_____ 18. Who will administer the tests?
_____ 19. Concern with children doing quite differently based upon teacher's or test administrator's style of administering tests.
_____ 20. Concern with teacher indirectly communicating test-taking style to children.
_____ 21. How might we create appropriate test-taking attitudes for children?
_____ 22. What methods can we use to motivate children and to establish a supportive atmosphere?
_____ 23. How do we answer questions from children before and during testing?

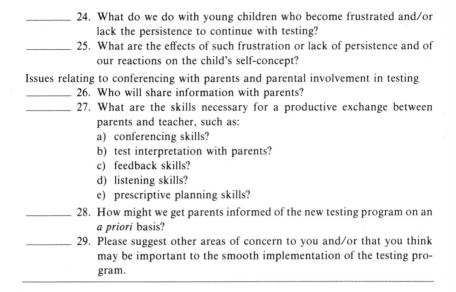

_____ 24. What do we do with young children who become frustrated and/or lack the persistence to continue with testing?

_____ 25. What are the effects of such frustration or lack of persistence and of our reactions on the child's self-concept?

Issues relating to conferencing with parents and parental involvement in testing

_____ 26. Who will share information with parents?

_____ 27. What are the skills necessary for a productive exchange between parents and teacher, such as:
   a) conferencing skills?
   b) test interpretation with parents?
   c) feedback skills?
   d) listening skills?
   e) prescriptive planning skills?

_____ 28. How might we get parents informed of the new testing program on an *a priori* basis?

_____ 29. Please suggest other areas of concern to you and/or that you think may be important to the smooth implementation of the testing program.

Keller of Syracuse University) was used along with a group meeting of representative faculty before an all-day in-service training session on Standardized Tests and Parent Conferencing. This procedure allowed the use of some of the teachers' own words in our presentations and the provision of some specific and relevant examples. This same session, however, also highlighted how different groups within a system have differing needs. The administrators wanted the workshop emphasis to be on the affective side of parent conferencing. They had many public relations problems with which to deal. The teachers, on the other hand, were far more interested in hard facts about stanines, grade equivalents, and the appropriate interpretation of the computer printouts they received. The group's different concerns reflected particular difficulties in the process of dissemination. A delicate balance must sometimes be struck between satisfying the people who are paying for the training and the people who are taking the training. Never, however, do a training sequence that is merely some system's "party-line" or propaganda unless you are a believer. Personal enthusiasm and investment in the topic are critical for the success of such an endeavor.

External consultants should make explicit all of the following:

1. Fee—how much per day, per hour, for the planning time?
2. Expenses—which of these are covered?
3. Who makes the reservations for hotels and rental cars?
4. Who does the typing and duplicating of materials?

Table 6.3. On Planning an In-service Training Workshop

1. What is the source of the request?
   a. administrative level
   b. large vs. small group problem
   c. self vs. other initiated
   d. motive behind request

2. What topic(s) are to be covered?
   a. consultant expertise
   b. needs assessment procedures
   c. history of problem(s) to be dealt with
   d. key people already involved in the area

3. Where, when, for what, and whom?
   a. voluntary vs. nonvoluntary
   b. credit vs. noncredit
   c. consultant fee or not
   d. during working day or not
   e. district gathering, or building, or classroom level

4. Materials preparation
   a. who types, duplicates, staples together, delivers
   b. who pays for these services

5. Evaluation
   a. what variables will be identified for evaluation procedures
   b. how will evaluation proceed
   c. who gets results
   d. for what is information used

5. Is the consultant expected to be available during meals (i.e., eat with participants) and after the training for evening consultations?
6. Evaluative data—does the agency have a procedure? All evaluative data should be shared.

In table 6.3 is a summary of some of the planning questions that must be considered before the implementation of the training. New trainers may find it a helpful checklist of issues to consider and things to do. Appendix 6.A is a list of topics for training sessions that are relevant to schoolwork.

IMPLEMENTATION

Once the arrangements have been made and topics selected, the trainer's second stage of work begins. There is no substitute for hard work and preparation involving reading, audio-visual production, sequencing of activities, and scheduling. Some people are able to "wing it." Most of the time this process falls flat, however, and participants feel indignant that their time was wasted by an unprepared, disorganized, blatantly uninformed, or irrelevant trainer. Teachers, in particular, report that they have suffered through some "awful" in-service training hours. Preparation does not imply over-structuring or overloading the participants. In fact, preparation (and some experience) allows for flexibility and correct estimation of content domains that can be covered.

Good training usually involves a particular body of information, appropriate media support, and self-confidence about the topic. There is no need to be *the* expert in a field to do a good presentation. The key elements of implementation are the identification of the right amount of information to present, helpful audio-visual devices for organization and/or impact, and a smooth sequencing of didactic and experiential or activity elements.

In terms of *amount of information*, less is usually better than more. Training participants tend to complain if they are overloaded and overwhelmed by information. They seem less likely to negatively evaluate learning a few important, helpful facts. There are limits, of course, on how little can be taught and still be worth the time spent. New learning that also demands new skills needs to be presented in small amounts with time allotted for practice. In the training of consultation skills, for example, it is quite common that the participants *say* they already do a lot of consulting. Role-play practice has often revealed, however, just how unskilled the participants really are. Table 6.4 is an outline of a day-and-a-half training sequence in consultation. Notice the relatively few topics introduced and the amount of time devoted to practice.

Another training strategy is to provide an overview of what the field contains. This is sometimes helpful in raising participants' awareness of what their training priorities should be. While raising the interest level, this strategy is not very effective in actually changing participants' behavior. If an organization development consultant provides an overview of organizational behavior, it is unlikely that the next staff meeting will be run any differently. However, the participants could realize that there are *possibilities* for change.

In addition to carefully circumscribing content domain, the trainer should also develop an explicit list of targeted objectives or competencies. These might be made available to the participants. The trainer can then link the lecture and the activities to each of the competencies. This seems to increase participant willingness to engage in activities. The process of identifying training objectives also provides the participants with a standard against which to make helpful evaluations. No matter how careful the planning has been, there may be a participant who wanted more or different experiences. If the trainer's agenda is clear, then it helps make clear the trainer's expectations of what equals success, and provides an avenue for input into the

Table 6.4. Consultation Training

Friday Evening 6–9 p.m.
1. Introduction and Overview 6–7 p.m.
    a. what is consultation?
    b. why do it?
    c. how is it different and better than other service delivery strategies?
                7.00–7:15 p.m. Break
2. Models of Consultation 7:15–8 p.m.
    a. what is a model?
    b. mental health consultation
3. Demonstration Role-Plays 8–9 p.m.
    a. trainer with volunteer
    b. groups of 4
Saturday Morning 9 a.m.–12 noon
2. Listening Skills 9–10 a.m.
    a. reflect
    b. paraphrase
    c. summarize
    d. elaborate
    e. clarify
2. Feedback Skills 10–11 a.m.
    a. giving
    b. receiving
                10:30–10:45 a.m. Break
3. Sample Methodology 11 a.m.–12 noon
    a. i.d. problem
    b. analyze problem—ABC's of behavior
    c. generate solutions
    d. implementation
    e. evaluation
                12 noon–1:30 p.m. Lunch
Saturday Afternoon 1:30–5 p.m.
1. Continue with Sample Methodology 1:30–2:15 p.m.
2. Sample Role-Plays 2:15–3:45 p.m.
    a. trainer with volunteer
    b. groups of 4
    c. problem solving sessions
                3:45–4:00 p.m. Break
3. Barriers to Implementing a Consultation Program
    a. personal
    b. organizational

---

training experience. It is frustrating to read at the end of five days of training that a particularly important topic was omitted. Letting people know at the outset what will be covered and seeking their input immediately can reduce the probability of that happening. A caveat is in order. It is our experience that participants will sometimes try to change the content of a meeting because of their own anxieties or unresolved organizational difficulties. It seems best not to completely overhaul a format until some quick, whole-group consensus has been discerned, perhaps through a write-in procedure. Then the change should come after a break in the action and be integrated smoothly with other planned activities.

Once while giving in-service training on applied behavior analysis, a teacher aide kept pressing the trainer to devote the time to the discussion of individual, troublesome cases. The trainer's first internal response was to "dump" the planned activities and move to a case-consultation format. Fortunately, a co-presenter had picked up cues from the rest of the group that they preferred to learn an array of new techniques. The afternoon session was modified slightly to contain one case presentation with a group effort to identify antecedent and consequent conditions and to brainstorm potential strategies. The final evaluations indicated generally very high satisfaction with the workshop. (Appendixes 6.B through 6.J contain some handouts or overhead possibilities for a workshop on applied behavior analysis.)

A not-so-successful outcome was measured after a workshop on consultation for social workers and psychologists at a children's center. The pretraining planning group insisted that the group needed conceptual, didactic inputs on consultation. It was pointed out that their real-life workloads made experiential elements and role-play redundant. The trainer reluctantly bowed to this analysis. During the three days of training some role-play was introduced. This turned out to be the most popular part of the training. The workshop, though generally well received, was criticized for information overload and not enough examples. One of the evaluators understood the planning error in the stressing of strict information giving. After the workshop she encouraged the trainer "not to believe a group under stress," urging future in-service training to engage in more experiential learning that would cause further cohesiveness in the staff. The trainer should have realized that the participants were fearful of encountering each other because of poor organizational history. In fact, this group was a microcosm of the agency, a product of two recently merged systems with the old guard and the new staff on uneasy terms over treatment philosophies and agency mission. None of this had anything to do with the training per se, but all of it had an effect on the entire experience.

These examples are given to stress the importance of balancing the trainer's experience and expertise with valid group input before and during the training experience. It is important to stay flexible enough to modify a format or to give up "sacred cows" of training. It is equally important to be *in charge* of the training.

Audio-Visuals

Audio-visuals can be helpful in training sessions if operated smoothly. Most universities offer courses in media production that are helpful for learning the absolute basics, for example, getting the machinery to run. They are also useful in teaching slide production and sequencing slide and sound presentations. The how-tos of media are not within the scope of this chapter. However, once the basics are mastered, there are still some important process rules for media use. These rules are often overlooked by the beginning trainer.

1. Arrive early to check equipment, placement, and general room conditions.
2. Have all the collating accomplished *before* the presentation.
3. Put only one or two thoughts per slide or overhead transparency.
4. If the equipment breaks down during the training, seek help, but be ready to quickly go on without it.
5. Handouts should be carefully planned as content supports and potential action sheets. They should be of excellent quality.

We have broken and/or disregarded each of these rules at some time and regretted it.

> Once planning a workshop on aggressive children with 120 participants, all the important information was secured except for how the room was shaped. When the trainers arrived, the overhead projector was in place, but the room was a long, narrow, and windowless one with only one light switch. We were in total darkness or total brightness, rendering the overheads useless.

Participants seem to like to go home with something. The somethings are usually handouts. These should be plentiful, but not overwhelming, and provide sources of related or additional information. One handout to include is a brief bibliography of readings in the area. Another helpful one is a breakdown of the targeted competencies and the schedule. In addition to summaries of what the presenter has said, the handouts can be action-oriented. Worksheets that can be used immediately on-the-job seem particularly popular. Such handouts provide bridges between training and a change in work behavior. (There are examples of worksheets in Appendixes 6.K through 6.N.)

The best method for distributing the handouts is to have the training packet together in a folder. The folder might have the participant's name or the name of the training topic. Do not spend valuable time handing out sheets. Leave them piled separately on a table for participants to retrieve. If you must hand something out, go very slowly, starting at the same spot and specifying the route that the pages must take. Have just enough so that the person at the end is not deluged with extra pages—many of which will probably get lost. It is very distracting to watch seven or eight pages being sent around with people checking with each other to see that they have all the appropriate information. Stop the action of the training to allow all of that to settle down. Do not be shy about asking for help from the audience to accomplish a distribution task. Allow them to worry about getting page 5 to someone in the eighteenth row! Very often people are happy to move around a little.

A final word on handouts and other visuals is that at least some of them should be personalized for the group in some way. The schedule and use of an overhead with their system and organizational subsystem names, for example, are helpful. Figure 6.1 is an example of one such overhead used for a training experience aimed at improving group productivity and process. The overhead was meant to illustrate the complexity of the system in which the participants worked and highlight the needs for skills in dealing with groups of people. The fact that the trainer had done the requisite "homework" about the system was evident.

Use of sound effects in training depends on the quality of the original recording and the play-back equipment. Bad sound is worse than no sound. Participants become frustrated by not hearing or understanding a tape. Audio tapes can add dramatic elements to a presentation. Training dealing with child-related topics can be greatly enhanced by the taped voice of a child. It seems a particularly focusing experience for participants to hear an actual child's voice.

Training experiences should be composed of somewhat diverse teaching strategies. Good lectures that are supported with good audio-visuals can keep the attention of a serious adult group for 1 1/2 to 2 hours and can give important basic information.

Participant Involvement

Participant-generated learning is another strategy that puts the participants in simulations of the problems or skill areas that have been discussed in the lecture. Such small group activities are invaluable, but must have face validity to the participants' present situation and must not be too anxiety-provoking. The apparent relationship between the activity and the training goal is engineered through careful study of the participating organization and through linking knowledge domains with practice. The anxiety generated by the small group exercise depends on who the participants are, the exercise, its timing, and the climate that has been set by the trainer.

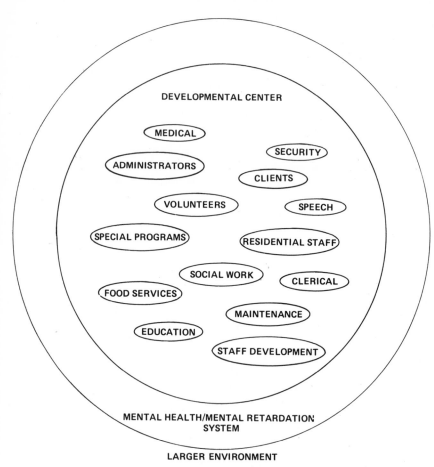

Fig. 6.1. A Personalized Overhead Transparency to Highlight System Complexity.

Some groups find role-playing easy, while other groups are quite frightened by it. Some groups are used to group simulations of staff meetings, for example, and so need little introduction. It is usually true, however, that most people are somewhat anxious about practicing new skills in front of others. Trainers can mitigate this anxiety by demonstrating what is being asked and by inquiring about the content and process of previous training events. This helps establish the experience level of the participants, and helps put current training content needs in context.

Some exercises are very scary no matter what the group. For example, telling people to choose a group or partner using a process that involves the systematic exclusion of some members is always anxiety-provoking unless the trainer insists that it be done in just one or two minutes. Exercises involving feedback are often frightening, especially if they are very unstructured. People are usually afraid of being rejected or being criticized in front of others.

Many trainers use warm-up or ice-breaker activities to get the group relaxed enough to begin the training process. Ice-breakers may be easy, fun activities (some examples are given in Appendix 6.O), or be just a few words of personal information about the trainer. A few humorous remarks at the outset is a time-honored way to begin a speech. The goal of this is to put the audience in a favorable frame of mind for what will follow. It is probably wise not to tell jokes unless you tell jokes well. There is no point in beginning a training session by looking incompetent. More than jokes, participants appreciate spontaneous wit and good-naturedness. It is never appropriate to use sarcastic or biting humor that takes advantage of a participant for a laugh. A defensive, cautious stance will ensue. This is not an atmosphere conducive to learning. Other obvious pitfalls are off-color, sexist, or racist "humor." It is easy to offend. The only person a trainer can safely derogate is him or herself.

Long exercises can be more frightening than short ones. If the trainer says to (1) think of what is important in a teammate, (2) interview those people who seem to have those qualities, (3) list top choices, (4) go back for another interview, and (5) choose a teammate, some of the participants are likely to find it a very upsetting exercise. Compare that with, "You just have a minute. Find someone to work with you on some of the day's activities." The product (i.e., teammate) is the same in both processes, but the time and the consciously accept/reject structure of the first process makes it a far more risk-taking exercise. With the increased risks may come concomitantly increased learning. If the learning is not doubled by doubling the risk, however, the anxiety generated may be a bad bargain.

Timing

Decide in advance at which point in the training sequence to introduce a particular activity. Some trainers use a gradually-increasing-risk formula while others create a situation that is risky immediately, thereby somewhat desensitizing the participants. The danger in the latter strategy is scaring off some of the learners or putting them in needlessly frightening situations.

A weekend encounter group training exercise was entitled "Power and Rejection." The focus was on self-consciously building personal power and owning up to or increasing individual influence in a group. One of the exercises involved a long team-formation and then team-building process. Suddenly, the trainers announced that one person from each group must be excluded. The exclusion process resulted in the formation of another group of "rejects." Years after this training, at least one of the "rejects" reported carrying psychological scars. He said that he'd learned "not to take part in such groups." Obviously, this was not the intended learning.

It is hard to know how or if to protect trainees. What matters is to learn from yours and others' experiences in terms of trainee comfort levels. Training should generally operate a little beyond where people are comfortable.

If a climate of trust and acceptance can be established by the trainer almost any activity will be gallantly attempted by trainees. This climate is established by:

- sharing something personal about yourself at the outset
- sporadically sharing personal process concerns (e.g., I'm worried that you're not understanding this.)
- treating the trainees with deference and respect
- responding to feedback openly and nondefensively
- learning names as quickly as possible
- laughing at your own mistakes

It is wise to plan some variety in the workshops. Didactic units can be followed by small group, dyad, or individual activities. There is usually one long exercise. Participants report it easier to listen in the morning and "do" in the afternoon. It is advisable, therefore, not to schedule the longest lecture input during the last hour. A smooth flow among lecture, audio-visuals, small group or individual activities, debriefing, and discussion/question-and-answer segments allows for different types of learners to experience a preferred mode for at least part of the training.

Final Implementation Notes

Moving around the room keeps an audience's attention as you speak. Modulating voice tone and rate of speed is helpful in keeping the participants alert. Trainers must be willing to be performers. A slightly exaggerated use of gestures and facial expression is important in front of a group. The larger the group, the greater the effort should be to engage them. Eye contact and knowing names will keep a small group involved with a trainer. When the numbers climb over 30-40, however, the trainer must expend considerable energy just to make the participants focus on him or her. The media may not be the *entire* message, but it is very influential, especially as a group grows larger.

Table 6.5. Implementing a Training Experience

1. Housekeeping
   a. Provide schedule   —————
   b. Point out restrooms and/or refreshment availability   —————
   c. Allow 1 1/2 hours for lunch, if possible   —————
2. Process
   a. Introduce new people (e.g., student observers)   —————
   b. Clarify the trainers' roles (i.e., teacher, observer, facilitator) —————
   c. Avoid (if at all possible) large group confrontations   —————
   d. Debrief with other leaders or observers during breaks   —————
   e. Clearly divide leadership responsibilities   —————
   f. Give one instruction at a time   —————
   g. Reinforce participant risk-taking   —————
3. Content
   a. Share goals   —————
   b. Tie activities to stated goals   —————
   c. Provide high quality visual aids   —————
   d. Make paper and pencils available   —————
   e. Watch vocabulary for jargon and off-color words   —————

In table 6.5 is a checklist of implementation concerns. It may be helpful to review some of your past training experiences and add or delete items from this list.

EVALUATION

Implicitly and explicitly throughout the entire planning and implementation phases of training there is feedback and the chance to gather evaluative data. No training process is complete, however, without some sort of summative (i.e., final) evaluation process. Like the other phases, the evaluation method may range from quite simple to quite complex. A very simple, yet effective device is pictured as table 6.6. The decisions regarding evaluation depend on audience comfort, time, and money.

Few people enjoy filling out long, cumbersome evaluations. If there is a reason for an evaluation instrument being exceptionally long or detailed, the trainer might explain that to the participants before seeking the information.

Evaluations are usually distributed immediately after the training is over. There is an advantage to this method in that the participants are still somewhat captive and therefore the return rate is high. Immediate feedback is also not contaminated by memory problems and gives the presenter some quick reading of his or her success. The obvious problem with immediate feedback

Table 6.6. Evaluation Instrument

Please take a moment to share your reaction to the training with me.

1. Was the training relevant to your concerns?

2. Were the methods used effective?

3. Was the day well organized?

4. What was the best part?

5. What was the worst part?

6. What are your suggestions?

---

is that the trainees are responding to the training only and not the usefulness of the training for the on-the-job situation. Because the point of training is usually to improve performance in another setting, gathering delayed data is crucial. However, the time and expense of delayed data gathering often deters the trainer.

Sometimes the usefulness of a training sequence can be indirectly measured by the invitations a trainer receives to work with other members of the same organization or do follow-up training with the original group. This seems a powerful positive message; however, many factors outside of the trainer's expertise can affect return engagements. For example, the person arranging for training experiences may move to another position. That can result in a whole new list of trainers being drawn up. Or, the training priorities of an agency may change because of external mandates. If new legislation, a new test, or a new method of looking for oil comes on the scene, even popular training sequences will be dropped in favor of the new needs for information.

If the consultant/trainer worked with a planning group before the training, it is sometimes possible to meet with them again six weeks or six months after the training to gather follow-up data. This is also an indirect method, but one that may lead to further requests for training and consultation.

Perhaps the best training method for the consultant/trainer to implement is an intensive presentation period with follow-up sessions for a specified amount of time. Initially, the participants are given concrete guidelines on how to use the new skills, then the consultant/trainer can arrange for observation periods with the trainees. The trainer may also set up small trouble-shooting meetings over the course of four to six months to provide clarification and support of new behaviors. Such a package of training is often attractive to agencies that are rightfully skeptical of the long-lasting value of one-shot training methodologies.

Another possibility is to arrange for the provision of supervision of the new skills from on-the-job taped examples. The consultant/trainer agrees to listen and provide feedback to the participants based on taped examples of the targeted training competencies. This can become somewhat cumbersome, but is a possibility when distances make follow-up visits infeasible.

SUMMARY

This chapter has outlined the usefulness of training activities as part of a consultation program. Planning, implementation, and evaluation issues were covered. What seems important is to do training as a consultant would do it. Involve participants at every phase, remain open and flexible in the face of feedback, learn from each experience, and leave the organization better able to meet its own needs rather than more dependent on outside resources.

SUGGESTED READINGS

Bowles, P. E., Jr., & Nelson, R. O. Training teachers as mediators: Efficacy of a workshop versus the bug-in-the-ear technique. *Journal of School Psychology*, 1976, **14**(1), 15–25.

The implementation of behavior modification techniques relies on effective training of teachers as mediators. This is often done as a result of an in-service workshop conducted by a consultant. The early training of mediators involved a triadic model of consultant-parent-child. One of the more popular though costly techniques involved the bug-in-the-ear which enabled the consultant to advise the parent in a given situation.

The present study found that there is no difference, as far as effectiveness of implementation of modification programs in the classroom, between teachers in a control group who received no instructions and those in the in-service workshop. To counteract this problem, half of an experimental group received bug-in-the-ear training in their own classrooms. This group, as opposed to a control group, used praise and contingency statements more in accordance with modification principles and more effectively in the classroom.

The study demonstrated that just teaching the principles of behavior modification is often not sufficient to produce desired change. It is advised for the consultant to use bug-in-the-ear techniques where possible or at least role-playing situations that arise in the class.

Smith, P. L. Assertion training as an entry strategy for consultation with school administrators. *The Counseling Psychologist*, 1975, **5**(4), 79–84.

In this article, the author presents a program for school administrators which serves the dual purpose of an entry strategy and an aid to the consultees in being

more effective in their jobs. Assertiveness would appear to be an important character-
istic for those in positions of power, such as the school administrators. The author
claims that the demonstration workshop suggested here serves as an instructional
base for the assertiveness training while simultaneously conveying the message that
the consultant is interested in the whole system. A packet on the demonstration
workshop is available from the author. After the demonstration workshop, a five to
eight session training format is arranged with interested administration subgroups.

Stein, T. Some ethical considerations of short-term workshops in the principles and
   methods of behavior modification. *Journal of Applied Behavior Analysis*, 1975, **8**,
   113–115.

The author suggests that brief workshop or seminar format methods of teaching
behavior modification principles and techniques are inadequate. Professionals who
attend such sessions can only be poorly trained at best—ready to add bits and pieces
of behavioral methodology to already eclectic practice repertoires, without thorough
understanding of the theories behind the procedures, and little competence with the
procedures themselves. This situation has led to charges of "unethicalness" leveled at
behavior modification by its critics. Stein gives some suggestions for improvement.
Perhaps his comments are applicable to all such "brief exposure" formats, whatever
methods they purport to teach.

Wetzel, R. J. Behavior modification techniques and the training of teachers' aides.
   Psychology In The Schools, 1970, **7**, 325–330.

This article presents a training program for classroom aides and a description of
measures used to evaluate its effectiveness. Five trainee groups, each composed of a
teacher and two aides, participated in a four-week training program that stressed
setting behavioral goals, contingency management, and evaluation of methods and
procedures. Training took place in a lab and in the regular classroom and included
teaching observing behavior, modeling by training staff, providing corrective feedback, and discussing behavior. A variety of evaluation techniques were used following training. Video tapes pre- and post-training appeared to show positive training
effects. Behavioral measures of training effects showed an overall significant pre-post
increase in recorded approval and decrease in disapproval dispensed by aides in the
classroom. Instruction in a behavioral task and an attitude measure also showed
positive effects after training. The principal effect of this training program, according
to the author, was that it brought verbal behavior regarding reinforcement and the
use of reinforcement in the classroom into congruence.

Although this article describes a training program for classroom aides, it seems
applicable to teachers as well. Its value lies in the description of training procedures
and suggestions for evaluation of training effects.

APPENDIX 6.A
IN-SERVICE OPTIONS FOR CONSULTANTS

Following is a list of possible topics for workshops or consultation sessions.

_____ Teaching to student needs
  _____ developing instructional alternatives for individual learners
  _____ diagnostic teaching
  _____ structuring space for classroom control
  _____ structuring time
_____ Learning Centers
  _____ designing centers
  _____ setting up centers
  _____ introducing students to centers
  _____ record keeping
_____ Contracts
  _____ writing academic and behavioral objectives
  _____ advisory conferences with students
  _____ writing contracts
  _____ evaluating and modifying contracts
_____ Peer and cross-age tutoring
  _____ selecting tutors and students to be tutored
  _____ training tutors
  _____ materials and activities for tutoring
  _____ supervising and evaluating the tutoring
  _____ developing a "learning through teaching" program for an entire class
_____ Affective Education
  _____ integrating affective goals with academic tasks
  _____ creative expression
  _____ raising self-esteem in students
  _____ encouraging self-expression in students
  _____ Human Development Program ("magic circle")
  _____ classroom meetings
  _____ cooperative classroom program
  _____ role-playing
  _____ experiential and value clarification exercises
  _____ bibliotherapy
  _____ teacher advisory conferences with students
  _____ materials and media for affective education
_____ General Classroom Management
  _____ setting up rules, expectations, consequences
  _____ establishing routines

———— general classroom management strategies for teachers
———— monitoring systems: teacher, peer, self
———— class courts
———— stimulating student involvement
———— Social Relations in the Classroom
———— assessing your classroom (sociograms and other measures)
———— interventions to promote social relationships
———— intervening in social problem situations
———— Behavior Modification
———— identifying appropriate behaviors to be reinforced in children
———— identifying inappropriate behavior to be changed
———— using praise systematically
———— using varied reward systems
———— rewarding individual students
———— rewarding groups of students
———— peer reinforcement
———— planned ignoring
———— using behavior checklists
———— evaluating and revising the behavior modification system
———— Punishment
———— knowing when to punish
———— knowing how to punish
———— combining rewards and punishments
———— withdrawing rewards and privileges
———— time-out procedures
———— in-class suspension
———— in-school suspension
———— early dismissal plan
———— Crisis-intervention
———— general procedures
———— reality therapy
———— responding to specific problems
———— attention seeking
———— testing limits
———— withdrawn behavior
———— social immaturity
———— hyperactivity
———— aggressive behavior
———— negativism: defiance and work refusal
———— lying and cheating
———— stealing

_____ "sexual" acting-out
_____ anti-authoritarian behavior
_____ "bizarre" behavior
_____ "the scapegoat"
_____ phobias
_____ absenteeism
_____ Ethnic Studies
_____ cultural differences in learners
_____ capitalizing on a child's ethnic background in the classroom
_____ language
_____ family experience
_____ community experience
_____ developing positive ethnic self-concept
_____ cultural awareness
_____ art
_____ music
_____ literature
_____ food
_____ dress
_____ history
_____ ways to involve the community and parents in school
_____ understanding your feelings about different ethnic groups
_____ identifying stereotypes
_____ values clarification in relation to ethnic issues
_____ Other areas
_____ for schools
_____ developing interpersonal relationships
_____ facilitating communication
_____ defining goals and priorities
_____ general problem-solving
_____ setting discipline procedures and codes
_____ for teacher teams
_____ developing interpersonal relationships
_____ facilitating communication
_____ defining goals and priorities
_____ general problem-solving
_____ setting discipline procedures and codes
_____ giving and taking feedback
_____ for teachers
_____ value clarification
_____ meeting teacher needs
_____ setting goals for change

———— assessing your teaching
———— personalizing your classroom
———— developing helping skills
———— developing interpersonal communication
———— coping with stress

APPENDIX 6.B
SUMMARY OF BEHAVIORAL
MANAGEMENT STRATEGIES

Principle 1. A behavior that is followed by a reward is more likely to recur or increase.

Principle 2. If small steps toward a final new behavior are rewarded, it is likely that the child will eventually be able to perform the entire new behavior.

Principle 3. A behavior that is not followed by a reward (is ignored) is likely to decrease or stop.

Principle 4. To stop or decrease a behavior, rewards should be withheld, not taken away.

Principle 5. To stop an undesired behavior, reward an alternative behavior that cannot be performed at the same time.

Principle 6. Rewarding a nearby child who is behaving properly while ignoring a misbehaving child is likely to stop or decrease undesired behavior.

Principle 7. To stop a behavior that can no longer be ignored, calmly and without judgment state the rule.

Principle 8. To stop a behavior that can no longer be ignored, calmly and without judgment redirect the child's behavior by suggesting an alternate activity.

Principle 9. Removing a child from a highly rewarding classroom to an isolated area with no rewards is a way to reduce dangerous or otherwise unmanageable behavior.

APPENDIX 6.C
STEPS IN BEHAVIOR MODIFICATION

1. SELECT SPECIFIC TARGETS FOR CHANGE.
   - targets must be observable, countable, measurable
   - "dead man" targets are not allowed
   - identify what behaviors are to be increased as well as decreased
2. DEFINE THE CONDITIONS UNDER WHICH THE TARGET BEHAVIORS ARE MOST APT TO OCCUR.
   - curriculum—instructional program
   - social context
   - reward contingencies
3. REINFORCE THE TARGET BEHAVIOR AS SOON AS IT OCCURS AND OFTEN ENOUGH FOR THE BEHAVIOR TO SUSTAIN ITSELF.
   - a reinforcer is something that increases the rate of a behavior
   - a reinforcer is automatic
   - use reinforcers often at first but less later on
4. COMPARE BEGINNING AND ENDING RATES OF THE BEHAVIOR TO SEE WHETHER THE STRATEGY FOR CHANGE WAS EFFECTIVE.
   - behavior is always "right"
   - only the data can tell if the program was effective

APPENDIX 6.D
RULES FOR REINFORCEMENT

1. Be sure you know what you are going to reinforce and what you are not.
2. Be sure you are reinforcing an appropriate behavior.
3. At first, reinforce very frequently.
4. Reinforce as soon after the behavior occurs as possible.
5. Be sure the task for which you are reinforcing the child is within his or her reach.

APPENDIX 6.E
TYPES OF REINFORCERS

1. Thing to eat (e.g., candy, raisins, cereal)
2. Things to play with or handle (e.g., small toys, puzzles, games)
3. Things to look at or listen to (e.g., movies, puppet shows, cartoons, records, tapes)
4. Praise or attention (e.g., noticing with a smile or word a desired behavior, spending time with children contingent on appropriate behavior)
5. Tokens or points (e.g., stars on a chart, stickers, chips)
6. Preferred behaviors of child before intervention (e.g., TV watching, moving around classroom, talking to friends)

APPENDIX 6.F
HOW TO FIND THE RIGHT REINFORCERS

1. *Ask!*
2. *Past history*. What is already known about particular age groups?
   a. Younger children: They consume large amounts of energy, need carbohydrates (e.g., candy, food, fruit). Social reinforcers are parents, teachers, and other adults.
   b. Adolescents: Peer approval, social status, freedom of choice, time to themselves, symbols of independence, activity rewards.
3. *Observation*. Behavior is an arrow pointing to the child's critical reinforcer. A critical reinforcer is any event essential to a person's physical or psychological survival. Given a free operant situation does the child prefer:
   a. social or alone activity
   b. adult or peer contact
   c. single companion or group
   d. active or passive activity
   e. large or small muscle activity
   f. continuous or varied stimuli
   g. some idiosyncratic activity (e.g., washing table tops)

APPENDIX 6.G
PUNISHMENT: GENERAL PRINCIPLES

Events that follow behavior and weaken the likelihood that the behavior will be repeated are called *punishing stimuli*. When these events are used to control the behavior of others, they are called punishment.

Punishment is the opposite of reinforcement but tends to operate in the same manner regarding how often it is used and how much is needed to effect a response.

Punishment may have the ability to produce strong and lasting effects on behavior, but using it may have negative side effects.

Punishment should be avoided because:

1. People learn to either avoid or escape from sources of punishment.
2. Those using punishment become associated with punishment (conditioned punishers).
3. Punishment tells only what NOT to do, not what TO DO.
4. The punishing person (teacher, parent, aide, etc.) becomes a model for aggression. Children imitate aggressive acts in their relationships with each other and younger siblings.
5. Punishment interferes with learning as it produces high-level anxieties.

Effective punishment must do these things:

1. Prevent avoidance and escape from the source of punishment (always provide clear-cut steps for earning reinforcers back).
2. Minimize need for future punishment. Use a warning signal so that the child will eventually be able to respond to the warning alone AND be sure to reinforce the incompatible, desired behavior.
3. Avoid the use of an aggressive model. Withdrawing reinforcers is preferable to presenting painful stimuli as it ensures that the child does not learn to imitate aggression as a way of solving problems.

APPENDIX 6.H
BEHAVIOR CONTRACTS

A behavior contract is a written agreement between you and your child. Both parties should sign it and both should have copies of it. Children usually like behavior contracts; signing a contract is usually a new, grown-up thing to do. They also feel more sure that with the whole thing down in writing we adults will not be able to sneak out of our end of the bargain.

A good behavior contract should:

1. Be explicit.

    It must say exactly what behaviors are rewarded and what behaviors are not rewarded or are punished. Everyone should be absolutely sure they are clear on the agreement. It is usually good to role-play with the child to ensure clarity. If you say something like, "This is what I mean when I say you will not get a reward when you insult your sister . . . ," then say or do whatever the child usually does.

2. Include what both people will do.

    It is not a behavioral contract if you just list 30 things the child must do. You must include your part too.

3. Include reward arrangements.

    Say what the reward will be, how often the behavior will be rewarded, and when the reward can be collected.

4. Include how it will be decided if the necessary level for a reward has been reached.

5. Most important of all: KEEP YOUR PART OF THE DEAL!

    A contract that is not followed through on is worse than no contract at all.

APPENDIX 6.I
ACCEPTABLE TEACHER RESPONSES

Reinforcers
  A. Verbal—Any praise of work, effort or appropriate behavior which tells the student what he has done.
    1. Your work is improving.
    2. You did a fine job on that, (*name*).
    3. I'm pleased with your project.
    4. I appreciate your help.
    5. I feel great when you try like that.
  B. Non-Verbal
    1. Smiling, arms relaxed, hands open.
    2. Touching arm or back of chair.
    3. Physical nearness.
    4. Eye-level contact.
    5. Head nod.

Punishers
  A. Verbal—Any statement which expresses your negative feelings about a specific inappropriate behavior and not the person, or which points to the disruption the student's behavior is causing.
    1. I feel upset when you disrupt the class.
    2. It bugs me when you continually talk.
    3. Your talking is disturbing Joan's work.
    4. The class cannot concentrate when you behave that way.
  B. Non-Verbal
    1. Superior posture, looking down.
    2. Arms on hips or folded.
    3. Stern look, not mean or hateful.
    4. Physically distant from student.

Unacceptable Teacher Responses

Inappropriate Reinforcers
  A. Verbal—Any statement which evaluates the person rather than his behavior.
    1. *You* are a good boy.
  B. Non-Verbal—Any ambigious response which may have "extra" meaning.
    1. Touching an opposite sex high school student
    2. Double-meaning winks (possibly sarcastic)

Inappropriate Punishers
  A. Verbal: Any statement which evaluates the person rather than his or her behavior. Any question-type response, or yelling.
    1. You're stupid.

    2. Why are you doing that?

    3. Why aren't you working?

B. Non-verbal: Any aggressive touching, shaking, slapping.

APPENDIX 6.J PRELIMINARY REPORT OF DATA GATHERING EDUCATIONAL PLAN

Student _____ Birthdate _____ Date _____

1. Best Learning Modalities: (Check)   2. (a) Strengths:
   Input: Output:
   _____ Auditory   _____ Oral
   _____ Visual   _____ Written
   _____ Tactile   _____ Non-Verbal
   _____ No Identifiable Difference _____

3. Amount of Structure Needed in: (Check)   (b) Weaknesses:

	Open	Moderate	High
Time			
Room space			
Activities			
Materials			

4. Areas to be emphasized: Reading ___   Arithmetic ___ Spelling ___
   Other ___ Affective ___ Behavior ___
   Comments:

5. *Suggested management* and teaching strategies* (groups often overlap—check)

Instruction	*Classroom management*	*Affective*
___ Enrichment experiences	Rewards:	___ Discussion group (e.g., Magic Circle)
___ Language development	___ Tangible (e.g., Pencil)	___ Tutor peer
___ Language assessment	___ Privileges (e.g., free play, line leader)	___ Assignments that guarantee success
	___ Praise	___ Recognize for effort (not just accomplishment)
Remediation In:	___ Non-verbal (e.g., smiles, eye contact)	
___ Auditory discrimination	___ Shorten assignments	___ Art communication
___ Auditory memory	___ Checklist	___ Puppet play, dramatic activities, role play
___ Visual memory	___ Contracting, job sheets	
___ Visual discrimination	___ Alternate activities (e.g., seatwork with physical movement)	___ Leadership role
___ Abstract reasoning		___ Buddy system (e.g., call or accompany to school)
___ Gross motor		
___ Fine motor	___ Receive tutoring	___ One-to-one counseling
___ Perceptual motor	___ Reinforce directions	___ Feeling chart
___ Career education		

___ Multisensory
___ Concrete approach
___ Manipulative
material
___ Pictorial aids
___ Tactile experiences
___ Emphasis on direc-
tionality/sequencing
___ Audio tapes
___ Programmed
___ Activity cards
___ Self-directing
___ Non-self-directing

___ Seat close to black-
board (visual)
___ Seat close to
teacher (auditory)
___ Needs consistency
___ Drill
___ Learning centers
___ Quiet place
___ Time out

* Further information is available from Psychology Consultant.

APPENDIX 6.K
BEHAVIORAL WORK SHEET

Step 1

Describe the undesirable behavior that is to be eliminated or reduced. Try to answer the questions:

- What would this behavior look like to an outsider?
- What would they see or hear going on in the classroom, playground, etc?

_____

_____

_____

Next, estimate how often the undesirable behavior occurs.

- Once a day   _____
- Between two and five times   _____
- Between six and ten times   _____
- More than ten times a day   _____

Step 2

Describe the behavior you would like to take the place of the undesirable behavior.

Try to think of that behavior which, if increased, would automatically reduce the frequency of the undesired behavior. (Again, try to tell what this behavior would look like or sound like to an outsider.)

_____

_____

_____

Try to estimate how often this last behavior occurs each day:

- Once a day   _____
- Two to five times a day   _____
- Six to ten times a day   _____
- More than ten times a day   _____

APPENDIX 6.L
A MAP FOR ALTERNATIVE ROOM ARRANGEMENTS

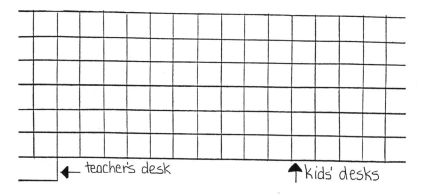

TRY:
- Cut out desks in groups of 2, 4, 6, or 8
  —put the desk groupings in one part of the room
  —scatter the groupings throughout the room
- Cut out the number of desks in your room in a horseshoe shape
- Cut out the desks in long rows that run down the center or either side of the room
- Any other ideas

ASK:
- Where does the teacher's desk fit into any arrangement?
- Will the arrangement help or hinder what I value in my room?

APPENDIX 6.M
BEHAVIORAL DESCRIPTION WORKSHEET

Write what is wrong with the following targets:
1. Jerry does not feel good about himself.

_____

_____

2. I want Jimmy to be quiet.

_____

_____

3. I want Patty to enjoy doing her homework.

_____

_____

4. I want Johnny to be nicer to his little brother.

_____

_____

5. I want Marcia to stop being so sad.

_____

_____

APPENDIX 6.N
SPACE UTILIZATION IN THE CLASSROOM

"Qualities Most Highly Valued"

Quality		Space Structure Indicators
1. _____	*	_____
		_____
_____		_____
		_____
		_____
2. _____	*	_____
		_____
_____		_____
		_____
		_____
3. _____	*	_____
		_____
_____		_____

"Qualities Least Valued"

Quality		Space Structure Indicators
1. _____	*	_____
		_____
_____		_____
		_____
		_____
2. _____	*	_____
		_____
_____		_____
		_____
		_____
3. _____	*	_____
		_____
_____		_____

APPENDIX 6.O
ICE BREAKING ACTIVITIES

1. Break into groups of 3 and each person tell the earliest childhood memory or funniest childhood memory.

2. Each participant gets a lemon (apple, banana) and examines it carefully. The fruits are then collected. Each member must try to retrieve his or her fruit from the collective pile.

3. Family groups are divided into small teams and asked to draw a picture of the team.

4. Members learn each others' names by presenting their names with an alliterated adjective. Each member tries to repeat all the previous names and adjectives.

5. Members of the group are asked to share their fantasies about what they expected to happen at this particular workshop.

6. The leader involves group in a relaxation fantasy journey.

7. Participants receive 6 to 10 small sheets of paper. They are told to write a key, self-descriptive phrase on each sheet and pin the sheets to their clothes. The group is then told to mill around (cocktail party fashion) reading each others' phrases but not speaking. A whole group debriefing can follow.

8. Members break into groups of 4, each receiving pieces of a jigsaw puzzle. The entire group has the pieces to make four squares but must nonverbally cooperate to solve the puzzle. No one may take a piece without it being offered. Each member must be attentive to the others' needs.

7

Moving from Direct to Indirect Service Delivery

BARRIERS

A number of forces can be operative in inhibiting the development of a consultation program in a setting (see fig. 7.1). Particularly important among these forces are:

1. The principal "actors" in the setting just do not believe in the efficacy of consultation.
2. Appropriate training or practicum experiences have not been included in the professional socialization of the mental health worker.
3. The press for direct service is so great that no time or way is seen to enlarge a direct service role to include indirect services.
4. The consulting role appears threatening to decision makers.

Each of these barriers to implementation deserves some extended attention. Following a discussion of each, some strategies to accomplish the addition of consultation to a professional repertoire will be given.

Does It Work?

Perhaps the greatest obstacle to doing good consultation is a pervasive belief among professional mental health people that they must be in direct remedial contact with "The Pathology." They are, after all, the ones who trained for years to treat mental illness. Two assumptions are operating here. One is that pathology resides within the client or between the client and his or her small group. The most extreme dynamic position has been called "intrapsy-

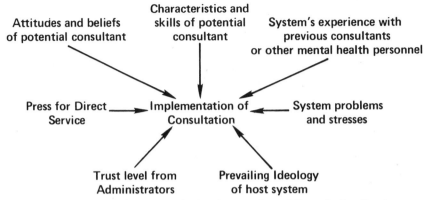

Fig. 7.1. Forces Acting Upon the Implementation of Consultation Services

chic supremacy" (Levine, 1973). That is, what is important to know about persistent, dysfunctional human problems is what cannot be known directly. A highly skilled practitioner must plumb the depths of the unconscious and be able to use mythology, religion, anthropology, literature, and Freudian and Neo-Freudian theory to interpret the unconscious symbolic content that becomes manifest. No small task! If a practitioner believes that the important stuff of the human condition is the unconscious mind and the inevitable conflicts among the id, ego, and superego, then consultation is seen as quite superficial. Caplan's (1970) exposition of mental health consultation was revolutionary in its recognition of the intrapsychic, interpersonal, organizational, and societal contributors to dysfunction. Even this new model of service delivery, however, relied mainly on educative and indirect therapy-like activities.

The second assumption that interferes with consultation is that there will be an inevitable watering down of effect when consultees are used as intermediaries of treatment. This assumption is made by practitioners from any theoretical position. Behavioral specialists may find that their publication-perfect-plan is applied inconsistently. Humanistic therapists might be put off by an evaluative or sarcastic consultee style and see no way to have influence upon it.

Both of these beliefs may be accurate in certain situations. They are related in that they are building blocks of professional identities: "I do something that is very difficult and that is best done by me. Others who attempt to do what I do without proper training and credentialing are charlatans and potentially dangerous." It is unfortunate that the state-of-the-art in mental health is such to make "professional preciousness" (Sarason, 1973) unjustified to say the least.

In fact, what state-of-the-art information is available points to the importance of coordinated, available, congruent, but not particularly highly trained, services. Some people in therapy do get better. Most people who feel the need for help never approach a mental health expert (Christensen, Birk, Brooks, & Sedlacek, 1976; Christensen & Magoon, 1974; Horwitz, 1978; McKinlay, 1973). Their choices for helpers are clergy, family, and friends. Many problems facing us are clearly not amenable to therapeutic intervention—poverty, racism, uprootedness, and the changing role of the family. Those who do come for help are offered an expensive hour per week. The $60.00–$100.00 hour may work for those who can pay but it cannot be *all* we have to offer.

The other way that beliefs in intrapsychic supremacy and inevitable watering down are related is their focus on remediation rather than prevention. "Doctors" are supposed to *fix* things. In the United States, physician-healers are our most prestigious group. To invest time in an activity that does not result in a cure is often seen as trivial—even not reportable on some standard time management accountability sheets. Despite long years of rhetoric about the need to prevent dysfunction (and some promising programs that have accomplished just that, e.g., Allen, Chinsky, Larsen, Lochman, & Selinger, 1976; Cowen, 1973), we are still a nation of first aid technicians. The entire technology for prevention is not at hand. However, the entire technology for remediation is also not at hand, but it, rather than prevention, continues to receive societal and professional support.

In summary, beliefs that the professional mental health worker holds about the site of pathology, the potential competence of non-professionals, professional territoriality, and the role of the professional as healer and/or preventer all have influence on his or her openness to consultation as a service delivery system. The research on the efficacy of consultation (e.g., Mannino & Shore, 1979; Medway, 1979) is at least as positive as psychotherapy outcome research.

Role of Training

The obviously related issue to the ones raised above is lack of training. People become as they are taught. Many graduate schools offer no formal training in consultation through either courses or specially arranged practicums (Meyers, 1978). Consultation is a relatively new area of study—with perhaps 25 years of literature. This is part of the training problem. The other aspect is a notion that consulting is a natural outgrowth of knowing something very well. No formal course work is needed in consulting, only in what the consulting is about. Anyone who has seriously tried to serve as an internal or external consultant to a system knows the inaccuracy of such a notion. *It is not enough to know.* All human communication occurs on multiple levels. The consultant must be an expert in human communication, systems theory, and relevant content areas, and have the necessary personal and interpersonal skills. This particular combination probably does not occur serendipitously with any high frequency. The actual effectiveness of training programs to teach consultation has received consistently positive support (e.g., Alpert & Rosenfield, 1981; Alpert, Silverstein, & Haynes, 1980; Bergan, 1977; Goodwin, Garvey, & Barclay, 1971). This area needs further attention, however, as there is evidence that we can teach consulting skills, but limited evidence that we actually produce people who do a lot of consulting as part of their professional role functions.

Practitioners from a number of disciplines have identified consulting as a priority training need (Apter, 1978; Meyers, 1978). Consultation is a popular topic in continuing education formats. This is helpful, but is unlikely to be very influential because the typical workshop format does not allow for follow-up supervision of new skills. Workshops do excite many people to seek new skills, however, and so should not be underestimated as catalysts for changing attitudes and beliefs about service delivery.

Clinical Press

Even those who believe in the conceptual rightness of consultation and have had appropriate training often have difficulty implementing consultation programs. The press to do direct service is often very great in schools, mental health departments, and other human service agencies. Often these agencies see direct service to a client group as their primary mission. Professionals who ask to include other indirect activities during the workday can be seen as not "pulling their weight." Agencies that mandate a consultation/education (C & E) service may allocate less than 5 percent of their resources in that area (Snow & Newton, 1976). Professionals who find themselves identified as "C & E" people also often find themselves as permanent back-ups and stop-gaps. That is, the lack of or a reduced *clinical* caseload makes the person seem completely available to fill other positions during times of stress (C. W. Conoley, 1978; C. W. Conoley & J. C. Conoley, 1981). The times of stress often greatly outnumber the calm times with the resulting demise of the consultation service.

Sometimes consultants face very upset consultees who want something done (i.e., remove the problem) immediately. In the face of such crises, the chance to be a consultant is greatly reduced. Consultation can provide a supportive, crisis intervention effect, but is really not conceptualized as such a technique. Consultation is by definition a long-range, preventive, educative, ecological strategy. If it were used effectively the clinical press might be reduced (e.g., C. W. Conoley & J. C. Conoley, 1981; Ritter, 1978) but only over the span of a few years. The pressure to give up on consultation becomes very strong. Sometimes the end result of consultation is not equally pleasing across subsystems within an agency. For example, in the previously cited Conoley and Conoley chapter one of the "successes" of consultation was the handling of mild to moderate clinical cases by community caregivers in a rural county. This left the outpatient team with no waiting list but a significantly more disturbed clientele. This was a goal of the C & E team, but was a less popular outcome among outpatient team members who lost much of their professional reinforcement. This anecdote illustrates how the "clinical press" could originate and be maintained by vested interests within an agency that professes a commitment to consultation.

Consultation as Threat

Ironic as it may seem, some decision makers may see consultation or consultants as threats to their systems. Because the function of the consultant is to assess the status quo and work to improve system functioning, there is likely to be some systemic upset with the appearance of a skilled consultant. Administrative paranoia about the consultant is usually associated with fears that the consultant will 1) learn more about the system than the administrator knows; 2) discover weaknesses in the system or administrator; 3) align with malcontented staff members and facilitate unsanctioned change; or 4) waste the time of staff members by taking them away from regular client duties in order to consult.

Successful consultation almost always depends on positive administrative backing. Organization development consultants know that they must gain approval from top administrators. Often, more case-centered consultants overlook this fact of organizational life and fail to give priority to activities aimed at building a positive relationship with top administrators.

Administrators must value the contribution a consultant can make to a system. They necessarily have a different perspective on organizational functioning than do staff members and may foresee or imagine a number of problems arising from a consultation effort. They deserve a careful description of the hows and whats of consultation. They have a perfect right to place limitations upon the scope of the consultant's work. Consultants may find that extremely stressed systems do not have the welcome mat out for them. Although they may be in desperate need of additional input, the decision makers may feel that they cannot absorb any more change or disruption. It is also true that extremely autocratic administrators may demand such control over a consultative effort that there is practically no chance for success. Such administrators often cannot tolerate the idea that their staff is going to talk to an outsider over whom they have only limited control.

Consultants can assure administrators of their commitment to confidentiality and to positive change. Consultants can explain that they will know the system from only their own perspective—a perspective no more true than any other now in operation. They can also remind administrators of consultant's ethical responsibilities to the very clients the agency may serve. In addition, consultants can "sell" the idea of consultation as a way to improve service to clients without expanding staff. All these strategies can be attempted to help an uneasy administrator rest more comfortably with a stranger in the house. Consultants are often irritated at any but immediate, unconditional, positive regard from the top people in a system. Such openness may actually be a danger signal. Administrative decision makers are charged with protecting the system. Some interrogations and controls are signs of a system gatekeeper who is appropriately performing his or her role. Extreme openness may indicate a malfunction in the gatekeeping role with no one protecting the system from outside inputs or assaults. On the other hand, extreme openness may indicate a very positive history with previous consultants.

When the administrative control or suspicion concerning a consultant is an outgrowth of positive gatekeeper concern, it will abate as consultants prove themselves to be reliable and helpful to the system. If the administrative concern is really based on a general pattern of autocratic style and extreme needs for control, there is little the consultant can do initially to mitigate the administrator's fears. Consultants who work in such systems must accommodate to administrative controls as nearly as possible until a consulting relationship can be developed with the administrator. When such a relationship is established, consultants can focus on changes in administrative style as a consultation target.

The last sentence in the preceding paragraph may strike some readers as representing questionable ethics. If consultants are invited into a school, for example, to assist teachers in managing student learning and behavior more expertly, how is the transition from teacher to principal made? The principal asks for teacher change. Is targeting the principal for administrative consultation initiating unsanctioned change?

Consultants must be personally clear about what their contributions to a system can be. They must also be "systems-thinkers." If the autocratic, unpredictable principal emerges as the primary contributor to teacher difficulties, then the professional consultant must target the principal for consultation in order to accomplish contractual goals to assist teachers. How should this be done? Should consultants burst into a principal's office to confront the administrator with the damning evidence? This hardly seems an effective strategy.

Systems thinkers realize that any identified problem in a system has multiple forces maintaining it. Consultants are hired to tease out the driving and inhibiting forces surrounding organizational issues. If the principal is part of the problem, assistance should be offered in the same way it is offered to other consultees. A relationship must be built, helpful questions or advice offered, confidentiality strictly maintained, easy access established, and obvious caring communicated. No deception is attempted. Consultants merely make themselves available to people (all the people) who seem to need their assistance.

Now, compare what has just been described with what is called *unsanctioned change*. Unsanctioned change involves the consultant in: 1) hiding personal agendas for change in order to be hired; 2) creating or exacerbating unrest among staff members in order to disrupt the system; 3) being *genuinely* available to only some of the people (or none of the people) in a system; or 4) failing to exhaust or develop planned change procedures before increasing internal or external stresses upon a system.

Consultants are hired to be advocates for the system that pays them (Chesler & Arnstein, 1970; J. C. Conoley, 1981). If the system that has hired them is engaged in hurtful activities—is not really fulfilling its stated mission—it is part of the consultant's job to get the system back on the right track. This, in most cases, involves collaboratively planned changes. If, after a series of consultation activities of increasing directiveness, a system administrator refuses to suspend unethical activities, the consultant must withdraw from the system and work according to his or her own ethical principles in terms of continued action. This is a very complex ethical area. Most of us need the advice of a peer supervisor and some very clear personal values to navigate through such a situation. Here are some of the issues:

1. How long does a consultant remain after unethical practices have been discovered? Part of the consultant's job is to be a self-correcting force upon the system. Consultants cannot leave a system every time they see something going wrong.
2. Are there really ethical principles at stake or merely different political ideologies? Autocratic, graceless administrators may be bothersome, but are they really hurting client services in a meaningful way? How are staff members implicated in supporting the autocracy of their supervisors?
3. Are seemingly quick, dramatic confrontations being planned to heighten consultant power and influence rather than facilitate change? Some people enjoy the excitement of conflict and intrigue as a life-style, not merely as a response to unbearable situational stress. Consultants must not *be* such people and should avoid overidentifying with such a group or person when learning about a system.
4. Finally, what a consultant should be able to do better than other system members is take the role of the others, that is, be able to walk in the proverbial moccasins of all the system factions. Such an imaginary stroll often results in a better picture of how each group is contributing to system dysfunction in some way. Progress is made mainly through conflict. Being involved in conflict is not unethical. Blind, uninformed loyalty

to any particular group is, however, particularly unprofessional and unhelpful to the overall system.

If top administrators suspect the consultant of unsanctioned change activities, they have two choices. One is to nondefensively inquire as to the purposes of the activities and try to incorporate the answer into an organizational feedback loop so as to make use of the information in a helpful self-renewing way. The second response is to fire the consultant. Let there be no doubt as to which choice is more frequently chosen. The easiest way to get fired by a system is to be seen as an unhelpful troublemaker. Well-run systems extrude deviants because deviants interfere with smooth running. In fact, it seems to be the nature of societies to extrude deviants (lepers, mentally ill, deformed, religiously different, intellectually impaired).

Often, the consultant's role in a system is to make it more able to absorb differences. For example, a consultant may assist a teacher in dealing with a very heterogeneous class; or, an organization development consultant may assist a group to constructively manage conflict in order to increase creativity. This function is not best accomplished, however, by the consultant seeming "different" or deviant. Pure ideology is no match for clear goals and well developed pragmatics.

BEYOND THE BARRIERS

Each of the concerns discussed as barriers to consultation seems amenable to change. Professionals who seriously want to be consultants should seek training. They should especially acquaint themselves with systems theory (von Bertalanffy, 1966); and the practice and theory of consultation (Bergan, 1977; Caplan, 1970; J. C. Conoley, 1981b; Cummings, 1980; Gallessich, 1974; Goodstein, 1978; Mannino & Shore, 1975; Meyers, Parsons & Martin, 1979; Zusman & Davidson, 1972). They must establish professional support networks that serve a peer supervisory function in order to receive input on complex ethical issues; and, they must be able to resist temptations to merely meet the clinical press for direct service. They must engage in long-range, preventive, systems thinking and help others to do the same.

In addition to these global guidelines, there are numerous specific behaviors to be aware of when moving from an exclusive direct service model to a consultation model (Conoley, Apter, & Conoley, 1981). For example, get to know consultees by establishing proximity to them. "Hang around" gathering places and social gatherings and appear approachable. Schedule meetings with consultees to show interest in what they are doing. Be sure that the meetings conform to the norms of the system in terms of times, places, and people present.

Focus priority attention on relationship building. Take the time to ask enriching questions and then wait to hear the whole story. Foster consultee self-respect by avoiding premature judgments about them and by preventing them from looking foolish just because they do not know something. In addition, model calm problem solving without reassurance during case discussions. This will reduce consultee anxiety without reducing his or her self-esteem. Consultees are also anxious about consultants so it is important to be ready for constant testing. This is the way it is—not a reason to make negatively evaluative judgments about a consultee.

Be aware that consultants are role models to consultees. By modeling empathy, tolerance for feelings, and a conviction that all human behavior is eventually understandable, consultants perform a very valuable function within a system.

Make sure the services available through consultation are clear to all those concerned. If a psychologist, for example, has been mainly doing assessments for a school district, an increase or change in services should be preceded by some verbal or written announcements. The psychologist might visit faculty meetings and explain consultation, emphasize confidentiality, identify the goals or improvements anticipated, and generally educate the consultee to use consultation services. Such an announcement should have elements of one-downmanship included. The consultant should show deference to the consultees' expertise and emphasize a desire to lighten the load on the consultees.

Because early consultation efforts might be misunderstood as attempts at offering psychotherapy, the consultant must use techniques to avoid the provision of psychotherapy. If this is not done, direct service to clients might be replaced by direct service to caregivers. Some useful guidelines include:

1. Ask mainly objective, not personal questions.
2. Discuss problems by discussing the client, *not* the consultee.
3. Do not let the consultee's anxiety over a case control consultant responses. Being empathic does not imply being unable to tolerate strong emotions surrounding problem solving.
4. Learn tactful but quick interruptions when a consultee is disclosing too much personal information. For example, "There's so much going on in your life at home! How is it affecting you at work?" Or, "You are sounding somewhat overwhelmed. Would it be helpful for me to recommend some good counselors to you?"

There are certain consultation postulates that must be gradually taught to consultees. When consultees come to see problems as consultants do, the chances for consultation becoming well established are very much improved. These postulates are:

1. The setting is always part of the problem.
2. Effective problem solving behaviors can be learned.
3. Help must be located near the setting.
4. The help offered must have the potential for being established on a systematic basis using the natural resources of the setting.
5. Errors are inevitable.
6. Efforts will be misunderstood.

A final strategy is to blend direct and indirect services in some systematic fashion that regularly relies on consultee insights and actions. Such a blend might be accomplished by conceptualizing the steps necessary to deliver high quality services (as in figure 7.2). When a case is referred for consultant intervention, the first step might involve a meeting with the referring consultee. The goal of this meeting would be to clearly identify the problem, the strengths of the client, what has been done previously to alleviate the problem, and to establish the goals of this new intervention attempt. In addition, other critical personnel connected with the client might be identified. Following this first meeting, the consultee and the consultant gather data directly from client observation, from the key personnel identified earlier, from new appraisal techniques, and from already written reports concerning the client.

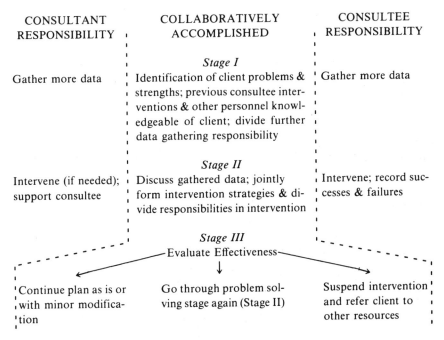

CONSULTANT RESPONSIBILITY	COLLABORATIVELY ACCOMPLISHED	CONSULTEE RESPONSIBILITY
	Stage I	
Gather more data	Identification of client problems & strengths; previous consultee interventions & other personnel knowledgeable of client; divide further data gathering responsibility	Gather more data
	Stage II	
Intervene (if needed); support consultee	Discuss gathered data; jointly form intervention strategies & divide responsibilities in intervention	Intervene; record successes & failures
	Stage III Evaluate Effectiveness	
Continue plan as is or with minor modification	Go through problem solving stage again (Stage II)	Suspend intervention and refer client to other resources

Fig. 7.2. Overview of Consultation Sequence

A second meeting is held to integrate the information and develop joint hypotheses about effective intervention strategies. These are carefully planned out with both the consultee's and consultant's roles clearly specified. The strategies are tried. Both successes and failures are recorded. Consultant support is available during the intervention phase.

A third meeting is held to evaluate the effectiveness of the plans. The consultee and consultant decide to (a) recycle through the problem solving process to develop more interventions; (b) continue the plan as is or with minor modifications; or, (c) suspend the intervention and refer the client to other resources.

The process involves the consultant and consultee in collaborative steps throughout the intervention. Direct services might be offered to a client in the form of diagnostic assessment, counseling, medical examinations, or behavior modification plans, but both consultee and consultant collaborate on planning and evaluating these services. Consultants should avoid temptations to take over cases too quickly. If they do offer some direct services it should be understood that the consultee will receive input regarding these direct services. Teachers, for example, report frustration over knowing a child is receiving therapy (of any sort) but not knowing if they should be performing special activities or expecting certain child reactions to the therapy. It is difficult for some therapists to talk about their work with clients for fear of violating confidentiality agreements. Some facility must be gained, however, in advising consultees of behaviors they might attempt, environments they might modify, and crises they might encounter with a client during critical phases of therapy. A spirit of partnership should prevail rather than one of adversarial blaming. An adversarial atmosphere drains energy away from problem resolution. Consultant and consultee may gain some short-run satisfaction out of identifying each other as culprits; but, in the long run, the problematic client remains problematic.

Chronic client problems facilitate a blaming mentality among helpers. The helpers may blame the client's family or other helpers for malicious or incompetent activities. Consultants who have a particularly resistant case must stay aware of the tendency to project blame when a first, second, or third series of interventions do not succeed. It is important to remember that everyone does what they feel they *can* do. It may seem a pittance from the consultant's perspective, but that is part of the consultation problem—to help people do more than they thought they *could* do. It is not a reason to give up on consultation implementation and resume direct personal services. The meagerness of a consultee's contribution to case resolution only shows how much consultation is needed. Our tendency to *give up* when others do not *live up* to our expectations is a little like small children who gather a group about them to play a new game. Often their cognitive and language limitations make it impossible for them to explain the rules, so they leave in disgust because the others are not "doing it right." Consultants must look inward as nondefensively as possible when they perceive that no one else is "doing it right." Collaboratively planned rules of the game, even if slightly imperfect, will facilitate success.

> A young consultant, fresh from an in-depth course in behavioral techniques, observed a disruptive child in a classroom and compared his frequency counts with those of the teacher. The teacher had been using a behavior checklist at the suggestion of the consultant. The frequencies were widely disparate with the teacher greatly "overestimating" the child's disruptive periods. The consultant considered that the teacher might have some personal vendetta against the child and was trying to have the child referred out of the classroom. He also wondered if the teacher might be just incompetent in the use of simple behavioral checklists. Over time, what seemed most true was that the teacher was very concerned about this child for many reasons in addition to disruptive behavior. The consultant had given the teacher just one way to communicate concern (i.e., tallies of behavior) and so the teacher abided by the rules and simultaneously broke them. Some more flexible consulting style resulted in a much more comprehensive description of teacher caring and competence, and a final successful resolution of the case.

NO FINAL SOLUTIONS

There is no way to accomplish a particular service delivery system in a final static form. The service delivery system must be responsive to systemic developmental changes and flexible enough to utilize the diverse talents of different service providers. There are some published descriptions of systemwide service delivery methods (e.g., Bergan, 1970; Fairchild, 1976; Meyers, 1973; Reilly, 1973; Snapp, Pells, Smith, & Gilmore, 1974) that may be helpful prototypes for those in the position of designing completely new methods or modifying old procedures. The consultant is necessarily always in a dynamic state of tension concerning how to best assist a particular organization because the organization is always in a dynamic state of tension maintained by internal changes, external demands, and interface exchanges. There is a tendency to create structures in response to system needs and then see them as eternally correct. The developers feel unwilling to change something that has worked in the past. Living systems *always* change. Nothing is constant except change. The changes occurring may be, at any one moment, imperceptible. Sensitivity to these changes, and ability to assess and compare organizational needs over time are crucial aspects of successful service delivery. The emphasis given direct and indirect services may shift in response to system shifts. A sudden influx of new clients (e.g., children of illegal aliens heretofore denied public education) may move a psychological service delivery system toward increased direct services to children and families. That move must be remembered as a response to an historical event, not as a new policy.

Public Law 94-142 has instigated numerous changes in public education. One of the less desirable outcomes has been the use of school psychologists paid by special education as gatekeepers *for* special education. Two issues are apparent. First, this function should become a smaller and smaller contributor toward the entire role of the psychologist over time. At some point, the overwhelming wave of previously unserved or severely segregated children will have been absorbed into the system and should require only periodic reevaluations. Most of the in-depth reevaluations should be ongoing and shared between special education teacher and parents as specified by the Individualized Educational Plans (IEPs) (see Appendix 3.D for suggestions about IEP development).

The second issue is a systemic problem that should be obvious to everyone involved. Psychologists paid *by* special education to identify children *for* special education who then generate additional income for the special education component are involved in a potentially serious conflict-of-interest position. How can they *not* feel pressure to continue a direct service assessment role? Psychologists presently involved in such a situation must look beyond their own skills and preferences and specifically target systemic change in terms of their funding base.

The source of funding may be the major obstacle to delivery of a complete range of services. If that is so, steps should be taken to adjust that problem. For example, a number of states have minimum foundation funds (regular education funds) for psychologists. Much of this money has gone unused simply because no one asked for it. Sometimes the person in charge of asking for the funds simply does not understand what other services are possible. Often there is no press from regular education teachers for psychological services because what they have experienced has been irrelevant to their daily functioning. These two situations can be targeted for change.

In planning for change in service delivery, the planners are balancing a vision with a context. Neither the vision nor the context is more or less real. Awareness of both is necessary. Without a vision of how the world *should* be, the planners have no way to make plans. Without a knowledge of their particular moment in history, they have no chance to see their dreams realized.

SUGGESTED READINGS

Berger, N. Beyond testing: A decision-making system for providing school psychological consultation. *Professional Psychology*, 1979 (June), 273–277.

The author presents an alternative approach to testing in the schools. She has devised a six-step decision-making process involving all the people actively involved with the child. The role of the psychologist is that of facilitator, encourager, clarifier, and information giver. The model consists of three decision-making stages and four action stages.

Berkovitz, I. H. Mental health consultation to school personnel: Attitudes of school administrators and consultant priorities. *Journal of School Health*, 1970, **40**(7), 348–354.

This article highlights some very important factors which should be considered when consultation services are rendered to school personnel: 1) Administrators, especially superintendents, principals, and guidance directors, can play important roles in facilitating or impeding the establishment of the consultant within a school system. To be effective, the consultant should be aware of the formal and informal structures and processes of the administrative staff. 2) The consultant should have in mind a flexible set of priorities by which to determine sequence and proportion of consultation services to groups of school personnel, teachers, special auxiliary personnel, and administrative staff. Whenever a limited amount of service is offered to a large group of individuals, the problem of allocation arises. Variables influencing these priorities are: budget and goals of the consulting agency; size of school district; available supply of experienced consultants; receptivity of the various groups of school personnel; and attitudes, motives, and agenda of key administrators in the school district.

Gallessich, J. Organizational factors influencing consultation in schools. *Journal of School Psychology*, 1973, **11**, 57–65.

The author feels that the key to success in school consultation lies in the consultant's skill at assessing the organization in which he or she is working. Gallessich describes four organizational factors which must be considered: external forces; internal forces; the school's trajectory; and staff perceptions of the consultant's role. The way in which each of these will influence the desired outcomes is considered. The consultant is seen as a change agent and some very useful change strategies and their implications are discussed.

Grundle, T., Emiley, S., & Webb, D. Entry credentialization and role change in consultation to a consultation program in a school system. *Journal of Community Psychology*, 1973, **1**, 383–386.

The problems of entry and credibility in a parochial school system are discussed, and solutions are suggested. The role change from client to consultee to organizational-centered consultation is described, with examples of successful *and* unsuccessful role changes. Successful change in roles occurred when the consultants operated within the consultee expectations and perceptions and did not impose their own values.

Heller, K. Facilitative conditions for consultation with agencies. *Personnel and Guidance Journal*, 1978, **56**(7), 419–423.

Postulating that psychological professionals should recognize the need for both individual and social change skills, Heller analyzes the consultant's role in community change efforts. While he emphasizes the need for a responsive community as a prerequisite for lasting change, Heller initially focuses the consultant's energies on the analysis of the agency-community interaction dynamic. In order to then develop appropriate change strategies, he has developed a 2x2 model. The model, with lengthy textual explication (complete with very helpful examples) and the inclusion of several well-developed examples of strategies for analyzing and cultivating agency and community readiness for extreme change, is informative and easy to read.

Katz, F. E. The school as a complex social organization. *Harvard Educational Review*, 1964, **34**, 428–455.

The school is described as a complex social organization which, in many respects, conforms to the definition of a bureaucracy. The school has specific structures and individuals play specific roles in order to carry out the mission of the school. However, Katz wants to show how the informal activities of the school have their own structures and functions as well and are not merely idiosyncratic deviations by individuals. Katz focuses on "autonomy" as one such structure which may, in itself, define the behavior of individuals within an organization.

Rappaport, J., Davidson, W., Wilson, M., & Mitchell, A. Alternatives to blaming the victim or the environment. *American Psychologist*, 1975 (April), 525–528.

This article presents a description of how a set of conceptions about community intervention has been translated into a set of goals, strategies, and actions in the form of a training program for community psychologists. The author's basic thesis is that a simple rejection of the medical model either conceptually or stylistically, or both, is insufficient to bring about the sort of impact and understanding that community psychologists seek. In addition, the authors state that it is necessary to go one step further and to eliminate blaming the victim and blaming the environment ideology. A more sensible approach for the community psychologist lies in seeking community strengths and aiding in the development of those. The program strategy includes an attempt to establish "minisocial systems." A central component of the strategy is creating a setting that enhances independence rather than dependence. Emphasis is placed on the process of creating alternative settings rather than solving specific social problems.

8

What Do We Say When We Say, "Consultation"?

The following are annotated transcriptions taken from taped interactions between psychology trainees and their consultees. These are provided not because they represent perfect examples of consultation. They may provide some concretization of the principles that have been presented in earlier chapters.

Each transcript represents one of the consultation models discussed previously. The annotations were added to highlight the verbal processes that illustrate consultation decision points or as our own editorial comments. The names and parts of the situations described in each of the transcriptions are disguised in order to protect the privacy of the consultees and clients who gave permission for their situations to be used as educational tools. We are grateful to our students for enduring the anxiety of taping their efforts and to their consultees for their willingness to share their experiences.

TRANSCRIPT I: MENTAL HEALTH CONSULTATION

These conversations represent portions of the first few meetings between a consultant (C) and a consultee (T).

Session I

C: Hello, my name is James Jones.
T: I'm glad to finally meet you, Dr. Jones.
C: Please, call me James, May I call you Mary?   one-downsmanship
T: Oh, of course.   rapport building

C: I saw your note today (about wanting to see me) and I wondered if you might have some time now to meet or, if you're too busy, we could meet at some other time.

one-downsmanship

T: Oh, no. Now is a good time. I wanted to see you about Phillip. You know I've just taken over this class this week.

C: I heard Sue left. It can be tough to take over a class in the middle of a semester.

empathy

T: Yes, I feel like there's a three-ring circus going on and Phillip is the leader.

C: Phillip is leading them astray, huh?

problem definition

T: Yes, he's always making wisecracks or misunderstanding the assignments and getting the other children laughing and not doing their work.

C: So, the whole class gets into the act.

problem definition

T: Yes.

C: That certainly sounds like a tough situation. I think it's neat that you feel that you have the time to work on Phillip's behavior. I'll bet there's a lot of other things on your mind what with being new.

validate problem; reinforce teacher concern

T: I talked with Fran [principal] and she thought that you could help me. I feel like I'm so new here that I don't want anything to go wrong. If I had started with this class maybe I would understand all the children better and how the school operates.

C: I don't know if you've worked with a consultant before, but I want to let you know how it generally goes. We won't need to get a permission slip from Phillip's parents unless we decide that it would be helpful for him to receive special services outside of the classroom. Initially, we can try to work on Phillip's disruptiveness while he's in the classroom so we won't need to contact his parents unless we need their cooperation. Also, I will fill out a form that indicates how I spend my time. You know, accountability. On this form I just list the amount of time I spend in your class. That way, what we talk about and whom we talk about is confidential.

explain consultation, make school more understandable to new teacher; explain consultation parameters; emphasize confidentiality

Anything you mention to me is confidential.

T: I appreciate your telling me all of that. There are lots of rules and regulations to be aware of—all separate in some ways from teaching. It's a little scary to me. I am really afraid of doing something wrong.

theme becomes apparent: I am new and inexperienced; this child's bad behavior will cause others to negatively evaluate me

C: I just wanted to let you know that what you and I discuss here is not reported to anyone, you know. Unless there's a law broken that we have to report, like child abuse or something.

limits of confidentiality

T: Yes, that makes sense.

C: Now, after all that, it would be helpful to me to hear more about what Phillip is doing.

problem definition

T: What do you mean?

C: Well, can you give me a typical example of what Phillip does when he misbehaves? What is the rest of the class doing and what situation might you be in?

problem analysis

T: Let me think. It would most probably be while the class is supposed to be doing some assigned work. Phillip will throw an eraser at one of his friends, or drop his book on the floor to make a loud noise. He'll make some wisecrack when I try to correct him, and then the whole class gets involved.

C: So, when it comes time for Phillip to do his work, he causes a disturbance to get you involved and then makes the situation into a stage to get the attention of the whole class?

problem analysis

T: Yes, that's right.

C: How hard is it to settle the class down when they all get started?

problem analysis

T: The class settles down pretty quickly. Just Phillip stays wild.

C: That's good that the rest of the class seems responsive. What do you tell them that seems to work the best?

reinforce teacher efforts; problem analysis

T: Well, I guess what has worked the best is somelike, "Children, if you want Phillip to be the teacher in this class, we'll just see what the principal will say when you visit her."

C: Being faced with going to see the principal

problem analysis

settles them down, huh? How about its effect
on Phillip? Does he settle down when threatened
with a visit to Fran's office?

T: Yes, but not for long. He just starts something
up again in a little while.

C: It sounds like a power struggle with Phillip. He
isn't recognizing your authority in the classroom.

interpretive statement
testing for teacher
emotional involvement

T: I feel like he's always challenging me.

C: I'm impressed by how well you understand
what is happening in your classroom. You
really have a good idea of Phillip's desire to
get attention and be liked by the class. It's
going to be a challenge for us to guide him so
that he will want your positive attention and
get attention from the class in more acceptable
manners, too. How often does the attention
seeking occur?

reinforce teacher
concern; reframe
problem from rebel-
lious child to lonely
child

T: Seems like all the time.

C: Is there any pattern, that is, more in morning,
or after lunch, or doing seatwork?

problem analysis

T: Well, as I said, it's mostly when the children
are given an assignment to do alone. The time
of the day doesn't seem to matter. He is
quieter when he's working in a small group.

C: He really seems to like attention and interaction
with peers.

reframing statement

T: Yes, I guess so. I hadn't thought of it exactly
like that.

C: What kinds of things have you tried with Phillip
so far?

define previous
strategies

T: Well, the first day I was here, I moved him
away from his friends and made him sit with
some girls who seemed quiet. But that hasn't
helped because now he just throws things or
shouts across the room.

C: That was a good strategy, but it didn't pay off
with Phillip.

reinforce teacher
effort; suggest that
programs must be
individualized

T: No.

C: What else have you tried?

T: Well, when he's misbehaved, I've made him sit outside the classroom for 10 or 15 minutes; but he doesn't seem to mind that at all. He just parades in front of the class and happily sits outside.

C: So that didn't stop his misbehavior.

T: No.

C: It's funny how a punishment to one child is not a punishment to another. When I was a child I hated for people to see me sitting out in the hall but it doesn't bother Phillip, huh?

> reframe failure of strategy as new information for case work; share self-disclosing information with consultee; provide perspective that even troublesome children may "turn out all right"

T: No, he seems to like the opportunity for people to see him, he's trying to get attention.

C: Yes, you're right. That's sure there, trying to get attention even if it's in a negative manner. What else have you tried?

> reinforce teacher

T: Well, I finally sent him to the office. That's when they suggested that maybe you could help me with him.

C: Well, you've been busy trying different strategies. Have you tried anything else?

> reinforce teacher

T: No, that's all I can think of right now.

C: Did sending him to the office help?

> problem analysis

T: Yes, for a while he did settle down.

C: How long would he stay "settled down"?

> problem analysis

T: Oh, for about a day and a half.

C: That's interesting to know that he knows how to behave appropriately if we can just meet some of his needs to be special. What do you think? Does that sound like a reasonable goal, to find a way for Phillip to get attention or be special to you and the kids that's appropriate?

> point out the existence of positive behaviors in child's repertoire; preliminary goal setting statement

T: Yes, that sounds good.

C: Let me think. Hmm. Do you have any ideas about what we might try?

> build on teacher preferences

T: Well, no. I can't think of anything either.

C: Is there anything in the classroom that you allow the children to do for you if they've been good? Something special.   *problem analysis*

T: I guess so. I will let one person be first in line when the children go to lunch or recess.

C: That's a nice custom. I bet the children like that honor. Being the first in line is exciting for them at this age.   *reinforce teacher*

T: Yes, they do really seem to feel important when they get to be first.

C: It probably wouldn't be fair to the other children for Phillip to be first in line all the time, even though that would make him special in an appropriate way.   *empathy for teacher reluctance*

T: No, it wouldn't.

C: What would you think about allowing Phillip to choose the leader of the line? Maybe impressing upon him the importance of choosing the students using the same decision process you use. Like who has been working hard and hasn't led the line recently.   *strategy suggestion*

T: Well, that would be OK, but I don't know that I want to reward him for all the bad things he's been doing.

C: That's true, you wouldn't want Phillip to think he has gotten into the position of getting good things from you by acting inappropriately. We want to put him in a position of getting appropriate attention for acting in a way that you think is good. Is that right?   *reinforce teacher concern; reframe reluctance*

T: Yes, he should *earn* the rewards.

C: So, if he were to behave appropriately, you could honor him with that special position.   *test possible strategy*

T: Yeah, that sounds fine.

C: OK, but of course the trick is to find him working on-task for five minutes so that you can reward him and move him into a role of getting attention from you in a way you like.   *begin to specify strategy*

T: Yes, it won't be easy to catch him working.

C: It will be challenging. First thing in the morning might be the best time. Especially if you could give an assignment in a small group that you think he could handle and stand nearby in a   *specify strategy; connect strategy with previously shared information* way that he knows you're watching him. Do you think that will work?

T: It might. But I can't just stand around him all day. How many days would he have to be good before he got the reward?

C: Well, that's up to you. In the beginning it's good to reward right away and very frequently so that the new behavior becomes established. What if you talked with Phillip to see if he's willing to work for the line privilege?

defer to teacher; provide information

T: Maybe I could make up a chart for him to tape to his desk. That worked with one child I had. I'll tell him that if he's behaving well I'll compliment him and he should put down a check. If he's being good and I don't notice, he can raise his hand and ask for a compliment. If he has, say, 5 checks at the end of the day, he gets to choose the line leader.

C: That sounds like a great idea. Do you have written down anywhere what the criteria or rules for line leader are? I was thinking that some teachers have the kids develop rules, one a day, for awhile and have the children say them aloud together until they know them.

reinforce teacher idea; further specify plan

T: You know, I did that once and I just forgot about it this year. I actually had the rules on strips of paper pasted around the room like Big Brother is watching. When a kid would act up, I'd ask him or her what rule was being broken.

C: That's terrific. That way Phillip could get some specific guidance about what to look for in a line leader and also have some goals to be working toward. Would it be OK if I dropped in from time to time to observe Phillip? Sometimes when I observe a child in class it helps me understand better.

reinforce teacher; set up expectation of cooperative working

T: Sure, that would be fine. I would welcome any ideas on keeping him in line.

C: Well, it's time for me to get to a meeting. Today's Tuesday. Could we meet again on Friday?

schedule next meeting so teacher can expect continued involvement

T: Sure.

C: Good. Now if you will try to arrange it so that you can assign Phillip the positive attention role of choosing who is first in line, I will come in and observe him. Maybe through this initial effort we can see how well he handles positive attention and adjust our plans accordingly. How does that sound? *further specify consultant involvement*

T: It sounds good.

C: Good. I've enjoyed getting this chance to meet you. I don't want to wish you bad luck but I hope we have more time to visit. *rapport building*

T: Thanks. I do too. It's been nice meeting you and I'll talk to you again soon. Good-bye.

C: Good-bye.

Session II

C: Good morning, Mary. How are you?

T: Good morning, James. How are you?

C: Just fine, thanks. Hey, I like your bulletin board. It's really striking. *rapport building; reinforce teacher*

T: Yes, thank you. I feel like I'm settling in more now and getting the classroom in shape.

C: It's nice, isn't it, when the room can take on more of your own personality and you can settle in and feel more comfortable. *consultant mentions teacher's newness and puts it into a temporary time perspective*

T: I really am feeling more comfortable here. Things in the class are going much better now.

C: That's great, Mary. You've got Phillip headed down the straight and narrow, huh? *give teacher credit for improvement*

T: Well, let's say we're having some improvement.

C: Yes, when I observed Phillip yesterday it sure seemed like you were having a good relationship with him. *reinforce teacher effectiveness with child*

T: Yes, after we talked last time, I spent some time the next morning talking with Phillip about his hobbies. He seemed to really enjoy talking about soccer. Then, when it came time for lunch, he had been good all morning so I chose him to be the leader of the line. He does seem to be coming around.

C: So, you've really got him working more for your positive feelings than for getting negative attention. Haven't you?

label teacher strategy in positive behavioral terms

T: Yes, he does seem to enjoy it now when we talk. He seems pretty eager to please me.

C: Say, that's great. You must be very good at talking with a child individually in such a way that the child feels really special about you.

reinforce particular teacher strength

T: Do you think so?

C: Well, what do you think? It sure seems to me that you got Phillip to talk about what he was interested in and when he did he felt like you were genuinely interested in him.

reassure teacher of effectiveness

T: I guess so.

C: I know kids have a way of falling back into bad habits but it seems like Phillip will usually respond to your way of taking him aside to talk with him. It's especially insightful of you to talk with him about positive things. That's probably the difference between how his parents treat him and how you handled him.

give teacher expectation that there are rarely any "final" solutions; reinforce teacher special efforts with child

T: Oh, yeah.

C: This kind of thing is exciting to me. The difference is that you spent some time giving him positive attention and probably at home he gets the most attention when he's misbehaving.

provide teacher with another time perspective, i.e., time spent controlling acting-up child versus time spent reinforcing appropriate child.

T: Yeah, that makes sense.

C: Does it seem like a lot of work to keep giving the positive attention?

check on teacher perceptions of demands of the behavioral program

T: Well, it's hard to say now. But I don't think it will be too bad.

C: That's nice you have so much energy. You really do enjoy getting to know about each child, don't you?

reinforce teacher involvement

T: Yes, it is nice. That's what I like about elementary school.

C: What do you do to keep up your energy when things start going badly in the classroom? Like, if you felt they didn't appreciate you?

> consultant probes in area where he believes the major issue lies, i.e., teacher inexperience, isolation, and anxiety over work performance

T: I'm not sure. I guess I feel like I would need someone to talk to about it.

C: That sure makes sense. I wonder at times how to help teachers, such as yourself, who give so much. Are you close to any of the other teachers yet? Close enough to support each other when your energy for your students is low?

> further probes to test hypothesis about consultee involvement

T: Yes, I believe so. Jane Smith and I have visited some. She seems like a nice person.

C: I know Jane, too. She seems nice to me also. I was thinking about getting a group of teachers together to give each other support. Doing some problem solving about classroom problems but also sharing in the ups and downs of teaching. Do you think you'd be interested in trying it out?

> tentatively suggest consultee–centered intervention

T: Sure, I'd be willing to try it.

C: Good! You might mention it to Jane. I'll talk with her, too. I'd like to find a group of about five or six teachers who might enjoy this kind of idea.

> further specify new intervention

T: That sounds good.

C: Well, I'm glad Phillip is doing better. What if I touched base with you next week to see if he's still making progress?

> specify continued involvement with teacher

T: That would be fine.

C: Well, I sure enjoyed our conversation.

> rapport building

T: I did too. See you later.

Session III

C: Hi, Mary. How are you doing today?

T: Fine, fine, James. And how about you?

C: Oh, its going well. How's Phillip doing?

T: Well he had a setback Monday, but he's coming around.

> teacher seems to show good perspective on child behavior

C: Ups and downs, huh?

T: Yes, he's a little like a roller coaster. No, really he seems to be doing fine.

C: I'm glad to hear that. When I observed he seemed to have some redeeming qualities. It is nice he's building on those.

consultant shows willingness to become reinvolved with Phillip

T: Yes.

C: By the way, I wondered if you could tell me the times you'd be willing to meet with a group of teachers?

specify consultee-centered intervention aimed at reducing teacher isolation

T: Sure.

C: I'll let you know about the times.

T: OK.

C: See you later.

TRANSCRIPT II: BEHAVIORAL CONSULTATION

The consultant (C) and consultee (T) have known each other for some time before this consultation takes place.

Session I

C: Hello, Frank. How are you today?

T: I'm fine, Barbara. And you?

C: Things are going smoothly today. Your football team is really doing well this season.

individualized rapport building; consultant knows something about this teacher's work

T: Yes, this is the year for the Superbowl.

C: If their defense keeps holding up against the pass I bet they can make it, too.

further rapport building indicating particular knowledge of out-of-school activities

T: That's the truth.

C: I got your note about Fred. It sounds like a tough situation.

show interest and validate teacher request for help

T: Fred is really not doing well in class. I give him a whipping almost every day.

C: Sounds like a difficult situation. It would be helpful if we could discuss what is the most troublesome aspect of Fred's behavior.

> empathize; begin problem identification

T: He's disrespectful. I think that's the worst part.

C: How does he express his disrespect in class?

> specify inappropriate behavior

T: Well, today when I corrected him he cussed at me. You know, not directly at me. Just loud enough so everyone coud hear.

C: He cussed at you, huh?

T: Yes, it really burns me up—that kind of attitude.

C: So the most important change that Fred can make is to stop his cussing out loud in class. Is that right?

> set priority behavior change goal

T: Yes, he doesn't get into more trouble than some of the other kids. But when he does then his cussing starts up. Yes, it's his cussing that's the real problem with Fred.

C: OK. Good. Let's focus on this. As you think back on the cussing, when does it occur? You mentioned when you correct him for misbehaving.

> specify antecedent conditions

T: That's right. He cusses when I correct him.

C: Are there any other occurrences?

> specify context of behavior

T: No. Well, sometimes when the other children tease him, he cusses. But I correct him and then he stops.

C: So, it sounds like we should be most concerned with the times he cusses after you correct him?

> specify target behavior within a particular context

T: Yes.

C: OK. It's helpful to solve a difficult problem like this by trying to understand as much as we can about what occurs just before he cusses. Can you recall if it's something in particular that you correct him about when he cusses?

> specify antecedent conditions

T: That's hard to remember. Well, generally he's just out of his seat picking on other kids, getting into trouble.

C: Then every time you correct him he begins to cuss?

specify antecedent conditions

T: Yes. Well, almost every time.

C: Can you think of what makes the difference between the times he cusses and doesn't cuss?

specify particular discriminant stimulus

T: No, just how he's feeling I guess.

C: OK. How long does he keep the cussing up?

specify duration of behavior

T: Well, just a sentence or a few words.

C: So, a short blurt?

further specify target behavior

T: Yes.

C: Have you found any response from you that controls or stops his cussing?

probe for previous strategies

T: No, not really. He just blurts it out. Like I said, I've tried everything, but even the paddling doesn't faze him.

C: So paddling doesn't work. What else have you tried?

identify ineffective strategy without invalidating teacher's use of it; further probe for other attempts

T: Well, of course, I tried warning him, but that didn't work.

C: It seems like you've tried a lot of things but they haven't been effective. So we can drop those things you've tried off the list. You know something interesting that I've discovered about paddling is that many times it backfires on us. It's really strange. I've tried to figure it out. I'd like to hear your guesses about why it doesn't work and other things work better. My best understanding with my experience is that many times the kids will actually endure a great amount of pain to reap the benefits paddling brings with it. Things like seeming real tough, getting a stage to act on, getting all the children's attention. It's odd. It seems like the kids that would really be affected strongly by a paddling are the ones who can be controlled pretty easily with less severe measures. And the kids that don't respond to the less severe punishment are the ones that get the most mileage

reinforce teacher effort; try to move teacher into a more flexible array of intervention strategies; consultant injects minilesson on the relativity of punishers; highlights teacher's special expertise; consultant thinks that teacher may be somewhat dogmatic and authoritarian and need substantial support to change; frames comments as relative to personal experience in order to encourage

out of a paddling. So, some kids use a paddling as a platform to become worse kids rather
than better kids. They start acting worse and
worse. That's what I've thought about. What
kind of ideas do you have about why paddling
doesn't work?

teacher to discuss
issue; information and
opinion sharing aimed
at reframing consul-
tee's perceptions of
problem children and/
or paddling as an ap-
propriate intervention
strategy; ask for
teacher input

T: Well, I don't know. I just think if paddling
won't work, won't teach him respect, I don't
know what will.

C: You know you might be right—nothing might
work. It's frustrating to think you might be
wasting a lot of time on this kid. I hope some-
day Fred could look back on this year and
know the effort you were willing to put in to
make up for his parents or whoever. Do you
ever think about that kind of thing? I know it
seems funny. But sometimes I try to imagine
what would be the fate of so many of these
children if their teachers weren't so dedicated.
Oh, no. I guess, I got carried away. Well, let me
see—I'm afraid I got us off track. You were
telling what happens before Fred cusses and
how long it lasts. We haven't come up with the
right consequences to get rid of the cussing yet.
Is that right?

validate teacher's
concern over the
intractability of some
problems; reframe
teacher's frustration
with child as sign of
his concern and caring;
consultant catches
herself sounding
moralistic; one-downs-
manship; summary of
previous conversation

T: That's right, we haven't come up with any
answers.

C: This is a tough case and I'm not surprised that
we didn't come up with the answer because
you're good at handling these sorts of problems
just by talking to the kids. I really believe that
if it was going to be easy for us you would have
already solved it. But before we try anything,
let's measure how often and how much Fred is
cussing now. So when we try different things
we can see if there is any progress. OK?

validate complexity of
problem and teacher
expertise in handling
most difficult behav-
iors; reinforce teacher
expertise; establish
baseline procedures

T: How will we measure Fred's cussing? Do they
have a cussing test or something?

C: No! No! It's just an index card. I have some

specify data collection

here. See, you can just put the date up at the top here and Fred's name and cussing as the behavior at certain hours but, for Fred, maybe we could keep tabs on it all day since it doesn't happen often. In this column, marked frequency, you could put down the number of cuss words he says at that time. What this does for us is give us a baseline measure. So when we attempt new ways of stopping the cussing, we have an idea of how much its helping or making it worse. Would you be willing to keep these measures for 4 days?

process; explain process of validating the problem

T: Sure, it doesn't seem like it will take too much time.

C: Good, now I'd like to observe Fred if I may.

establish observation as consultant interest

T: Sure I'd like you to see him in action.

C: Thanks. Now, one thing I forgot to ask you about is the time during the day he would be most likely to cuss.

specify context of behavior

T: Well, that's hard to say. I imagine that its probably more likely to happen after lunch or just after the afternoon recess.

C: Then tomorrow I'll observe right after lunch. Then on Thursday I'll observe after recess. How does that sound?

specify consultant involvement

T: Sounds fine. The way things are going with Fred now he probably will act like an angel when you're there.

C: Just to make it harder on us, huh?

T: No doubt.

C: Well, so our plans are for you to keep a record of Fred's behavior for the next week. And I will come in and observe so that I get first-hand knowledge of Fred like you have. Then, next Wednesday, we can get together and think of some interventions to help stop Fred's cussing.

summarize responsibilities; set up next appointment

T: Sounds good.

C: OK. See you tomorrow after lunch.

Session II

C: Good morning, Frank.

T: Good morning, Barbara.

C: How's the teaching business going?   rapport building

T: It's getting a little wild with the holiday season almost here.

C: That really makes the tempo pick up around here.   rapport building

T: Yes, by the time the holidays get here we'll really need them.

C: Well, how's Fred been doing?

T: He's keeping it up. Here are the cards.

C: Let's see, out of the seven days, the cussing occurred five times. Each occurrence was either after lunch or after recess.   validate problem

T: Except when you're in the room. Maybe you could just stay in the classroom at those times.

C: Or get an inflatable doll that looks like me. It's not unusual that having a stranger in the room can change the way children act. But you know the timing that you pointed out is interesting. I was wondering about the activities he would be involved in when he would come back into the classroom after those two high energy times. But the activities didn't seem to support his acting wild; but then I noticed that the boys he was grouped with both times I was here. They seemed like a pretty rowdy crew compared to the group he was with just afterwards. Is that a regular grouping for him after lunch and recess?   assure teacher of consultant knowledge of reactivity; further specify antecedents to behavior; suggest hypothesis; specify antecedents

T: Yes, that structure is the same although there is some change in the schedule on Tuesdays and Thursdays because of music, but not at these times.

C: So that's pretty much the same group every day?

T: Yes, it is. Maybe I could just try switching the children in each group or the timing of each group.

C: That's a good idea. If it is the rowdy group of boys that are somehow setting the stage for Fred, that could do the trick.   reinforce teacher suggestion

T: That mixture of boys could be causing Fred's cussing.

C: Do you feel like it will be difficult to change Fred's group?   probe for teacher responses to tentative plan

T: Well, it will be difficult because that is the slow group for math facts, but I think I can form two groups out of that one.

C: And put the less rowdy kids with Fred, huh? specify process

T: Yes, I think that would do it.

C: Good. What I would like you to do is to keep monitoring his behavior for the next week. And I'll come by and observe twice again. Then we can meet next week at this time to see what the results are. OK?
explain need for further data collection; specify continuing consultant involvement; set up next appointment

T: Sounds good to me.

C: OK. I hope this works but, if not, we'll try something else. See you later.
give teacher expectation that first strategy may not be effective, but many more are available

T: Goodbye.

Session III

C: Hello, Frank. How are you?

T: Hi, Barbara. Fine, just fine. I have some good news about Fred. He's cussed one time this week but it wasn't at his regular time.

C: Well, your idea about forming a new group worked pretty well, huh? give teacher credit for intervention

T: Yes, except for that one time, the second day. Here it is on the card, 2:30 in the afternoon.

C: And no more?

T: No more.

C: That really is good news. Instead of it being a regular occurrence that you could almost set your watch by, now it's down to once a week.
reinforce teacher success

T: And probably less. He and I are seeing more eye-to-eye on many things now.

C: Well, you're just full of good news. reinforce teacher involvement with child

T: Yeah, I guess we've got this wrapped up.

C: Well, I'll talk to you later, Frank. Thanks for the good news.
suggest continued interest in case

T: Thanks for your help, Barbara. Good-bye.

C: Let me know if Fred suffers any big setbacks. Good-bye.
reinforce consultant availability for follow-up

TRANSCRIPT III: ADVOCACY CONSULTATION

This transcript represents one portion of an advocacy effort undertaken for children in a program for the visually impaired. It is May and the adoptive mother of a visually impaired child has just been informed that her son is to be "left back." The child's report card showed no failures throughout the year and the mother feared that her already timid son would be devastated by being separated from his long-time friends. Following the advocate's advice, the mother (an invalid) has requested a meeting in her home to discuss the apparently sudden decision concerning the child's educational programming. The advocate (C), three teachers ($T_{1, 2, 3}$), the special education director (SED), the mother (parent) and the child (client) are in attendance. This meeting was just one of many that the consultant had attended. A number of the families involved with the program had expressed concerns and displeasure with the teachers and educational philosophy of the program.

C: Does everyone know everyone else? Mrs. Jackson, have you met all these teachers and Mr. Justiss, the special education director?

consultant takes lead to gain some power at meeting

Parent: Let's see, I've talked with Mrs. Barnes and Mrs. Taylor on the phone but don't know the other people. Glad to meet you.

C: Before we begin, I'm wondering if, perhaps only for my benefit, you could say how each of you is involved in this decision. I'm a little surprised to see four of you here, as Mrs. Jackson had asked that only Mrs. Barnes and Mr. Justiss attend.

challenge school district's apparent attempt to overwhelm the parent

SED: Well, Dr. Hays, I asked the other two teachers to come because I thought they had worked with Ricky and knew something about his strengths and weaknesses. We know you don't like to be outnumbered by school people at meetings, but in this case I think it's the best idea.

C: We definitely want all the possible information we can get. If I weren't here, though, Mrs. Jackson would be facing some pretty heavy guns in a very anxiety provoking situation with no support. I think that this kind of set-up causes some

pursue issue, framing it as a potential obstacle to good problem solving

of the emotion and defensiveness that we've all talked about before and want to avoid. I'm wondering if Mrs. Jackson is comfortable.

Parent: Yes, I'd like to get on with it. I've called and called you people and always get the runaround. Maybe with everyone in the same room we can get something accomplished. Now I want to know why Ricky is being left back. This is supposed to be an ungraded program. I've spent a whole lot of time working on his plan and so don't know why he can't move into another classroom with his friends and still work on what he needs to work on. Why didn't anyone tell me sooner that he was failing?

T_1: Ricky seems immature compared to the others. He's small and this would be a good time to leave him back. He would really benefit from it.

T_2: It's not that he's failing. It's just that he's not moving as quickly as we'd hoped he would when we wrote the IEP. The other kids are better prepared for seventh grade.

C: I'm a little confused. Ricky and all the other special kids are being taught according to IEPs. How does the graded situation fit into an IEP?

[margin] pursue teacher's generalization; highlight purpose of IEP

T_1: Well, it really doesn't fit exactly. It's just that Ricky would spend part of the day in regular education in a certain grade. His special program is competency based.

C: What classes does he have with regular education?

[margin] probe for relevant information

T_1: He has art, music, and PE.

Parent: What difference does it make what grade he's in for art and PE and music? This is the most ridiculous thing I've ever heard of!

T_1: We really know what's best here, I think. Ricky needs more time with the program and, if we leave him back now, he'll be able to stay longer.

Parent: I think I know what's best. He hasn't failed

and he's real embarrassed about being left back. He says all of his friends will call him a dummy.

C: I think this is a new issue. We're probably all in favor of Ricky getting as much educational training as possible. Your program is housed at the junior high school and serves junior high school-aged children, right? So you are suggesting that Ricky could get an extra year at the junior high, where he fits in because of his size. Of course, your program is probably responsible for him until he's 21 years old anyway, right?

> ignore emotional exchange and move the group back to what appears to be the critical issue facing the district

T₂: That's right.

C: So somewhere along the line he's going to be "left back"—just as many of the children may be "left back" who wish to take advantage of as much public education as possible. Does that seem accurate?

> identify the underlying issue as affecting many of the children, not just this client; show openness to input and expertise of others

T₂: Well, we don't have any twelfth graders yet so we haven't faced that problem yet. But I guess it's possible that a number of the students would get through the grades before they were ready to graduate. We really hadn't thought of it.

SED: Now, I'd thought about this. You know grades don't mean very much for these kids. They all start off so behind and move so much slower than the regular children.

C: I think that's part of the problem here. Although you all agree that Ricky's not failing and that grades are kind of meaningless, you suddenly inform the parent of a decision. You probably are aware of how upsetting this would be to the child and the parent. This kid feels like all other kids, I guess, that it's a disgrace to be left behind. What do you think, Ricky?

> recast problem as not belonging to the child, but to the policies of school district; emphasize generic needs of child; focus on organization's needs to become more humane in its dealing with people; illustrate by asking client's opinion of situation

Client: I don't want to be left back. I want to be with my friends.

C: I think the idea of developing a way to deliver meaningful services to kids for the extra three or so years mandated by law is a good one. But the way you've gone about it seems somewhat arbitrary and inhumane. I think that a procedure needs to be developed that keeps the kids with age appropriate peers as much as possible, and prepares the children and the parents that the program is geared for service until age twenty one. I'm sure it's complicated because obviously some kids can finish all they need to know by eighteen. But, surely, the children and the parents deserve some notice about what all the constraints are.

specify new problem to be considered

T₁: If Mrs. Jackson would visit the program, she would see that the sixth grade program is just right for Ricky.

Parent: How do you suggest I visit the program? I haven't left the house in 15 months.

T₃: Well, Mrs. Jackson, we can hardly make home visits every time a parent wants to talk.

C: I don't know if we'll gain anything by blaming each other for why there's been a communication breakdown. Why not try to salvage this area and get some people working on preventing breakdowns in the future. Here are my suggestions: (1) Ricky should have his IEP reviewed for adjustments of activities and time lines sometime before the first day of school next academic year; (2) he be allowed to continue with regular education age-mates in music, PE, and art; and (3) a group of parents and teachers get together next year to decide how to handle the time problem in a way that won't be demoralizing to anyone.

short circuit potentially unhelpful anger between participants; specify plan

T₃: He's going to be left back sometime! Why put if off? We're going to have the same problem next year.

C: I think the term "left back" is an unfortunate one. We've all said that grades are pretty irrelevant in this situation. I don't think the same problem will appear next year if a partnership is developed among all the people concerned.

Parent: Ricky is really looking forward to high school graduation. He wants what the other kids have.

C: I think we all need some education and preparation for how to structure this experience. Obviously, we want Ricky to get all he can from the public schools. But that should be delivered in a sensitive, humane way.

SED: Okay. What I'm hearing is that Ricky's program will progress as usual and steps will be taken to prepare him, parents, and other kids for unavoidable or facilitative extra time at a particular level.

Parent: I hadn't been thinking about twenty-one before he got out of high school. I guess I knew about it, but I didn't really understand what it meant. I mainly want Ricky to be like the others (pointing to some grown children seated in another room).

C: That's what we all want. Could I be of any service in organizing the parent-teacher group that will discuss future policy and procedures concerning time lines?

SED: Yes. Let's plan a meeting for early August. Why don't you round up three to four parents and I do the same with interested teachers?

C: I'll call you August 1st with a list. In addition, Mrs. Jackson and I will write you a letter concerning the decisions reached at this meeting. If you remember as we remember, that letter could be put into Ricky's file.

SED: Okay! Well, thanks, we'll see you all again soon.

Margin notes:

try to move teacher to newly specified problem; emphasize need for cooperative efforts

dispel blaming mentality

label group as having common, not adversarial, goals

specify consultant duties; establish expectation that the decisions reached at this meeting are binding

TRANSCRIPT IV: PROCESS CONSULTATION

As part of her work on a grant project, the consultant was asked to facilitate staff development of the newly enlarged staff. A recent grant had resulted in five new members joining (all student assistants) and the return of an old-timer. There were six regulars on the project. The staff development took the form of miniworkshops on various topics, third-party consultation, administrative coaching, and help with the group process at the weekly two-hour staff meeting. What follows is a transcript representing the last few minutes of a staff meeting.

Staff: You're supposed to be observing our process [to consultant]. Why not tell us what you saw?

C: Which aspect of your group process are you interested in exploring?

show willingness to respond while asking clarification of exactly what is being asked for; avoid being placed in "all-knowing expert" role

Staff: Oh, I don't know. I'm interested in knowing what you saw and if we were doing okay.

C: This seemed to be a meeting where lots got accomplished and a number of important decisions were made. How did you all feel about the decisions?

reinforce participants for their efforts at meeting; identify one process for discussion

Director: Well I'm glad to get some things decided upon. I assume people said what they felt during the discussions.

C: Let's check that out. Did everyone have the level of involvement they wanted during the discussions? (Murmurs of agreement; some heads nodding.)

model asking others rather than making assumptions

Staff: I did, but I noticed that none of you [pointing at student assistants] said anything.

Student Assistant 1: Well, there is really not much to say. You all know more than we do about

	the stuff you're talking about. We'll just go along with what you say.	
C:	Do all of you [student assistants] feel the same way that Dorothy expressed? That is, that you're all pretty inexperienced and your roles are to carry out decisions.	model asking for individual input rather than allowing one person to speak for the group
Student Assistant 2:	Yeah, pretty much. I think I'll talk when I know everyone better. I'll be more comfortable then. (Others nod and say, "yeah.")	
Director:	That makes some sense, but remember you all were hired to be a part of this project. In some ways we are all new. We need everyone's active input.	
C:	Has anyone here [looking all around the table] ever said something wrong or stupid? (Lots of smiles and laughter.)	attempt to bring the entire group into the discussion
Staff:	At least once or twice that has happened.	
C:	What happens or should happen to people who make mistakes or sound silly?	probe for explication of the organizational norms
Staff:	Well, what has always happened is that we talk things over and everyone learns something and that's it. Should something else be happening?	
C:	Not sure. What do you want to happen to accelerate your feeling [to student assistants] more comfortable and able to participate fully in the group?	avoid expert role; inquire about what particular people want for this particular group
Student Assistant:	Well, I really feel that there's nothing to do. It just takes time at the beginning to get to know what everyone thinks of everyone else.	
C:	Let me do something unusual and give you all a two–minute lecture. Dorothy is right. Time is a great help in terms of getting a group working at top efficiency. One reason time can be of help	introduce lecture as an unusual event so that teaching role of consultant is deemphasized; present infor-

is because we get to know each other and are interested in what each person has to say. So, we ask him or her. If a member is quiet, we check out what's happening by saying things like, "I'm wondering what you are thinking," or "You've been quiet and I'm really interested in what you have to say about this." This makes people feel included and important because others care enough to ask. It, therefore, makes it more likely that people will spontaneously contribute. Of course, if time goes by and some people get into the habit of not speaking, then their input might be lost from the group. Sometimes people like that feel uninvested in the decision that's been made, because they had so little to do with it. That's bad, of course, for top efficiency in a group. End of lecture.

mation relevant to group participation and problem solving; share information about gatekeeper role in group; specify the positive outcomes associated with high levels of participation; specify negative outcomes of not gatekeeping or encouraging others to participate in group discussions

Staff: I see that talking in a group is mainly the responsibility of the individual but that others can help the quiet ones along. Watch out you guys [looking at student assistants], now your opinions will be asked until we can't keep you quiet!

Director: Well, if we don't stop talking about being quiet pretty soon it'll be past lunch. Let's all eat here together. I'll get some stuff sent over from the deli. Who wants what?

A number of such low-key social events were facilitated among all the staff members. This effort, spurred by some administrative coaching, soon added to a high sense of cohesion and morale among most of the group. The process consultant was rarely very active during group meetings. The returned old-timer to the group remained somewhat aloof. This distance contrasted so sharply with the high social interaction among the other members that it became somewhat of an issue between the old-timer and one of the newer staff members. After a few caustic interchanges at staff meetings and growing staff gossip about a rift, the director asked the consultant to intervene. The director met with the two principals and the consultant and made his wishes clear that because the disagreements were hurting the project the people involved must manage a workable truce.

Old-timer:	There's really nothing to talk about. I'm doing my job. I don't understand what the big deal is all about.
Staff:	You're so condescending all the time. At meetings I feel like you think you should have the last word on every-thing.
Old-timer:	That's ridiculous! I say what I have to say, that's all.
C:	There seem to be some feelings here that are hard for me to sort through. When you [staff] say that Ted is con-descending, what do you mean?
Staff:	He's uninvolved until the last moment, then he says something and expects it to be the law of the land.
C:	So, there's something about his timing and his tone of voice that irritates you. Ted, were you aware of the effects you were having on Joanne?
Old-timer:	No, I didn't mean to irritate her. She probably knows that I'm an old stut-terer. I always wait until other people stop talking before I talk, otherwise, I have trouble getting all the words out.
Staff:	No, I didn't know. I feel stupid about that, but I really don't feel I'm com-pletely wrong, Ted. You just seem dis-approving and critical. I know that's pretty vague, but I really feel it.
Old-timer:	Well, I guess you'd be disapproving if you were me, too.
Consultant and Staff:	What do you mean?
Old-timer:	Let's face it, this place is not what it used to be. Most people working here are just doing that. They're not here for a purpose—just here to earn mon-ey. It wasn't like that before.

Marginal annotations:

(beside the first C entry) probe for behaviors rather than derogatory judgments

(beside the second C entry) restate concerns in be-havioral terms; check for response of feed-back receiver

Staff: I'm sorry that I don't measure up to your exacting standards, but I do have a family to support, you know!

C: I'm wondering if the problem is money or if what Ted is feeling is lack of investment or involvement from the staff and/or a very common nostalgia for the ways things used to be. ignore tangential anger to bring participants back to major issue

Old-timer: I am nostalgic. That may be dumb, but. . .

Staff: I resent the implication that I'm not as invested in this work as you are! I would love to see some proof of that. And as for nostalgia, a lot of good things happened while you were here before *and* happened while you were gone. Maybe that's what's bugging you!

C: Joanne, you seem to care an awful lot about what Ted thinks. Why is that so important? reframe anger as concern for approval

Staff: He's held up as kind of the living legend around here. Of course, I care what he thinks. I admire his work, past and present, very much.

Old-timer: Living legend?!?

Staff: Yeah . . . everyone is always talking about when you and Dave confronted that hospital administrator in Seneca and about the way you adopted the autistic child.

Old-timer: I didn't know I was so well-known. I guess what we're doing now is harder in a way. Not so much publicity, just grinding out cases one after the other. It takes a lot of perseverance. I know this will sound phony, but I really do admire your work, too.

Director: Ted, would you provide a half-hour program at the next meeting giving everyone kind of an oral history of this Center? You know, how it started, what it was doing . . . kind of its evolution since 1970.

Old-timer: Well, maybe you could do that better than I could.

Director: Let's both do it. Next week. Who's the agenda person? Let's get it on before we forget.

C: It's important to be seen as valuable. We all need that. I think at least part of what's been going on between you two is two valuable people wanting the other to appreciate them. Do you feel like we've made any progress? (Tentative nods and then some nervous laughter.)

summary of issue as it may now be understood; abandon need to blame one or the other for the situation; check for readiness to end discussion

Old-timer: I'm pretty ready to join the present moment, but I won't stop criticizing if I see something wrong.

C: And won't stop praising what you see right? How about you, Joanne?

give concrete suggestion for behavioral change; check for readiness to end discussion

Staff: I do feel better. Ted, would you talk with me about a case? I've got the stuff upstairs. Is this meeting over?

Director: Go in peace!

C: Amen!

9

Ethical Considerations In Consultative Practice

COMMON DILEMMAS

Each reader will, no doubt, be cognizant of the professional and personal ethical codes binding his or her behavior. The translation of these codes into everyday behavior is difficult. In this chapter, some of the ethical dilemmas faced by consultants are presented. Consultants do not have a particular set of rules that govern their behavior apart from the rules in effect for their other professional functions. The situations they find themselves in, however, are often complex because of the intrinsically triadic nature of consultation. It is an impossible task to answer, in an *a priori* way, all ethical problems. Careful consideration of predictable dilemmas before they arise, however, allows for some straightforward, self-confident action if and when the situation calls for it (e.g., Lambert & Cole, 1977).

Perhaps the situation that the consultant finds most uncomfortable and difficult to handle without becoming disenfranchized from some group in an organization is the observation of an infraction that ethically requires the consultant to intervene.

An external consultant to the school has finally gotten the opportunity to work with a teacher who has been regarded by the principal as the least skillful, and most personally troublesome teacher. During the consultant's first observation, the teacher hits two of the children who failed to complete their assignments.

This case example is trite. What is worse than trite is that this example continually occurs. A variation of this case example is probably in the future of every consultant (Hyman, 1975).

The critical variables when this problem occurs are: ethical responsibility of the consultant; the legal responsibilities of the consultant; the contract with the primary administrator; and the contract with the teacher. Knowledge of the ethical and legal responsibilities are a requisite for working in the field as a consultant. The legal and ethical responsibilities can vary with the client population, and the organization and state in which the consultant is working. The spanking or hitting of children in school is unlawful in some states. Changing states, organizations, or client population may cause the same event to be an infraction of the organization's rules but not the law, or completely within the state and organizational guidelines. Ethically, the consultant is responsible to the hiring party, the consultee, and the client. The amount of ethical consultant behavior runs the gamut from the least involving responsibility—considering the effects on a given party—to the most demanding—actively representing or warning a given party. At all times, the effects of an intervention upon all concerned must be considered.

A guiding principle is, generally, that the more helpless or unaware the client is, the more carefully the consultant should consider or monitor the goals and strategies of the consultee. For instance, when working in elementary schools, the clients are usually young children. A consultant would surely balk at devising an elaborate punishment system for a classroom if there were not at least equal attention given to positive possibilities. To be punitively motivated toward young children is clearly inappropriate and likely to result in socializing them to be punitive. The consultant would encourage the consultee to consider more carefully his or her general goals for the students and how the problems experienced in the classroom could be viewed within those general goals. Intending to lead the consultee to another understanding of the most beneficial intervention, the consultant would actively redirect the consultee in deference to the client children.

While not easy to perform, the previous example is relatively simplistic because the ethical dilemma could perhaps be avoided and could be altered by working with only the consultee. The dilemmas become more complex when the consultant has to negotiate between the hiring party, the consultee, and/or the client. When the consultant needs to work with two or all of the parties because of the unlawful or unconscionable activity of one of the parties, the initial consultation contract becomes of paramount importance. Typically, it must be understood that the consultant holds every action or word of the consultee in confidence from the hiring supervisory administrator *unless* the consultee is chronically and stubbornly involved in unethical activities toward the client. Words and actions of the administrator are equally held in confidence *unless* there is a clear (How clear, you may be asking?) violation of staff or client rights. Consultants must first work to reeducate and then confront an inappropriate party and then move to inform appropriate supervisors.

In some instances, administrative and staff consultees are in collusion to infringe upon client rights. This imposes an ethical responsibility upon the consultant to find the leverage point within or outside of a system to facilitate change. Advocacy activities may be called for.

Not all contracts are of this nature. Sometimes there is an understanding that the "consultant" is collecting information for administrative review. Consultees must be thus informed and then can make informed choices as to what to disclose to the "consultant."

A reason we have codes of ethics is that what has just been described is very difficult to do. A hundred mitigating qualifications or justifications can (and will) be conjured up by all the participants or observers of an unethical event, policy, or procedure. These will be used to excuse or delay action on an inappropriate situation. The codes, as incomplete as they may be, serve as reminders of "bottom lines" that cannot be crossed while using the title of physician, psychologist, social worker, or educator.

Another common though less dramatic situation has to do with guardian consent for treatment and consultation procedures. The laws opening educational records to parents and students over 18 have had an important and beneficial effect on school personnel's consciousness about confidentiality issues. In addition, the due process safeguards which mandate parent notification when a child suspected of having a handicapping condition is to be discussed by the Committee on the Handicapped or evaluated by a psychologist have greatly involved parents in the educational process.

These regulations are meant to protect the rights of children and their families. Their intent is not to prevent professional problem solving from occurring about learning, behavioral, social, or emotional concerns of children. Good teaching has always involved using educational resources, whether materials or people, to the fullest. Educators have historically consulted with each other across grades and departments to clarify their thoughts about a child or to generate additional strategies for meeting each child's unique needs.

This problem-solving function is the role of the school consultant. This consultant, like all other mental health workers, is bound by strict rules of confidentiality. The teacher/child concerns brought up in consultation are examined by the consultant and teacher searching for new alternatives, a different perspective, or the existing strengths of a child. In order to increase their understanding of a problem, consultants may wish to observe in classrooms. No direct services are offered to the child without parental notification and permission. No decisions about changing a child's educational program or placement are made by a teacher and a psychological consultant. Decisions concerning new teaching or behavior management strategies may be made by teachers following consultation. These decisions and changes are typically within the province of teachers to make in order to enlarge their skills as educators. If consultation suggested that direct work with a child was necessary (e.g., evaluation, counseling, change in program) parent permission would be necessary to follow through on the appropriate course of action.

Typically, consultation interviews result in no reports or written records that must be added to the child's cumulative folder. The teacher and consultant may note down important points in their discussion, promising strategies or plan components, but no diagnostic classification concerning the child is ever recorded.

This discussion should not be interpreted as a way to avoid getting parent permission about important elements in the educational process. In the best situation, the school consultant would be introduced at a Parents' Night or PTA meeting, and be available to explain the consultation role to parents. Confidentiality would be less stressed. Schools that have consultation services might very well notify all parents of the new resource in that building. Parents can be told that the consultant will be used to facilitate professional problem solving about their children's educational needs.

Children's and families' rights to confidentiality and informed consent are best protected by a professional staff that is committed to protecting these rights, is careful of the quality of the information included in written records, and which discusses children in problem-solving, professional ways. Staffs need to refrain from unkind or thoughtless evaluative comments which color the perceptions of others about a child or family. The intent of open records legislation is best served by a faculty that concentrates on the strengths of its children and shares information only with those who have a need to know in order to better educate a child.

There are school district policies in some areas that prevent a psychologist's observation or teacher consultation until the child has been referred for special education placement consideration. This is a mistake. Psychologists should educate policymakers to the costs involved in this policy. Ysseldyke, Algozzine, Regan, and McGue (1981) have presented interesting data showing that the *act of referring* is the single best predictor of a child being given special education services. Because this is so, psychologists must be allowed to support teacher interventions with children before the referral process is begun. Special education is no panacea. In its present state-of-the art form, most children are better served with their peers in typical age-appropriate learning environments. These environments should be enriched and supported when necessary, but not denied to children. Erich Fromm once commented, "Everyone and anyone is much more simply human than otherwise; more like everyone else than different." Attitudes shaped by understandings like Fromm's will be ethically and practically correct.

BEHAVIORAL INTERVENTIONS

All treatment has ethical issues surrounding it. Important questions are: Is it safe? Appropriate? Best available? Interventions based on social learning theory have encountered particular scrutiny for a number of reasons. First, some behavioral interventions rely mainly or solely on environmental modification instead of personal change. This insults our human preference to feel as controllers rather than mere products of our environment. It also seems to make the client more of a target of the procedure than a partner in the treatment. Even our jargon represents this as we speak of target children or target behavior. Secondly, behavioral procedures are most successfully applied when the interveners have control over the environmental contingencies. This implies withholding and presenting positive and negative consequences in order to increase the likelihood that a particular behavior will be shaped or extinguished. (Again, notice the rather mechanistic language—behaviors are shaped or extinguished. Are people shaped and extinguished?) This seems to place extra ethical issues on the interveners because the clients, by definition, have limited opportunities to influence these environments. Skinner (1974) notes that people will not work or change for negative consequences and so there is little chance of aversive control becoming the preferred methodology. Children and other limited-informed-choice clients (e.g., prisoners, mentally retarded) are often not partners in choosing the treatment, however, and so it becomes unclear, even when positive contingencies are used, for whom the psychologist is working. Behavioral consultants are warned against "dead man" targets. That is, do not develop a management program that aims at promoting behaviors *best done* by dead people. Examples are sitting still, being quiet, stopping disruption. Dead man targets generally increase caretaker ease while not enhancing the coping abilities of the clients.

Well-conceived management programs must also examine what the minimal reinforcers and maximal aversives will be. It seems both practically and ethically sound to do less rather than more as long as "less" and "more" interventions are equally effective. Children should not be led to believe that unnecessarily dramatic positive outcomes will follow relatively routine behaviors. Neither should they experience extremely aversive consequences for minor infractions. If such large changes are necessary to establish a new behavior while extinguishing others, the fading of the contingencies should be carefully planned. Fading should *not* imply, however, that there is a return to a noncontingent environment. It is unfair, and perhaps unethical, to help create engineered environments and then not remain available to monitor the maintenance of the environments.

A third issue revolves around the actual usefulness of the behaviors targeted for change. Behavioral consultants are quick to notice what secondary gains follow from the occurrence of a behavior that in a *prima facie* way appears quite dysfunctional. Theoretical and applied work in family therapy have suggested that dysfunctional behavior in any system is related to that system's dysfunction rather than singularly residing within the labeled person (e.g., Hoffman, 1981). This understanding makes it important to conceptualize how deviant behavior is useful to certain systems and to plan system change efforts rather than merely accept the existence of one or two deviants within a system. From the general systems perspective, of course, a change in any part of a system will cause change in other parts. Sometimes changing a child is inefficient, however, because the system will constantly create new dysfunctional members. Research on families has shown that, when one identified patient is removed from the family, frequently another child or one of the spouses begins to show symptoms. Symptoms, therefore, have reinforcing consequences for more than the individual with the symptoms. Behavioral consultants must enlarge their sometimes rather microperspectives to entertain system hypotheses.

ADVOCACY CONSULTATION

The ethical dilemmas associated with advocacy have been presented in other parts of this volume. To reiterate our position: *We are always advocating for someone, some issue, or some position.* The question is not whether or not to advocate but how and for whom. Advocating for powerful people or majority views is relatively easy and usually goes unnoticed as such. In contrast, advocating for disenfranchised groups or unpopular views usually places the advocate consultant in quite a visible position.

Ends do not justify means in any situation. Advocates must remember that the only real moment is the present moment. As such, it must be lived with the integrity and humanness demanded of others. No just cause is inherently more noble than any other. However, not all causes are just. The advocate must be able to make distinctions between personal preferences and injustices. We are all tempted to label as wrong that which *we* feel distasteful or strange. Such myopic dogmatism is likely in the long run to cause ethical problems as it becomes easy to violate the rights of those we believe to be less righteous than ourselves.

Advocates must be honest—always honest to selves, consumers, and adversaries. This is *so* hard. As mentioned elsewhere, mistakes are inevitable and efforts will be misunderstood. Knowing this with certainty, the advocate consultant must have refuge with a support group to monitor and challenge decisions. Ultimately, as with all ethical dilemmas, the buck stops with the person. At times, the visible advocate may be an isolated person, making personal satisfaction with action of paramount importance (Hyman & Schreiber, 1975).

RESEARCH/SERVICE DILEMMAS

Consultation research carried out in natural settings creates all the typical research-related ethical issues. Informed consent, withholding of treatment to control groups, and maintenance of obviously failing treatments are a few examples of common dilemmas. Each of these can be resolved with careful planning.

In addition, more flexible, action-oriented research paradigms making use of process (formative) evaluation data need to be conceptualized. Consultation is supposed to depend on the circumstances presented. It underestimates the power of the models and badly serves the host organization to plan out strict lock-step procedures meant to enhance experimental rigor. Experimental rigor may be approached but external validity destroyed.

The relative amounts of energy and creativity devoted to well done research and well done service delivery must be carefully monitored throughout a project. Consultees should be aware of the major focus if one activity is, in fact, more highly valued than the other. With such information available, potential consultees can make better informed decisions regarding the consultation service. The consultees should also be included on a decision-making or policymaking board overseeing both research and service functions. In this way, their best interests are represented and their interest and commitment toward the research might be increased. In addition, the researchers' hypotheses are likely to become quite a bit more sophisticated as a result of consultee input.

Allen, Chinsky, Larsen, Lochman, & Selinger (1976) report on a study that involved consultation as one of its aspects. Their work is a good example of a happy balance between research and consumer needs. The many articles by Emory Cowen and his associates in Rochester (e.g., Cowen, 1973; Cowen, Dorr, Trost, & Izzo, 1972; Cowen, Lorion, & Dorr, 1974; Cowen, Trost, & Izzo, 1973; Zax et al., 1966) are other fine examples of university service to the community, resulting in high quality research.

DILEMMAS OR DIFFICULTIES

An ethical dilemma is the result of two codes coming into conflict. Can you steal medicine (break a law) to save your child (right to live)? Kohlberg's (1964) formulations about levels or stages in moral thinking highlight the complexity involved in making personal choices. He, like Piaget, conceptualizes people as moving through increasingly abstract and inclusive stages of thinking about moral decisions. It is, therefore, important to review all decisions for action, not only for their legalities, but also for what personal beliefs about rightness and wrongness are broadcast by the actions. Every action (and reaction) broadcasts a value.

There are, of course, hard things to do (for example, confront a consultee) that are not to be confused with moral dilemmas. Just because it is hard to do does not make it an ethical question requiring days of pondering and much expert supervision. All dilemmas are difficult, but not all difficulties are moral dilemmas. This point is perhaps belabored to suggest that it is not always comfortable to be a consultant. Difficulties arise and must be confronted directly and quickly. For example, if the consultant learns that a consultee is unhappy with his or her services, the thing to do is to approach that consultee to try to reestablish rapport and credibility. The thing *not* to do is be obsessed for days if that information should *really* have fallen into the consultant's hands.

In addition, just because it *is* hard to do (whatever it may be: offer services to an unappreciative consultee; get seemingly unfair feedback, or find resources for people you are sure will not read them) does not allow us not to try. Ethics add to tenacity (Newland, 1981). We perform difficult tasks under trying circumstances because we know we are doing right things. The circumstances do not define what is fair and just. Each of us living in certain circumstances defines the standards of goodness and justice. These standards are how others will know us.

SUGGESTED READINGS

Ad Hoc Committee on Advocacy. The social worker as advocate: Champion of social victims. *Social Work*, 1969 (April), 16–22.

The Ad Hoc Committee proposes that the professional code of ethics necessitates that social workers incorporate an advocacy role into their practice. Thus, primary commitment is to the client rather than the agency. This includes assistance to individuals experiencing retaliatory actions from employing agencies and/or communities. Good intentions are not enough. Effective advocacy requires technical competence, and knowledge of service delivery systems, institutional dynamics, and institutional change strategies.

Argyris, C. Dangers in applying results from experimental social psychology. *American Psychologist*, 1975, 30(4), 469–485.

Argyris explains the difference between an espoused theory of behavior (in X situation I would do Y) and a theory-in-use, which is what people actually do. He shows how much of a person's behavior is Model 1 theory-in-use, characterized by achieving perceived goals, maximizing winning, minimizing elicitation of negative feelings, and valuing rationality over emotionality. These four governing values result in a behavioral strategy of unilateral control of others and is evidenced by low desire for feedback, self-fulfilling prophecies, and single loop learning. All of these result in decreased effectiveness. Argyris advocates a Model 2 theory-in-use for social psychological experiments (win-win strategy and double loop learning) as a constructive demonstration of new ways to act.

Benne, K. D. Some ethical problems in group and organizational consultation. *Journal of Social Issues*, 1959, **15**(2), 60–67.

This is a description of some of the ethical problems which may arise during the consultation process. The author does not offer solutions to any of the problems but does suggest some ideas which may help in resolving these conflicts.

Bennis, W. G. A funny thing happened on the way to the future. *American Psychologist*, 1970, **25**(7), 595–608.

Reflecting upon predictions of the future which he made in 1964, Bennis portrays the need for more realistic methods of predicting and responding to change patterns. His scholarly approach to the analysis of organizational change as a reflection and integral part of sociological and political developments is fascinating and slightly disturbing. The value of this article is found in the provocative posing of ethical issues, both of sociopolitical and organizational variety. Bennis makes a strong statement for increased self and social consciousness with respect to organizational behavior and the responsibility of those directing the development of organizational futures to respond to the affective needs of the client systems. There is much to ponder in this article.

Chesler, M. A., Bryant, B. I., Jr., & Crowfoot, J. E. Consultation in schools: Inevitable conflict, partisanship, and advocacy. *Professional Psychology*, 1976, 7, 637–645.

Conflict is viewed as central to school life due to the bringing together of many diverse groups in one setting. It is suggested that this conflict can be used to examine and solve problems and establish new relations. The different roles a consultant can serve in a conflictual situation are examined, along with how and why the consultant chooses his or her values. Service to minority groups is stressed. The norms of society are to be questioned, according to the authors, and change implemented. Human potential can be wasted if consultants fail to question social situations.

Fanibanda, D. K. Ethical issues of mental health consultation. *Professional Psychology*, 1976, 7(4), 547–552.

Using a Caplanian paradigm of consultation, the ethical issues of responsibility, autonomy, client and consultee welfare, misrepresentation, remuneration, consultant and consultee relationship, and confidentiality are discussed and ethical positions recommended. This is done in an effort to delineate the necessary requisites to define consultation as a profession in its own right.

Kelman, H. Manipulation of human behavior: An ethical dilemma for the social scientist. *Journal of Social Issues*, 1965, 21, 31–46.

An excellent presentation of the ethical dilemma that all agents of change face. No simple solutions are presented, only ways of reducing the amount of manipulation employed. A classic article which should be read by anyone who works with people and is in a position to influence them.

McDermott, P. Law, liability, and the school psychologist: Malpractice and liability. *Journal of School Psychology*, 1972, **10**, 397–407.

The author defines malpractice and contrasts it to unethical behavior. Several law suits are presented as examples of school psychologists' involvement in court cases. The article concludes with three recommendations to be followed by school psychologists to avoid legal complications.

Walton, R. E., & Warwick, D. P. The ethics of organization development. *Journal of Applied Behavioral Science*, 1973, **9**(6), 681–698.

There are two value orientations that guide external consultants: an orientation toward organizational achievement, and an orientation toward improving the quality of work life. The dilemma of the OD practitioner is a product of his or her need to be both a management consultant whose primary concern is effectiveness and productivity, and a social reformer whose thrust is to increase humanistic values in the work place. The ethical dilemmas fall under three generic headings: power, freedom, and professional responsibility. Power relations include justice because an OD intervention will usually change or reinforce the current balance of power. The essential ingredients of freedom are an awareness of options for choice, knowledge of consequences, and the ability to act upon a decision. The authors question, for example, if participants in OD interventions give informed consent, are coerced or manipulated, or if OD data are misused. Finally, the issues of professional responsibility are addressed, including a code of ethics, the expectations of the client and the expertise of the consultant, excessive client dependency, consultant role contamination (OD practice of OD research), and violations of confidentiality.

Afterword

As mentioned in the preface, this volume is merely a beginning. There is much more to learn about the process of helping others do their work in satisfying ways. Doing consultation with the excitement and investment of a believer, and the caution and skepticism of a behavioral scientist is, perhaps, the best teacher. Individuals must be experts in something before they begin their consultation careers. In addition, they must care deeply about helping others with what they know. Risk taking, caution, knowledge, and compassion are some of the necessary combinations for effective consultation. Once these skills are in place, the world is waiting for action. There is a need for a critical mass of trained and motivated people to target primary prevention as a realistic goal. The remedial strategies always involve some pain or dysfunction prior to intervention. Why wait?

The school is the primary avenue to all children and most families. People serious about the delivery of psychological services must see the school, fraught as it is with conflicting missions, as the most desirable location for mental health workers. The time is past that allows for an elitism toward education. Only the best people can make meaningful mental health contributions while simultaneously dealing with difficult organizational issues. As our awareness of the interdependence among all human systems grows, it may happen that working for children will earn the prestige and support it deserves.

References

Abidin, R. Negative effects of behavioral consultation. *Journal of School Psychology*, 1975, **13**, 51–57.

Abt, C. *Serious games*. New York: Viking Press, 1970.

Alinsky, S. D. *Reveille for radicals*. Chicago: University of Chicago Press, 1946.

Allen, G. J., Chinsky, J. M., Larsen, S. W., Lochman, J. E., & Selinger, H. V. *Community psychology and the schools: A behaviorally oriented multilevel preventive approach*. New York: John Wiley & Sons, 1976.

Alpert, J. L. Conceptual bases of mental health consultation in the schools. *Professional Psychology*, 1976, **7**, 619–626.

Alpert, J. L. Consultation and the analysis of school faculty meetings. *Professional Psychology*, **10**(5), 1979, 703–707.

Alpert, J. L. & Rosenfield, S. Consultation and the introduction of social problem-solving groups in schools. *The Personnel and Guidance Journal*, 1981, **60**(1), 37–41.

Alpert, J. L., Silverstein, J. M., & Haynes, R. Utilization of groups in training for school consultation. *Journal of School Psychology*, 1980, **18**(3), 240–246.

Altrocchi, J. Mental health consultation. In S. E. Golann and C. Eisdorfer (Eds.), *Handbook of Community Mental Health*. New York: Appleton-Century-Crofts, 1972.

Altrocchi, J., Spielberger, C. D., & Eisdorfer, C. Mental health consultation with groups. *Community Mental Health Journal*, 1965, **1**(2), 127–131.

American Psychological Association. *Ethical standards of psychologists*. Washington, D.C.: American Psychological Association, 1979.

Amos, I. E. Child advocacy and the adversary system: Round peg in a square hole?, *Journal of Clinical Child Psychology*, 1981 (Winter), 56–58.

Apter, S. J. Results of a resource teacher survey. Unpublished manuscript, Syracuse University, 1978.

Apter, S. J. *Troubled children/Troubled systems*. New York: Pergamon Press, 1982.

Argyris, C. *Management and organizational development*. New York: McGraw-Hill, 1971.

Astin, A. W. & Holland, J. L. The environmental assessment technique: A way to measure college environments. *Journal of Educational Psychology*, 1962, **53**, 224–235.

Baker, B. N., & Wilemon, D. L. Managing complex programs: A review of major research findings. *R&D Management*, 1977, **8**(1), 23–28.

Barker, R. G. *Habitats, environments, and human behavior*. San Francisco: Jossey-Bass, 1978.

Barker, R. G. & Gump, P. V. *Big school, small school*. Stanford: Stanford University Press, 1964.

Barnes, E. *A checklist for an individualized plan*. Center on Human Policy. Syracuse, New York. Developmental Disabilities Project and Directional Service Project, 1978.

Barnes, E. *How to evaluate a school program*. Undated mimeo. Center on Human Policy. Syracuse, New York.

Barnes, E. *Suggestions for parents.* Center on Human Policy. Syracuse, New York.

Bassin, M. & Gross, T. *Organization development, a viable method of change for urban secondary schools: Assessment of a pragmatic model, High School Self Renewal.* Paper presented at annual meeting of the American Educational Research Association, Toronto, March 1978.

Bennis, W. G. *Organization development: Its nature, origins, and prospects.* Reading, Mass.: Addison-Wesley, 1969.

Bergan, J. R. *Behavioral consultation.* Columbus, Ohio: Bobbs Merrill, 1977.

Bergan, J. R. A systems approach to psychological services. *Psychology in the Schools,* 1970, **8**, 315–319.

Bergan, J. R., & Tombari, M. L. The analysis of verbal interactions occurring during consultation. *Journal of School Psychology,* 1975, **13**, 209–226.

Bergan, J. R., Tombari, M. L. Consultant skill and efficiency and the implementation and outcomes of consultation. *Journal of School Psychology,* 1976, **14**(1), 3–14.

Berger, N. S. Beyond testing: A decision-making system for providing school psychological consultation. *Professional Psychology,* 1979 (June), 273–277.

Berlin, I. N. Resistance to change in mental health professionals. *American Journal of Orthopsychiatry,* 1969, **39**, 109–115.

Berlin, I. N. Some lessons learned in 25 years of mental health consultation to schools. In *The Workshop of Mental Health Consultation,* 18–48. Washington, D.C.: National Technical Information Service, U.S. Department of Commerce, 1974.

Berlin, I. N. (Ed.) *Advocacy for child mental health.* New York: Brunner/Mazel, 1975.

Biklen, D. *Let our children go: An organizing manual for parents and advocates.* Syracuse, N. Y.: Human Policy Press, 1974.

Biklen, D. Advocacy comes of age. *Exceptional Child,* 1976 (March), 308–313.

Blake, R. R., & Mouton, J. S. *Consultation.* Reading, Mass.: Addison-Wesley, 1976.

Blake, R. R., & Mouton, J. S. Toward a general theory of consultation. *Personnel and Guidance Journal,* 1978, **56**, 328–330.

Borich, G. D. (Ed.) *Evaluating educational programs and products.* Englewood Cliffs, New Jersey: Educational Technology Publications, 1974.

Breer, P. E. & Locke, E. A. *Task experience as a source of attitudes.* Homewood, Illinois: Dorsey Press, 1965.

Browne, P. J., Cotton, C. C., & Golembiewski, R. T. Marginality and the O. D. practitioner. *The Journal of Applied Behavioral Science,* 1977, **13**(4), 493–505.

Burns, M. L. The effects of feedback and commitment to change on the behavior of elementary school principals. *Journal of Applied Behavioral Science,* 1977, **13**, 159–166.

Caplan, G. *The theory and practice of mental health consultation.* New York: Basic Books, 1970.

Chandy, J. The effects of an inservice orientation on teacher perception and use of the mental health consultant. Paper presented at the annual meeting of the American Psychological Association, New Orleans, August, 1974.

Chesler, M. A., & Arnstein, F. The school consultant: Change agent or defender of the status quo? *Integrated Education,* 1970, **8**(4), 19–25.

Chesler, M. A., Bryant, B. I., Jr., & Crowfoot, J. E. Consultation in schools: Inevitable conflict, partisanship, and advocacy. *Professional Psychology,* 1976, **7**, 637–645.

Chesler, M. A., & Crowfoot, J. E. Sociologists in the public schools: Problems and roles in crisis management. Paper presented at the National Conference of School Sociologists, Los Angeles, June 1975.

Chesler, M. A., & Lohman, J. E. Changing schools through student advocacy. In R. A. Schmuck & M. B. Miles (Eds.), *Organization development in schools.* Palo Alto, Calif.: National Press Books, 1971.

Chin, R., & Benne, K. D. General strategies for effecting change in human systems. In W. G. Bennis, K. D. Benne, R. Chin, & K. E. Corey (Eds.), *The planning of change* (3rd ed.). New York: Holt, Rinehart & Winston, 1976.

Christensen, K. C., Birk, J. M., Brooks, L., & Sedlacek, W. E. Where clients go before contacting the university counseling center. *Journal of College Student Personnel*, 1976, **17**, 396–399.

Christensen, K. C., & Magoon, R. N. Perceived hierarchy of helpgiving sources for two categories of student problems. *Journal of Counseling Psychology*, 1974, **21**, 311–314.

Colligan, R. C., & McColgan, E. B. Perception of case conduct as a means of evaluating school psychological services. *Professional Psychology*, 1980 (April), 291–297.

Collins, J. F., Porter, K., Beam, A., & Moss, D. *Sources and resources: An annotated bibliography on inservice education* (Rev. ed.). Syracuse, New York: National Council of States on Inservice Education (123 Huntington Hall, Syracuse University), 1979.

Conoley, C. W. Community based consultation. Paper presented at the American Psychological Association, Toronto, Canada, August 1978.

Conoley, C. W. & Conoley, J. C. Strategic consultation: Community caregivers in the schools. In J. C. Conoley (Ed.), *Consultation in schools: Theory, research, procedures*. New York: Academic Press, 1981.

Conoley, J. C. Psychology of leadership: Implications for women. In S. K. Biklen and M. Brannigan (Eds.) *Women and Educational Leadership*. Lexington, Mass.: D. C. Heath Books, 1980.

Conoley, J. C. Advocacy consultation: Promises and problems. In J. C. Conoley (Ed.), *Consultation in Schools: Theory, research, procedures*. New York: Academic Press, 1981(a)

Conoley, J. C. (Ed.) *Consultation in schools: Theory, research, procedures*. New York: Academic Press, 1981(b)

Conoley, J. C. Advocacy versus organization development: Consultation training dilemmas. Paper presented at the Annual Meeting of the American Psychological Association, Los Angeles, August, 1981(c).

Conoley, J. C., Apter, S. J., & Conoley, C. W. Teacher consultation and the resource teacher: Increasing services to seriously disturbed children. In F. W. Wood (Ed.), *Perspectives for a new decade*. Reston, Va.: Council for Exceptional Children, 1981.

Conoley, J. C., & Barnes, E. Program development for severely handicapped children in public schools. Symposium presented at the National Association of School Psychologists, Washington, D.C., April, 1980.

Conoley, J. C., & Clark, M. A. Consultation training: Issues and evaluation. Paper presented at the annual meeting of the National Association of School Psychologists, Washington, D.C., April, 1980.

Conoley, J. C., & Conoley, C. W. The effect of two conditions of client-centered consultation on student teacher problem descriptions and remedial plans. *Journal of School Psychology*, 1982, **20**(4).

Cormick, G., & Love, J. J. Ethics of interventions in community disputes. In H. Kelman, D. Warwick, & G. Bermant (Eds.), *Ethics of social intervention*. New York: John Wiley & Sons, 1976.

Cossairt, A., Hall, R. V., & Hopkins, B. L. The effects of experimenter's instructions, feedback and praise on teacher praise and student attending behavior. *Journal of Applied Behavior Analysis*, 1973, **6**, 89–100.

Cowen, E. L. Long-term follow-up of early detected vulnerable children. *Journal of Consulting and Clinical Psychology*, 1973, **41**(3), 438–446.

Cowen, E. L., Dorr, D., Trost, M. A., & Izzo, L. D. A follow-up study of maladapting school children seen by non-professionals. *Journal of Consulting and Clinical Psychology*, 1972, **39**, 235–238.

Cowen, E. L., Lorion, R. P., & Dorr, D. Research in the community cauldron: A case history. *The Canadian Psychologist*, 1974, **15**(4), 313–325.

Cowen, E. L., Trost, M. A., & Izzo, L. D. Nonprofessional human-service personnel in consulting roles. *Community Mental Health Journal*, 1973, **9**, 335–341.

Cummings, T. G. *Systems theory for organizational development*. New York: John Wiley & Sons, 1980.

Cutler, R. L., & McNeil, E. B. *Mental health consultation in schools: A research analysis.* Ann Arbor: Department of Psychology, University of Michigan, 1964.

Ellis, A., & Grieger, R. *Rational-emotive therapy: Handbook of theory and practice.* New York: Springer, 1977.

Fairchild, T. N. School psychological services: An empirical comparison of two models. *Psychology in the Schools,* 1976, **13**(2), 156–162.

Ferguson, C. K. Concerning the nature of human systems and the consultant's role. *Journal of Applied Behavioral Science,* 1968, **4**(2).

Fine, M. J. Applying transactional analysis to consultation training. Paper presented at the Annual Meeting of the American Psychological Association, Los Angeles, August 1981.

Fine, M. J., Grantham, V. L., & Wright, J. G. Personal variables that facilitate or impede consultation. *Psychology in the Schools,* 1979, **16**(4), 533–539.

Freidman, M. P. Mental health consultation with teachers: An analysis of process variables. Paper presented at the Annual Meeting of the National Association of School Psychologists, New York, April 1978.

French, W. & Bell, C. H. *Organization development* (2nd ed.). Englewood Cliffs, N.J.: Prentice-Hall, 1978.

Gallessich, J. Organizational factors influencing consultation in schools. *Journal of School Psychology,* 1973, **11**, 57–65.

Gallessich, J. Training the school psychologist for consultation. *Journal of School Psychology,* 1974, **12**, 138–149.

Gamson, W. A. *Simsoc: Simulated society* (3rd ed.). New York: The Free Press, 1978.

Goldstein, A. P. *Psychological skill training.* New York: Pergamon Press, 1981.

Goodstein, L. D. *Consulting with human service systems.* Reading, Mass.: Addison-Wesley, 1978.

Goodwin, D. L., Garvey, W. P., & Barclay, J. R. Microconsultation and behavior analysis: A method for training psychologists as behavioral consultants. *Journal of Consulting and Clinical Psychology,* 1971, **37**, 355–363.

Gross, S. J. A basis for direct methods in consultee centered consultation. Unpublished manuscript, Indiana State University, 1978.

Guetzkow, H. (Ed.). *Simulation in the social sciences.* Englewood Cliffs, N.J.: Prentice-Hall, 1962.

Gutkin, T. B. Teacher perceptions of consultation services provided by school psychologists. *Professional Psychology,* 1981, **11**(4), 637–642.

Halpin, A., & Croft, D. *The organizational climate of schools.* Danville, Ill.: Interstate Printers and Publishers, 1963.

Hare, A. P. *Handbook of small group research* (2nd ed.). New York: Free Press, 1976.

Hayman, J. L., & Napier, R. N. *Evaluation in the schools: A human process for renewal.* Belmont, Calif.: Wadsworth, 1975.

Haynes, S. N. *Principles of behavioral assessment.* New York: Gardner, 1978.

Hoffman, L. *Foundations of family therapy: A conceptual framework for systems change.* New York: Basic Books, 1981.

Horwitz, A. Family, kin and friend networks in psychiatric help-seeking. *Social Science and Medicine,* 1978, **12**, 297–304.

Hughes, J. N., & Falk, R. S. Resistance, reactance, and consultation. *Journal of School Psychology,* 1981, **19**(2), 134–142.

Hyman, I. The school psychologist and child advocacy. In G. Gredler (Ed.), *Ethical and legal factors in the practice of school psychology.* Harrisburg, Pa.: Pennsylvania Dept. of Education, 1975.

Hyman, I., & Schreiber, K. Selected concepts and practices of child advocacy in school psychology. *Psychology in the Schools,* 1975, **12**(1), 50–57.

Inkeles, A. Industrial man: The relation of status to experience, perception, and values. *American Journal of Sociology*, 1960, **66**, 1–31.

Isaacson, D. An investigation into the criterion related validity of the consultation analogue situation. Unpublished doctoral dissertation, Syracuse University, 1981.

Jason, L. A., Ferone, L., & Anderegg, T. Evaluating ecological, behavioral, and process consultation interventions. *Journal of School Psychology*, 1979, **17**(2), 103–115.

Katz, D., & Kahn, R. L. *The social psychology of organizations* (2nd ed.). New York: John Wiley & Sons, 1978.

Keller, H. R. Behavioral consultation. In J. C. Conoley (Ed.), *Consultation in schools: Theory, research, procedures*. New York: Academic Press, 1981.

Keutzer, C. S., Fosmire, F. R., Diller, R., & Smith, M. D. Laboratory training in a new social system: Evaluation of a consulting relationship with a high school faculty. *Journal of Applied Behavioral Science*, 1971, **7**(4), 493–501.

Kohlberg, L. Development of moral character and moral ideology. In M. L. Hoffmon & L. W. Hoffmon (Eds.), *Review of child development research*. New York: Russell Sage Foundation, 1964.

Kounin, J. S. *Discipline and group management in classrooms*. New York: Holt, Rinehart & Winston, 1970.

Lambert, N. M., & Cole, L. Equal protection and due process considerations in the new special education legislation. *School Psychology Digest*, 1977, **6**(4), 11–12.

Lawrence, P. R., & Lorsch, J. W. *Developing organization: Diagnosis and action*. Reading, Mass.: Addison-Wesley, 1969.

Levine, M. Problems of entry in light of some postulates of practice in community psychology. In I. I. Goldenberg (Ed.), *The helping professionals in the world of action*. Lexington, Mass.: D. C. Heath, 1973.

Levine, M., & Levine, A. *A social history of helping services: Clinic, court, school and community*. New York: Meredith, 1970.

Lewin, K. *Field theory and social science*. New York: Harper, 1951.

Lippitt, R. & Lippitt, G. Consulting process in action. *Training and Development Journal*, 1975, **29**, 48–54.

Mannino, F. V. *An experience in consultation as perceived by consultants and consultees*. Adelphi, Md.: Mental Health Study Center, National Institute of Mental Health, 1969.

Mannino, F. V., & Shore, M. F. The effects of consultation—A review of empirical studies. *American Journal of Community Psychology*, 1975, **3**, 1–21.

Mannino, F. V., & Shore, M. F. Evaluation of consultation: Problems and prospects. In A. S. Rogawski (Ed.), *Mental health consultation in community settings. New directions for mental health services*. San Francisco, Calif.: Jossey-Bass, 1979.

Martin, R. The ethical and legal implications of behavior modification in the classroom. In G. Gredler (Ed.), *Ethical and legal factors in the practice of school psychology*. Harrisburg, Pa.: Pennsylvania Dept. of Education, 1975.

Martin, R. Expert and referent power: A framework for understanding and maximizing consultation effectiveness. *Journal of School Psychology*, 1978, **16**, 49–55.

Maslow, A. H. *The farther reaches of human nature*. New York: Viking, 1971.

Massachusetts Advocacy Center and Massachusetts Law Reform Institute. *Making school work*. 2 Park Square, Boston, Mass., 1975.

Matuszek, P. A. Program evaluation as consultation. In J. C. Conoley (Ed.), *Consultation in schools: Theory, research, procedures*. New York: Academic Press, 1981.

McDonald, S. Checklist for hearing officers. Unpublished mimeo. Center on Human Policy, 1977.

McIntyre, D. Two schools, one psychologist. In F. Kaplan & S. B. Sarason (Eds.), *The psychoeducational clinic*. Massachusetts Dept. of Mental Health, 1969.

McKinlay, J. B. Social networks, lay consultation and help-seeking behavior. *Social Forces*, 1973, **51**, 275–292.

Mearig, J. S. On becoming a child advocate in school psychology. *Journal of School Psychology*, 1974, **2**, 121–129.

Mearig, J. S. *Working for Children: Ethical issues beyond professional guidelines.* San Francisco: Jossey-Bass, 1978.

Medway, F. J. How effective is school consultation. A review of recent research. *Journal of School Psychology*, 1979, **17**(3), 275–282.

Meyers, J. A consultation model for school psychological services. *Journal of School Psychology*, 1973, **11**, 5–15.

Meyers, J. Consultee centered consultation with a teacher as a technique in behavior management. *American Journal of Community Psychology*, 1975, **3**, 111–121.

Meyers, J. Training school psychologists for a consultation role. *School Psychology Digest*, 1978, **7**(3), 26–31.

Meyers, J. Mental health consultation. In J. C. Conoley (Ed.), *Consultation in schools: Theory, research, procedures.* New York: Academic Press, 1981.

Meyers, J., Parsons, R. D., & Martin, R. *Mental health consultation in schools.* San Francisco: Jossey-Bass, 1979.

Newland, T. E. School Psychology—Observation and reminiscence. *Journal of School Psychology*, 1981, **19**(1), 4–20.

Newmann, F. The use of psychiatric consultation by a casework agency. *The Family*, 1945, **26**, 137–142.

O'Leary, K. D., & O'Leary, S. G. (Eds.). *Classroom management: The successful use of behavior modification* (Rev. ed.). New York: Pergamon Press, 1976.

O'Leary, K. D., & Wilson, G. T. *Behavior therapy: Application and outcome.* Englewood Cliffs, N.J.: Prentice–Hall, 1975.

Pfeiffer, J. W., & Jones, J. E. *Stuctured experiences for human relations training.* Vol. I & II. Iowa City, Iowa: University Associates Press, 1969-1970.

Pipes, R. B. Consulting in organizations: The entry problem, In J. C. Conoley (Ed.), *Consultation in Schools: Theory, research, procedures.* Academic Press: New York, 1981.

Rae-Grant, Q. The art of being a failure as a consultant. In J. Zusman & D. L. Davidson (Eds.), *Practical aspects of mental health consultation.* Springfield, Ill.: Charles C. Thomas, 1972.

Redl, F. The concept of the life space interview. *American Journal of Orthopsychiatry*, 1959, **29**, 1–18.

Reilly, D. H. School psychology: View from the second generation. *Psychology in the Schools*, 1973, **10**, 151.

Rhodes, W. C., & Tracy, M. L. *Study of child variance.* Ann Arbor: University of Michigan Press, 1972.

Ritter, D. R. Effects of a school consultation program upon referral patterns of teachers. *Psychology in the Schools*, 1978, **15**(2), 239–243.

Robbins, P. R., & Spencer, E. C. A study of the consultation process. *Psychiatry*, 1968, **31**, 362–368.

Robbins, P. R., Spencer, E. C., & Frank, D. A. Some factors influencing the outcome of consultation. *American Journal of Public Health*, 1970, **60**, 524–534.

Robinowitz, C. B. Consultation in mental retardation and developmental disabilities. In A. S. Rogawaski (Ed.), *Mental health consultations in community settings.* New Directions for Mental Health Services No. 3. San Francisco: Jossey-Bass, 1979.

Rogers, C. R. *Carl Rogers on personal power.* New York: Delacorte, 1977.

Sarason, S. B. The school culture and processes of change. In F. Kaplan & S. B. Sarason (Eds.), *The psycho-educational clinic.* Massachusetts Dept. of Mental Health, 1969.

Sarason, S. B. *The creation of settings and the future societies.* San Francisco: Jossey-Bass, 1972.

Sarason, S. B. Social action as a vehicle for learning. In I. I. Goldenberg (Ed.), *The helping professions in the world of action.* Lexington, Mass.: Lexington Books, 1973.

Sarason, S. B. *The culture of the school and the problem of change* (2nd ed.) Boston: Allyn and Bacon, 1981.

Sarason, S. B., & Doris, J. *Educational handicap, public policy and social history: A broadened perspective on mental retardation.* New York: Macmillan, 1979.

Sarason, S. B., Levine, M., Goldenberg, I. I., Cherlin, D. L., & Bennett, E. M. *Psychology in community settings: Clinical, educational, vocational, social aspects.* New York: John Wiley & Sons, 1960.

Schein, E. H. *Process consultation: its role in organizational development.* Reading, Mass.: Addison-Wesley Publishing Co., 1969.

Schmuck, R. A. Process consultation and organization development. *Professional Psychology,* 1976, **7,** 626–631.

Schmuck, R. A., Runkel, P. J., Saturen, S. L., Martell, R. T., & Derr, C. B. *Handbook of organization development in schools.* Palo Alto, Calif.: Mayfield, 1972.

Schmuck, R. A. Improving classroom group processes. In R. A. Schmuck & M. B. Miles (Eds.), *Organization development in schools.* Palo Alto, Calif.: National Press Books, 1971.

Schowengerdt, R. V., Fine, M. J., & Poggio, J. P. An examination of some bases of teacher satisfaction with school psychological services. *Psychology in the Schools,* 1976, **13,** 269–275.

Secord, P. F., & Backman, C. W. *Social Psychology* (2nd ed.). New York: McGraw-Hill, 1974.

Skinner, B. F. *About behaviorism.* New York: Knopf, 1974.

Slaikeu, K. A., & Duffy, M. Mental health consultation with campus ministers: A pilot program. *Professional Psychology,* 1979 (June), 338–346.

Snapp, M., Pells, B., Smith, J., & Gilmore, G. E. A district wide psychoeducational services delivery. *Journal of School Psychology,* 1974, **12**(1), 60–69.

Snow, D. L., & Newton, P. M. Task, social structure and social process in the community mental health center movement. *American Psychologist,* 1976, 582–594.

Stein, D. D. Training needs in clinical psychology. Paper presented in symposium at the Annual Meeting of the Eastern Psychological Association, Boston, Mass., April, 1972.

Stein, H. The use of the consultants. *American Journal of Orthopsychiatry,* 1956, **26,** 249–251.

Steele, F. *Consulting for organizational change.* Amherst, Mass.: Univ. of Mass. Press, 1973.

Tannenbaum, R., & Schmidt, W. H. How to choose a leadership pattern. *Harvard Business Review,* 1958, **36,** 95–101.

Taylor, S. *Negotiation: A tool for change.* D. D. Rights Center of the Mental Law Project, 1979.

Taylor, S. J., & Biklen, D. *Understanding the law: An advocate's guide to the law and developmental disabilities.* Under H.E.W., Office of Human Development Grant of National Significance #54P71332/3-01, Syracuse University and The Mental Health Law Project, 1979.

Tollett, D. J. An analysis of the continuing consultation program and development of a profile of schools in Tennessee Appalachian Education Co-op. *Dissertation Abstracts,* 32-02-A p. 716, 1971.

Tombari, M. L., & Bergan, J. R. Consultant cues and teacher verbalizations, judgments and expectations concerning children's adjustment problems. *Journal of School Psychology,* 1978, **16,** 212–219.

Tyler, M. M., & Fine, M. J. The effects of limited and intensive school psychologist teacher consultation. *Journal of School Psychology,* 1974, **12**(1), 8–16.

von Bertalanffy, L. *General systems theory.* New York: Braziller, 1968.

von Bertalanffy, L. General systems theory and psychology. In S. Arieti (Ed.), *American handbook of psychiatry.* Vol. III. New York: Basic Books, 1966.

Walker, P. R. *The institutionalization of change and inservice in schools and colleges of education.*

Washington, D.C.: Far West Teacher Corps Network and the E. R. I. C. Clearinghouse on Teacher Education, 1978.

Walton, R. E. *Interpersonal peacemaking: Confrontations and third party consultation*. Reading, Mass.: Addison-Wesley, 1969.

Watzlawick, P., Weakland, J., & Fisch, R. *Change*. New York: W. W. Norton, 1974.

White, P. O., & Fine, M. J. The effects of three schools' psychological consultation modes on selected teacher and pupil outcomes. *Psychology in the Schools*, 1976, **13**(14), 414–420.

Wilcox, M. R. Variables affecting group mental health consultation for teachers. Paper presented at the American Psychological Association's annual convention, San Francisco, Calif., August 1977.

Ysseldyke, J., Algozzine, B., Regan, R., & McGue, M. The influence of test scores and naturally–occurring pupil characteristics on psychoeducational decision making with children. *Journal of School Psychology*, 1981, **19**(2), 167–177.

Zax, M., Cowen, E. L., Izzo, L. D., Madonia, A. J., Merinda, J., & Trost, M. A. Teacher-aide program for preventing emotional disturbances in young school children. *Mental Hygiene*, 1966, **50**, 406–415.

Zusman, J., & Davidson, D. L. *Practical aspects of mental health consultation*. Springfield, Ill.: Charles C. Thomas, 1972.

Author Index

Subject Index

About the Authors

Jane Close Conoley (Ph.D., University of Texas at Austin, 1976) associate professor of psychology at Texas Woman's University, has served on the psychology faculty of Syracuse University in New York State and been involved in elementary and secondary education as teacher, counselor, school psychologist, and consultant. She is the editor of another volume on consultation as well as coauthor of books on emotionally disturbed children and work with special needs children and their families. In addition, she is author or coauthor of several journal articles, chapters, and numerous papers delivered at professional meetings.

Collie Wyatt Conoley (Ph.D., University of Texas at Austin, 1976) assistant professor of psychology at North Texas State University, has been clinical director of an Austin, Texas day treatment facility, director of a New York State Mental Health Department Community Services Program, and senior staff psychologist at the North Texas State University Counseling Center. He is author or coauthor of several journal articles concerning consultation and psychotherapeutic interventions and chapters concerning community psychology and consultation research. In addition, he has an independent practice specializing in marital and family therapy from a systems orientation.